FROM THE HISTORY OF KL - AUSCHWITZ

New York · HOWARD FERTIG · 1982

Kazimierz Smoleń
Danuta Czech
Kazimierz Smoleń

Tadeusz Iwaszko

Władysław Fejkiel

Władysław Fejkiel
Zofia Posmysz
Wanda Koprowska
Danuta Czech

- The Concentration Camp Auschwitz
- The Auschwitz Sub-Camps
- The System of Punishments Used by the SS in the Concentration Camp at Auschwitz-Birkenau
- Escapes of Prisoners from the Concentration Camp Auschwitz-Birkenau
- Ethical and Legal Limits of Experimentation in Medicine - in Connection with Professor Clauberg's Affair
- Starvation in Auschwitz
- "Sängerin"
- Days of Horror
- Most Important Events in the History of the Concentration Camp Auschwitz-Birkenau

FROM THE HISTORY OF KL-AUSCHWITZ

First published in 1967 by
Państwowe Muzeum w Oświęcimiu
Howard Fertig, Inc. Edition 1982
All rights reserved.
First American Edition

Library of Congress Cataloging in Publication Data
Main entry under title:
From the history of KL-Auschwitz.
　Reprint. Originally published: Oświęcim, Poland:
Państwowe Muzeum w Oświęcimiu, 1967.
　1. Auschwitz (Poland: Concentration camp)
I. Smoleń, Kazimierz.
D805.P7F7613　1982　　　940.53'15'03924　　　81-5426
ISBN 0-86527-338-3　　　　　　　　　　　　　　AACR2

Printed in the United States of America

Translated from the Polish text by
KRYSTYNA MICHALIK Ph.D.

EDITORS' OFFICE:
Kazimierz Smoleń M.A. (Editor), Jadwiga Bezwińska Ph.D. (Secretary),
Jerzy A. Brandhuber, D. Czech, M.A. (Members of the Editors' Office).

Krakowskie Zakłady Graficzne Zakład Nr 6, Kraków, ul. E. Orzeszkowej 7
Zam. 241/67

KAZIMIERZ SMOLEŃ, M. A.

THE CONCENTRATION CAMP AUSCHWITZ.

I. ESTABLISHMENT AND DEVELOPMENT.

The town Oświęcim, which had circa 12 thousand inhabitants in 1939, is situated within the Cracow District (*Województwo*), in the bifurcation of the rivers Vistula and Soła. Its distance from Cracow is about 60 kilometres to the south-west, as the crow flies, and it lies about 30 kilometres to the south east of Katowice.

After the end of military operations in September 1939 the town Oświęcim, together with the adjoining area, was incorporated with the terrains of the Third *Reich* and the Nazis changed its name to Auschwitz. Towards the end of 1939 there originated in the Office of High Command of the *SS* and Police in Wrocław (with *SS-Grup-*

penführer Erich von dem Bach-Zelewski at its head) the initiative to establish a concentration camp in the area of Oświęcim. The author of that idea was *Gestapo* Inspector *SS-Oberführer* Wiegand, a subaltern of von dem Bach-Zelewski, who motivated his proposal by the necessity of making mass arrests among the Polish population of Silesia, incorporated with the Third *Reich*, and among the inhabitants of the remaining Polish terrains, then forming the so-called *General Gouvernement*.

The locale for the concentration camp was to be a suburb of Oświęcim, Zasole, with its military garrison buildings. The buildings being outside the town itself had the advantage of being isolated and of offering the possibility of a further development of the camp in the direction away from the town.

The Inspector of concentration camps, Richard Glücks, sent two commissions to Oświęcim in order to assess the possibilities of realizing the project. One commission, with custody camp commandant of the Sachsenhausen camp *SS-Sturmbannführer* Eisfeld at its head, came to Oświęcim in January 1940 and decided that the former military barracks were not suitable for the establishment of a camp. The other commission arrived at Oświęcim in April and stayed there for two days, April 18 and 19, 1940. At its head was Rudolf Höss, who had followed Eisfeld as custody commandant of the Sachsenhausen camp. Following Glücks' report Himmler issued an order, dated April 27, 1940,[1]) to establish a concentration camp in Oświęcim (*KL* Auschwitz) and to build it using future prisoners as man-power. Glücks nominated Rudolf Höss commandant of the camp and told him "to establish a transit camp for 10 thousand prisoners".[2])

Höss came to Auschwitz with 5 other *SS*-men on the last day of April 1940 and began supervising the preparatory work in the area of the barracks, done by 300 Jews who were sent by the Mayor of the town to work there.

---

[1]) Trial of Höss, vol. 21, card 27.
[2]) Commandant of Auschwitz, The Autobiography of Rudolf Hoess, Pan Books, London, 1961, p. 116.

Rapportführer Palitzsch had brought as early as May 1940 30 prisoners from the camp at Sachsenhausen. They were criminal offenders and their camp numbers were from 1 to 30. The first transport of political prisoners, Poles, came to the camp on June 14, 1940. It consisted of 728 persons with camp numbers from 31 to 758.

In order to isolate the camp from the Polish population, living in its vicinity, the *SS* deported in June 1940 circa 2 thousand persons. Other families were deported on the 8 th of July and in November, 1940. Thus almost the entire Polish population of the suburb Oświęcim-Zasole was ousted and 123 houses were demolished [3] by prisoners from the so-called demolition squad. The commandant kept the building materials from the demolished houses for further use in enlarging the camp. The Auschwitz concentration camp became thus surrounded within a radius of 5 kilometres by grounds owned by the *SS*.

At the moment of its establishment the camp had 20 buildings, 14 one-storied and 6 two-storied ones. In the years 1941—1942, prisoners were used to add one storey to all the ground-floor houses and to build further 6 buildings of 2 storeys, together with the camp kitchen. The building materials, obtained after demolishing peasant houses, were partly used again. All together the camp consisted of 28 two-storied buildings (not counting the camp kitchen and administration buildings). The average number of camp inmates fluctuated between 13 thousand and 16 thousand, with a tendency to mount up to 28 thousand prisoners in the beginnings of 1942. The prisoners were housed in blocks, using all available space from garrets to cellars, and temporary wooden barracks were added in the spaces between the brick houses. The barracks were demolished when, due to a high death rate, the number of prisoners had decreased and when the camp at Birkenau had been established.

In the early months of 1941 the commandant's office began negotiating with the concern *IG-Farbenindustrie* concerning a further extension of the camp. *IG-Farbenindustrie* was planning to build a factory on the site of the village Monowice (Monowitz), situated

---
[3] Trial of Höss, 12, cards 45—47.

near the town of Oświęcim. The main thing in the negotiations was for the *IG-Farben* the possibility of acquiring cheap manpower, i.e. the prisoners, as "within a small distance from Oświęcim a concentration camp is being established."[4]). The site of the future factory was in Polish hands. The Polish owners were deported, their lands were confiscated and given to the *IG-Farben* free of charge.[5]) The first prisoners of *KL* Auschwitz began working at the building of *IG-Farben*'s factory in the end of March and the beginning of April, 1941. They used to walk to their work at first (circa 4 kilometres), later on they went by train. It was probably in September or October 1942 that one part of the prisoners permanently settled in recently built barracks in the factory area. Such were the origins of the camp at Monowitz, later called Auschwitz III.

During the inspection of the camp on March 1,1941 by *Reichsführer SS* Himmler, it was decided further to enlarge *KL* Auschwitz. Participants in the inspection also were: *Gauleiter* of Upper Silesia, Bracht, inspector of concentration camps, Glücks, high officials of the *IG-Farben* and the Head of the Office of High Command of the *SS* and Police, Schmauser. The camp was to be enlarged to the extent of providing accommodation for up to 30 thousand prisoners, while in nearby Brzezinka (Birkenau) a new camp for 100 thousand prisoners of war was to be established. Himmler further decided that big armaments concerns should be located around the camp so that the *SS* take the leadership also in the field of rearming the Nazi army.

Commandant Höss said that the decision of establishing a camp for such a large number of prisoners of war had been most surprising to everybody. Then, in March 1941, nobody knew what prisoners of war were meant. This shows that the Nazis were even then preparing their plans for attacking the Soviet Union.

To realize the plans of building a camp at Brzezinka there came on October 1,1941, *SS-Sturmbannführer* Karl Bischoff from Berlin to Auschwitz, delegated by *SS-Gruppenführer* Ing. Kammler, to

---

[4]) Document NO. NI. — 11784, January 18, 1941.
[5]) *Wochenbericht* No. 39 (Weekly Report No. 39), February 24, 1942.

take over the office of manager of the Special Building Project to establish an *SS* camp for prisoners of war in Auschwitz.

Ing. Kammler arrived at the camp in the beginning of October 1941 with the news that Brzezinka was to be a camp for 200,000 prisoners of war and not for 100,000, as formerly decided. At the same time farmhouses at Brzezinka were being demolished and their Polish inhabitants were deported.

The *SS* used the prisoners of *KL* Auschwitz as man-power; the prisoners went on foot to Brzezinka (Birkenau), covering a distance of about 3 kilometres [6]).

The first prisoners and Soviet prisoners of war were settled in the first days of March 1942 at Birkenau. They lived in still unfinished barracks, devoid of running water or sanitary equipment. The sanitary, hygienic and living conditions at Auschwitz were deplorable, but those at Birkenau were truly hopeless. These conditions were never improved and persisted in the same state till the end of the Birkenau camp's existence (later it was called Auschwitz II). Circa 250 barracks of the type of horse stables (*Pferdestallbarraken OKH-Typ 260/9*) were built on the site. Each barrack was intended to stable 52 horses, but the *SS* managed to crowd about 800—1,000 prisoners into each of them.

As the above mentioned camps were being enlarged the number of their inmates was steadily increasing. They attained their climax in the years 1943—1944, and it was then that Auschwitz I had circa 13 thousand prisoners, Auschwitz II (Birkenau) circa 120 thousand prisoners (men and women) and Auschwitz III (Monowitz together with other sub-camps) circa 25 thousand. The highest numerical strength (in all camps in the Auschwitz area) amounted to about 150 thousand prisoners, men and women. The numerical strength of all the camps constantly fluctuated, decreasing due to a high death rate among the prisoners and increasing due to the arrival of fresh transports. The strength of the particular camps underwent similar changes, also due to the establishing of new sub-camps or to their liquidation. The strength of pri-

---

[6]) Situational plan of the camp at Birkenau, bearing the name: *"Lageplan des Kriegsgefangenenlagers in Auschwitz, OS"*, dated October 14, 1941, and confirmed by the camp administration on October 15, 1941.

soners in the sub-camps varied according to the demands of industry for slave man-power, exploited in order to press on the armaments production.

The entire camp area, called the camp interest zone, came to circa 40 square kilometres. This vast camp combine was divided into three camps by order of the *Reichsführer SS* Himmler (garrison order of 22.11.1943, No. 53/43), and they were:

Concentration camp Auschwitz I (base camp)
Concentration camp Auschwitz II (Birkenau)
Concentration camp Auschwitz III (sub-camp, together with the Buna-Monowitz camp.).

In consequence of that division the administration of the camps was to be conducted centrally in Auschwitz I, as we learn from the above quoted order, and its commandant being superior in rank he was in authority over the commandants of the other camps.

The commandant of Auschwitz I retained his position as commandant of the Auschwitz SS Garrison and by order No. 57/43 was also nominated director of works, being in authority, as such, over all *SS* enterprises located in this area (with the exception of the agricultural section).[7]

The establishment of the camp for women should be mentioned here. The first women prisoners were brought from the concentration camp Ravensbrück to the camp at Auschwitz I on March 26, 1942. The transport consisted of 999 women and was located in one part of the Auschwitz camp, divided by a concrete wall from the rest of the camp. Another transport with 999 Jewish women had arrived on the same day. And so that day should be considered as the starting point of the establishment of the concentration camp for women, located in blocks with successive numbers from 1 to 10.

---

[7] The above mentioned names of camps were changed again by later orders as follows: *Frauenkonzentrationslager* (at Birkenau) was changed to *Frauenlager, Lager Buna* (Auschwitz III) to *Arbeitslager Monowitz*, then (in 1944) changed again to *Konzentrationslager Monowitz*. The camp at Birkenau (Auschwitz II Birkenau) was incorporated with Auschwitz I (*Stammlager*) on 25. 11. 1944. All these changes were "rather repainting of signboards... the Birkenau Camp, notorious throughout the world as the biggest extermination camp, disappeared from the list of Nazi concentration camps". But the changes did not in the least influence or improve the fate of the prisoners. (Dr Jan Sehn, Concentration Camp Oświęcim-Brzezinka (Auschwitz-Birkenau). Warszawa, 1956, Wyd. Prawnicze, p. 20)

On August 16, 1942 all women prisoners were transferred to the recently built camp at Birkenau, to the so-called sector BIa. The strength of the women's camp amounted then to about 15 thousand women. It steadily grew with time and in August 1944 there were 39,234 women prisoners.[8])

II. THE ROLE OF THE AUSCHWITZ CONCENTRATION CAMP IN REALIZING HITLER'S PROGRAMME OF THE EXTERMINATION OF NATIONS.

An analysis of original documents dating from the period of the camp's existence shows that prisoners from all countries under Nazi occupation during World War II were brought to Auschwitz. There were, among others, Poles, Russians, Czechs, Frenchmen, citizens of Luxemburg, Norwegians, Danes, Italians, Rumanians. It should be stressed that the Jews, who were detained in the above mentioned countries, often were citizens of Switzerland, the United States, Great Britain, Sweden, etc. but their citizenship failed to protect them from being arrested by the Nazis. Also a group of Spaniards was put into the Auschwitz camp. They came from France where they had lived in exile as anti-fascists since General Franco's take over and were arrested in France after it was invaded by the Nazis. One should particularly keep in mind the fact that a transport of 1,170 French communists was brought to Birkenau on July 8,1942, under the cryptonym "Night and Fogg" (*Nacht und Nebel*).

The prisoners in Auschwitz belonged to various race groups, represented various political points of view, but always anti-fascist ones. They were arrested regardless of religious denomination, sex, age or occupation. Among those registered in the camp registers we find children below the age of 14 and old people.

The wave of arrests in the occupied countries rose particularly after the Nazis had attacked the Soviet Union. It was then that the Chief of the Security Police and Security Service sent a circular letter of August 27, 1941 to all posts under his command, with the following recommendations:

---

[8]) It should be added that approximately 30,000 Jews from Hungary (men and women) were at Birkenau on that day, though they were not as yet entered into the camp registers.

"The *Reichsführer SS* and Chief of the German Police, faced by the increasing inimical activities and utterances against the State after the beginning of war operations against the Soviet Union, has come to the basic decision that all subversive priests, Czechs and Poles, hostile to Germany, communists and similar rabble, should be detained in some concentration camp for a longer period of time."

Several hundred Soviet prisoners of war were brought to Auschwitz for the first time straight from the front lines in the beginning of July, 1941, and were located in Block No. 11. All together circa 10,000 prisoners of war were brought there up to November 1941. In November 1941 a Special Commission of the Police Office in Katowice had arrived at the Auschwitz camp, with its Chief, Dr Rudolf Mildner. They began interrogating all Soviet prisoners of war. After the end of the interrogations the Commission divided the prisoners into several pre-arranged groups, specified on special forms. Circa 9,030[9] prisoners of war had been interrogated, about 1,000 of whom were shot in the yard of Block No. 11 in Auschwitz. The action was conducted till the end of 1941 and the beginning of 1942.[10]

The criminal activity of the Commission was most probably actuated by order No. 8 of July 17, 1941, issued by Heydrich and concocted together with Keitel. Here is an excerpt of the order in question:

"The task of the Chief of the Security Police and Security Service in camps for prisoners of war is to pass in survey all prisoners of war in view of their political tendencies, then to eliminate and to subject to further "treatment":

a) individuals politically or otherwise unsuitable
b) all the persons that could be used for rebuilding the occupied terrains...

First of all, all the more important state or party functionaries,

---

[9] The difference between the number 9,030 and the number of the prisoners of war brought in October (circa 10,000) is the result of the fact that a certain amount of the prisoners of war had died in the period from 7.10. to 25. 11. 1942.

[10] Deposition of witness Kazimierz Smoleń in Nuremberg at the trial heard by the American Military Tribunal (Fall 12) — NO — 5849.

particularly former revolutionaries, should be disclosed... all commissars of the Red Army, leaders of the state... leaders of the industrial sector, the Soviet intelligentsia, all Jews and all those who will be found to be agitators or fanatical communists." [11])

The number of the Soviet prisoners of war was fast decreasing. This was caused by general exhaustion due to starvation, diseases and brutal killing of the prisoners by the SS during work hours.

From about 10,000 prisoners of war brought to the camp in the first days of October 1941, there remained about 9,030 on November 25, 1941.

On January 19, 1942	1,490 prisoners of war
On February 1, 1942	1,017 prisoners of war
On March 1, 1942	945 prisoners of war.

The camp of the Soviet prisoners of war at Auschwitz I was liquidated on March 1, 1942 and the remaining 945 prisoners were transferred to Birkenau which was then being built, to sector BIb. In spite of the fact that further 3,700 Soviet prisoners of war were brought to the camp in the years 1942—1944, only 92 prisoners of war had remained alive on January 17, 1945, according to the last roll-call in the camp.

The camp in Auschwitz was meant to be a concentration camp for Poles mainly, but as early as June 6, 1941 the first draft of Czechs (Aryans) was brought here. Successive larger drafts were to follow it. Almost immediately after the Nazis had attacked the Soviet Union (July 1941) Soviet prisoners of war were brought to the camp. The first mass transports of Jews from Upper Silesia arrived in January 1942, from France and Slovakia in March 1942, from Holland, together with Aryan women from Yugoslavia, in July, 1942, Jews from Belgium in August 1942, from Norway in November 1942, Gypsies in February 1943, Jews from Greece in March 1943, Jews from Italy in October, 1943. In those years transports were also arriving from Germany, Austria and other occupied countries. A mass deportation of Jews from Hungary began in May 1944.

It is of particular interest to note the fact that certain transports

---

[11]) *Materiały norymberskie* (Nuremberg Materials). Warszawa, 1948, p. 207.

of prisoners to Auschwitz are closely connected with particular events, and so:
1) April 6, 1942: the Nazis attacked Yugoslavia — the first Yugoslavs arrived at Auschwitz in September 1942.
2) September 10, 1943: as a result of Italy's capitulation the Nazi army invaded Italy. The first transports of Italian Jews arrived at the camp in October, 1943.
3) March 1944: the Nazis manned important strategic points in Hungary and the first mass transports from Hungary were sent to Auschwitz as early as May 1944.

III. EXTERMINATION THROUGH WORK.

All prisoners, arriving at Auschwitz up to 1942, were registered there without directly undergoing any selection. Since 1942, when mass transports of Jews started arriving at the camp, the SS-men selected the prisoners by dividing them into two groups. The one consisting (according to commandant Höss) of about 25—30%, sometimes only 15%, of the prisoners, comprised persons able to work. The prisoners belonging to this group were entered into the camp registers, i.e. their personal data were taken down and they were given their identification numbers which were sewn upon the left-hand side of the coat and upon the right leg of the trousers. Triangles in different colours were sewn above the prisoner's camp number. The colour of the triangle depended on the reasons for the detention.

There were the following categories of prisoners:
1) Political prisoners — with red triangles on which the first letter of the name of the prisoner's country was visible, the name of the country being in German translation. German citizens had no letter on their triangles. Sectarians had violet triangles.
2) Professional criminal offenders — green triangles, asocial types — black triangles, homosexuals — pink triangles, with the adnotation in their dossiers "Par. 175", which was the pertinent paragraph of the German criminal code dealing with such offenders.

3) Prisoners "in police custody" — had inverted green triangles and were denoted by the abbreviation *SV* or *PSV* (*Polizei Sicherungs Verwahrte*).
4) All Jews had David's stars and their yellow triangles were crossed with red triangles.
5) All Russians (excepting the prisoners of war) and Gypsies had black triangles and on them the letter "*R*" (*Russe*) or "*Z*" (*Zigeuner*).
6) Prisoners kept at the disposal of the Police Summary Court had no triangles, wore their civilian clothes and were detained in Block No. 11 which they were not allowed to leave. The letters „*PH*" in their dossiers denoted their status.
7) Prisoners who were commited to the camp to "be re-educated" (*Erziehungshäflinge*) had no triangles, only camp numbers beside which the letter "*E*" in red colour was placed.
8) Soviet prisoners of war had their camp numbers only.

A prisoner coming to the camp for the second time (after his release) had a special sign in the form of a beam above his triangle, of the same colour as his triangle. It denoted a recidivist.

Prisoners transferred to penal companies (*SK*) wore a white patch with a black circle, sewn or painted, above their triangles. Those suspected of planning to escape from the camp were distinguishable by a white patch with a red circle and the letters "*iL*" (*im Lager* — in camp), placed upon the left-hand side of the coat, on the back and on the leg of the trousers. They were not allowed to leave the camp, not even when escorted by the *SS*.

Besides the above mentioned distinctions the prisoners were tattooed, but only in Auschwitz. The first to be tattooed were the Soviet prisoners of war, in the autumn of 1941. They had their camp numbers tattooed on their left breasts. The other prisoners (with the exception of Aryan Germans) were tattooed under their left arms. The Jews had a tattoo of a triangle with the letter "*A*" or "*B*", besides their camp number, the Gypsies the letter "*Z*" (*Zigeuner*), besides their camp number. Tattooing was intended to prevent a possible escape from the camp and to facilitate recognition of a prisoner.

Since the winter of 1940 till about 1943 all prisoners, with the exception of Jews, had been photographed in the atelier of the investigation section. After that period only certain groups of prisoners were photographed.

The camp numbers were given in the order of arrival, there was only a differentiation according to sex and group, as mentioned above. The number of a deceased prisoner was never given again to a living one, neither were there any lacunae in the numeration. Therefore, knowing which was the highest number in each group, we can determine the amount of prisoners registered in the camp. Those, who after arriving at the camp were immediately sent by the SS to gas chambers, were not entered in the camp registers and their personal documents were destroyed.

The amount of prisoners entered in the camp registers is as follows:

	men	women
Ordinary numeration (custody prisoners)	202,499	90,000
Numeration of Jews, "A" series	20,000	30,000
„ „ „ "B" series	15,000	
Prisoners to be reeducated	10,000	2,000
Soviet prisoners of war	13,780	
Gypsies	10,094	10,849

Total: 404,222

Prisoners with camp numbers in Auschwitz: circa 404,222
Out of this total those who perished in the camp: circa 340,000

Prisoners were located in particular blocks situated within the camp wire fences which were charged with electric current. During the so-called quarantine they were taught various marching songs and how to report to superiors. They were also drilled in an exhaustive way (the SS ironically called the drill — sport exercises), were made to roll or crawl on the ground, etc. That kind of drill was accompanied with beating and maltreating the prisoners by the SS. Casualties and even cases of death were frequent.

After surviving the quarantine the prisoner would be assigned to one of the numerous work squads. The latter were called according to the kind of work done by the squad, e.g. joinery, carpentry squad, etc. The name of the place of work was also used to designate squads, e.g. *Königsgraben, Neubau*, etc. or the name of the firm for which the prisoners worked, e. g. *Hütte, Riedel, IG-Farben, Krupp, Union*, etc. There were several hundreds of work squads. Some were liquidated after they had done their work, new ones were formed to tackle new tasks.

The squads consisted of several prisoners only or of several hundreds of them.

Roughly they might be divided into squads serving:
1) the administration of the camp (clerks in offices, cleaners, block seniors working in the kitchen or store-rooms),
2) the building and enlarging of the camp, its farms and *SS* enterprises,
3) private firms and concerns.

The *SS* owned, among others, the following enterprises: *DAW (Deutsche Ausrüstungswerke), Deutsche Lebensmittel GmbH, DEST (Deutsche Erd-und Steinwerke), T.W.L. (Truppenwirtschaftslager)*. On the basis of fragmentary data it was ascertained that prisoners had worked 60,837 work days in the armaments industry in January 1943, and 537,000 work days in November 1943. The figures rose rapidly as the number of prisoners employed by the industry increased. The boards of industrial establishments asked of their own accord for prisoner man-power, placing their requests at the *SS* Economic Administration Head Office. Some firms dealt directly with the administration of the camp. In all factories, both in the *Reich* and in the occupied countries, the number of prisoners-employees amounted to about 500,000.[12]) Representatives of factories used to select workers from among the prisoners in the camp. To do so they received special permits to enter the camp terrain accompanied by its commandant.[13])

---

[12]) Trial of Gerhard Maurer (Vol. 6, card 23). Karl Sommer deposed that the industry had employed circa 500,000 prisoners at the peak period (Trial of Maurer, vol. 7, card 7.).
[13]) Vide footnote [12]). (Vol. 6, card 23).

Among the many Nazi documents, which had been preserved, those dealing with the employment of prisoners and the exploiting of their work, are particularly numerous. In one of his orders Oswald Pohl (*SS* Economic Administration Head Office) requested the camp commandants to take steps to make the prisoners' work "exhausting in the full meaning of the word, so that maximum results be obtained. There should be no time limits to work hours".[14]) In the first years of the war the work hours were 9—11 hours daily. In his circular letter to camp commandants of November 22, 1943, Pohl wrote, "I again call your attention to the fact that the work hours of prisoners, i.e. 11 hours daily, must be kept in winter months, too." [15])

The prolongation of working hours and the conditions of work led to the exhaustion of the prisoners and to diseases, thereby causing the death rate to rise.

The armaments concerns, mines and particularly the *IG-Farben*, had priority in securing man-power from the area of Auschwitz. In the message of Göring of February 18, 1941 [16]) and in the letter of the plenipotentiary for exceptional cases connected with the chemical output, of March 4, 1941,[17]) we find the following passage:

"The Inspector of Concentration Camps and the Chief of the Economic Administration Head Office is requested to get at once into touch with the Director of the Construction of the *Buna* Factory and to help him in every way whatsoever in his task of construction by detailing prisoners from the concentration camp to work there.

In all matters connected with the Auschwitz works the competency is in the hands of the Chief of the *SS Reichsführer's* personal staff, *SS-Gruppenführer* Wolf, who serves as liaison officer between the *Reichsführer SS* and the Auschwitz works."

---

[14]) Trial of Oswald Pohl (Economic Administration Head Office) vol. 4, documents, cards 12—13, Doc. NO — O — 129.
[15]) Doc. NO — 1290.
[16]) Doc. NI — 1240 (Trial of *IG-Farben*, vol. 72, cards 66—67, and trial of Maurer, vol. 7, cards 13—14).
[17]) Doc. NI — 11086 (Trial of *IG-Farben*, vol. 72, cards 113—114, and trial of Maurer, vol. 7, cards 25—27).

IG-Farbenindustrie (Dr Ing. Dürrfeld) in a letter of October 28, 1943, asked Pohl to permit more prisoners to be employed by the concern:

> "I take the opportunity to inform you that the employment of prisoners at *"Fürstengrube* and *Janinagrube"* had the best results. Our needs have been completely satisfied. The cooperation with the concentration camp authorities is progressing along most satisfactory lines." [18])

Ex-commandant Höss stated in his explanations [19]) that he had often heard that the employees of various factories had maltreated the prisoners working there and particularly that they had beaten the prisoners.

From a letter of September 14, 1942, which the *IG-Farben* sent to the firm of *Friedrich Krupp* in Essen, and which was written by Dr Dürrfeld, we learn that the camp administration got 4 *RM* for a skilled prisoner worker and 3 *RM* for an unskilled labourer. The *SS* received more than 20 million mark [20]) for the work of their slaves, the prisoners, over the period of two years and a half. The weekly report No. 90/91 from February 8 to February 21, 1943, tells us that Gerhard Maurer (*SS* Economic Administration Head Office) had visited the camp Auschwitz III on February 10, 1943 and had a conversation with the management of the *IG-Farben* (Werk Auschwitz). Ing. Faust (*IG-Farben*) made the following notes of the conversation:

> *"Obersturmbannführer"* Maurer next said that all the weak prisoners could be "removed" in order to ensure an almost complete efficiency of output."[21])

The expression "to be removed" meant with the *SS* to send the sick to gas chambers. The firms paid for a sick prisoner only for a fortnight while he was in the hospital. Therefore selections were often made in hospitals and even in the work squads, and weak or sick prisoners were killed with injections into the heart or were

---
[18]) *IG-Farben Auschwitz. Mossenmord. Dokumente zum Auschwitz Prozess.* (Mass murder. Documents of the Auschwitz trial), p. 74.
[19]) Trial of Höss (vol. 21, card 42).
[20]) Doc. No.NI — 9542, depositions of Otto Ambros (Trial of Maurer, vol. 7, card 135).
[21]) Trial of *IG-Farben* (vol. 93, documents, cards 23—28, and trial of Maurer, vol. 7, card 63).

sent to gas chambers. According to various statements of the prisoners the total of those killed only in Auschwitz III amounted to circa 30,000.

The hospitals in all Auschwitz camps were constantly overcrowded with sick and exhausted prisoners. The causes were manifold.

The calorie value of a whole day's food ration in the camp amounted to 1,300—1,500 calories.[22] Prisoners soon grew cachectic and the constantly increasing calorie deficiency led to starvation sickness. The general physical exhaustion was accompanied by psychic symptoms characterized by extreme apathy. After the reserves, stored in the body, were used up death due to starvation was inevitable. The prisoners who were in a state of protracted starvation were called "moslems" in the jargon of the camp. "Moslems" found it impossible to concentrate their thoughts, their memory failed them to such an extent that they were unable to remember their names.

Approximately 75 % of the prisoners in the camp were undernourished and therefore could survive from 3 to 6 months, depending on the kind of their work (light, moderate, or heavy). Medical examination of the prisoners, made after the liberation of the Auschwitz camp by the Soviet Army, showed that the weight of prisoners was circa 30—40 kilogrammes, that is 50—70% below their normal standards. "Moslems" were selected by the SS-men in the camp and sent to the hospital where the doctors and medical orderlies killed them with phenol injected into the heart.

It was mentioned before that selections took place in the hospitals also among those patients who, according to the SS, had been staying there too long or in order to quell epidemics. And so, among other instances of that kind, on August 29, 1942, 746 patients and convalescents were selected from the camp hospital for prisoners and were sent to Birkenau where they were gassed in bunkers.

---

[22] *"Hunger und Lebenserwartung in Auschwitz"* (Starvation and Expectation of Survival). Monograph by Dr Münch, ex-*SS-Untersturmführer* at Auschwitz. Archive of Państwowe Muzeum w Oświęcimiu.

Due to bad sanitary and hygienic conditions various epidemics were frequent in the camp (*typhus, diarrhoea*). Scabies, induced by the dirt, caused abscesses, considerable wounds, which in turn got infected and death was their result. Prisoners were afraid of being transferred to the camp hospital, not only because of the imminent selections, but also because of the experimenting illegally conducted there by *SS* doctors, who either wanted to acquire medical experience using the live bodies of prisoners or wished to test the action of new drugs. The following experiments, conducted on a large scale in Auschwitz, were particularly criminal:

1) Experiments conducted by Prof. Dr Carl Clauberg in Block No. 10 (Auschwitz I). He aimed at finding a quick method of the biological extermination of the Slavs. His experiments dealt with Jewish women, many of whom had perished,
2) experiments dealing with tumours, conducted by Dr Wirths,
3) experiments with uniovular twins conducted on Jewish and Gypsy children by Dr Mengele,
4) experiments testing the various drugs produced by the firm of *Bayer* (e.g. preparation *3582, Rutenol*, etc.), conducted by Dr Helmuth Vetter for *IG-Farben* or *Scheringwerke*.

It seems hardly necessary to add that all the experiments were conducted without the consent of those prisoners who were their victims and who very frequently died in consequence of them.

One occurrence should not be forgotten. In 1943 the representative of *"Ahnenerbe"*, Dr Bruno Beger chose 115 male and female prisoners as material for skeletons to be prepared in the Institute of Anatomy in Strassburg. The persons chosen in Auschwitz were taken to the concentration camp in Natzweiler and killed there. In 1944, when the Allies were already close to Strassburg, the Institute of Anatomy sent a letter to Hitler's personal staff asking what to do with the corpses of 80 prisoners still lying in the morgue of the Institute. In this letter we find the suggestion they would prepare the skeletons in a hurry so as to make recognition of the corpses impossible, but they were afraid that there

would be no chance of making casts for the anatomical collection.[23])
All the experiments conducted in concentration camps were pronounced to the criminal, both in Trial No. 1 (Suit against Physicians) and in the suit against *IG-Farben* (both suits were heard by the American Military Tribunal in Nuremberg). In the judgment against *IG-Farben* we find the following passage:

> "It is beyond any controversy that criminal experiments had been conducted by the SS physicians on the prisoners in concentration camps."

Great numbers of prisoners found death not only as the result of illness, starvation, selections, experiments and tortures. They were also liable to be shot or hanged. The executions took place in the yard of Block No. 11 in Auschwitz I. About 20,000 prisoners had lost their lives here being shot in the back of the head. Prisoners were also punished here by flogging. SS physicians were present both at the executions and at the floggings which is irrefutably proved by a document, namely the preserved diary [24]) of Prof. *SS-Obersturmführer* Dr Kremer, the camp physician in Auschwitz. Here are some passages from Kremer's diary:

"October 13, Was present at punishment and later on at the execution of 7 Polish civilians.

October 17, Was present at punishment and at 11 executions. Took material from quite fresh corpses, using pilocarpine injection."

The life of a camp inmate was threatened by constant dangers. The SS intended to exploit the prisoners to the utmost, even if it caused their deaths. Therefore it seems right to conclude that a prisoner in the camp was slowly but inevitably doomed to death.

VI. DIRECT EXTERMINATION

It was mentioned above that the SS had, since 1942, performed selections among persons of Jewish origin, brought to the camp at Auschwitz in special transports. The procedure was as follows:

---

[23]) Correspondence between Prof. Dr Rudolf Brand and Wolfram Sievers, also between Sievers and Eichmann (Doc. No — 087 and Trial of the members of the Auschwitz Camp Garrison, heard by the Supreme National Tribunal in Cracow) later quoted as Trial of the Auschwitz Garrison, Vol. 37, card 28

[24]) Archive of Państwowe Muzeum w Oświęcimiu. The quoted entries are from the year 1942.

After opening the doors of the freight railway cars the persons travelling in them got off and were told by the *SS* to leave their luggage in the cars or on the railway ramp. Next, men were separated from women and children, thus forming two groups. Each of the newcomers had to pass in front of an *SS* doctor [25] who decided on the fate of the person. There were no fixed criteria which would be obligatory for the *SS* doctors at selections.

If at the moment of the arrival of a fresh draft the camp was not overcrowded or if there was a greater demand for man-power or for certain skilled workers, the percentage of those deemed fit for work might be higher. Naturally, the best chances of being considered fit for work existed for young people, presenting a satisfactory physique and not for older people, children or pregnant women. The *SS*-men did not undertake any medical examinations at the selections, not even the most rudimentary ones.

The amount of persons unfit for work was always considerably higher than of those fit for work and on the average consisted of 70—75% of new arrivals. (There were 85% of those unfit for work among the Greek Jews.) Such a group was surrounded by *SS*-men who were on duty at the ramp. They led the group into the yard of one of the crematoria. There were cases of the sick or the weak being loaded into trucks and taken to the crematoria. There, the *SS*-men told the newcomers that they must bathe and be disinfected before entering the camp. They were told to remember where they had left their clothes, so as to preserve the necessary order. From the room where they had undressed they were led naked to a smaller room which looked like a bath because of the showers affixed to the ceiling. There were inscriptions on the doors in German: "bathroom". Nevertheless this was the gas chamber. Depending on the capacity of the chamber approximately 2,000 persons were crowded into it. The hermeticaly sealed doors were then closed and the gas Cyclon B (*HCN* in chemistry) was shaken in through vents in the ceiling. Cyclon B had the form of small

---

[25] "...the Jews had to pass individually in front of an SS doctor", said Höss in his Autobiography (Commandant of Auschwitz, The Autobiography of Rudolf Hoess, London, 1961 p. 214.

crystals. Death through suffocation was almost instantaneous and was accompanied by sensations of fear, dizziness and by vomiting.

After 15—20 minutes the doors of the gas chambers were opened and ventilators were put into action in order to scatter the poisonous fumes. The corpses were removed to another room where the hair was cut off, gold teeth were extracted and jewelry was taken (earrings and wedding rings). The corpses were then burnt in the crematorium ovens or on pyres. Personal documents of the murdered were burnt in the so-called *"Mühlverbrennungsofen"* (ovens for burning papers).

The whole process of extermination was top secret. Prisoners selected from recently arriving transports were detailed to work in the gas chambers and crematoria. The *SS* formed so-called special squads of such prisoners and their duty was to remove corpses from the gas chambers and to cremate them. Being "in the know" they were, after some time, in turn killed in the gas chambers and their places were again taken by fresh arrivals from next transports.

The process of extermination was a state secret and official documents dealing with it were full of cryptonyms, such as *"SB"* (*Sonderbehandlung* — special treatment), *"GU"* (*gesondert untergebracht* — kept in isolation). Cyclon B was produced by the firm *Degesch* (*Deutsche Gesellschaft für Schädlingsbekämpfung*) which formed part of the concern of *IG-Farben*. It was supplied to the concentration camps through the firm *Tesch and Stabenow* (*Testa*). Cyclon B was brought by trucks of the *SS* straight from the factory of that firm in Dessau, which fact is confirmed by preserved travel orders issued at Auschwitz.

The first attempt to use the gas Cyclon B for mass murders was carried out in Auschwitz I on September 3, 1941. Its victims were 600 Soviet prisoners of war and 250 sick inmates of the camp. The gassing took place in the cellars of Block No. 11. Commandant Höss admitted in his Autobiography that the use of Cyclon B "set my mind at rest, for the mass extermination of the Jews was to start soon and at that time neither Eichmann nor I was certain how these mass killings were to be carried out... Now we had the gas and we had established a procedure..." [26])

Since January 1942 the gassing was taking place at Birkenau in two country cottages specially adapted for the purpose („red house" and "white house"). The mortuary of crematorium I in Auschwitz I, with an area of circa 200 square metres, was also used as a gas chamber.

In 1942 the administration of the camp turned to German firms with the offer of having them build a crematorium. The firm *Lenz* refused because of the shortage of man-power. The firm *Hütte* (*Hoch und Tiefbau*) undertook the construction of a crematorium and its estimate, amounting to 133, 765/65 mark, was accepted. The construction of the crematoria and the gas chambers at Birkenau proceeded without delay. On January 29, 1943, Ing. Prüfer of the firm *Topf and Sons* had a talk with the Central Building Section of the *SS* and Police in Auschwitz and on the same day the director of the Central Building Section in Auschwitz was able to inform the *SS-Brigadeführer und Generalmajor der Waffen SS*, Dr Kammler in Berlin, that:

"The construction of crematorium II had been completely finished, down to the last details of construction, thanks to the use of all available means, working day and night, and in spite of untold difficulties and the frosty weather.

The ovens were put into action in the presence of Ing. Prüfer of the firm of constructors, *Topf and Sons*, from Erfurt. The ovens work faultlessly." [27])

The dates of finishing the construction of the crematoria at Birkenau and their capacity of cremating corpses in the course of 24 hours were as follows:

---

[26]) Commandant of Auschwitz, The Autobiography of Rudolf Hoes, London 1961, p. 165.
[27]) Trial of Höss, vol. 11, card 64.

Crematorium II	March 31, 1943	1,440 corpses,
Crematorium III	June 25, 1943	1,440 ,,
Crematorium IV	March 22, 1943	768 ,,
Crematorium V	April 4, 1943	768 ,,
Total		4,416 corpses in 24 hours.

Bearing in mind the need of camouflaging the extermination centres *SS-Obersturmführer* Bischoff (Building Section) sent the following instruction to the manager of the Agricultural Section in his letter of November 6, 1943;

"By order of the commandant *SS-Obersturmführer* Höss the crematoria I and II shall be surrounded by a belt of greenery forming a natural enclosure within the camp".[28])

As long as the crematoria were not yet put into action the corpses of the gassed were buried in common graves, later on they were burnt on immense pyres. Höss wrote about it as follows:[29])

"Towards the end of the summer (1942), however, we started to burn them — at first on wood pyres bearing some 2,000 corpses, and later in pits together with bodies previously buried. In the early days oil refuse was poured on the bodies but later methanol was used. Bodies were burnt in pits, day and night, continuously. By the end of November all mass graves had been emptied. The number of corpses in the mass graves amounted to 107,000."

The bodies were burnt on pyres because the crematoria could not cope with the quantities of people killed in gas chambers day by day (probably circa 30,000 persons were killed daily during certain periods of time). And so the director of the Central Building Section Bischoff [30]) wrote as follows in his letter to commandant Höss (February 12, 1943):

"Referring to the conversation of your correspondent of Jan. 29, 1943, with Ing. Prüfer from the firm *Topf and Sons*, we have considered the possibility of constructing crematorium VI (an open place of cremation 48,75 by 3,76 metres). The Central Building

---
[28]) Trial of Höss, vol. 11, card 67.
[29]) Vide The Autobiography of Rudolf Hoess, London 1961, p 211.
[30]) Trial of Höss, vol. 11, card 58.

Section had, in connection with the project, commissioned the firm *Topf and Sons* to elaborate a plan for an open place of cremation, which plan you will find enclosed."

The proposed crematorium VI was to be in the shape of an oven placed in a deep cavity, or rather a pit, with its slopes covered with bricks. Such an oven would combine the advantages of the immense capacity of the cremating pits with the economy in fuelling of the crematoria ovens, so that the huge amounts of wood, used up in the pits would be replaced by considerably smaller quantities of another fuel (coke, coal,).

In spite of all measures taken to make the extermination quicker, the administration of the camp could not cope with the killing of people during the Hungarian action (1944) and so those who were doomed to die in gas chambers often had to wait their turn in the so-called transit camp for several days.

In order to obliterate all traces of their crimes the Nazis had blasted the crematoria II and III and had burnt crematorium V in 1945. Crematorium IV was burnt down during the rebellion of the prisoners of the special squad on October 7, 1944. The ruins of the crematoria and gas chambers, as well as their preserved plans, clearly show the magnitude of these installations of extermination and the way they had been functioning.

V. THE STRUCTURE OF THE ORGANIZATION OF THE AUSCHWITZ CAMP.

The concentration camps were (since March 1942) under the administration of the *SS* Economic Administration Head Office, Group *D*. Formerly they were administered by the Inspector of Concentration Camps.

Group *D* was divided into *DI* — Central Office, *DII* — Employment of the Prisoners, *DIII* — Sanitary and Hygienic Matters in Concentration Camps, and *DIV* — Administration of Concentration Camps.

The activities of the Offices *DI* — *DIV* corresponded with those of similar administrative units in a concentration camp.

Commandant Höss presented the organizational scheme, describing the particular sections of the camp administration and their interdependence[31]).

Using this scheme and other preserved Nazi documents as the basis one can reconstruct the structure of the concentration camp at Auschwitz as follows:

Commandant's Office (*Kommandantur*) Section I.

The commandant of the camp stood at the head of the concentration camp and was responsible for all matters connected with it. He was at the same time commandant of the *SS* garrison in that area and director of all works, situated in the terrain and belonging to the *SS* (*DAW, DEST*, etc.) Further, the commandant's aide-de-camp, a staff N.C.O. (*Stabscharführer*), a judiciary officer, were also employed in the commandant's office and the Censor's Office was located there.

Political Section (*Politische Abteilung*) Section II.

The Chief of that Section was an SS Officer, delegated by the *Gestapo* of Katowice. His duties were: to file the personal documents of the prisoners, to correspond with the Reich Security Head Office and with the posts through which the prisoners had been committed to the camp, particularly the posts of the *Gestapo* and *Kripo* (Criminal Police), to receive the transports and to watch over the security of the camp (by quelling conspiracies among the prisoners). He also conducted inquiries during which tortures were used so that they often ended with deaths of prisoners. Further, he conducted the registrar's office and controlled the work of the crematoria. The camp investigating staff was part of the Political Section.

Administration of the Custody Camp (*Schutzhaftlagerführung*) Section III.

The most important task of this Section was the direct administration of the concentration camp. The head of the Section made reports concerning the strength of the camp, was responsible for

---
[31]) Trial of Höss, vol. 21 card 54 and following.

the order in the camp, was present at punishments, executions, etc. His helpers were the *Rapportführer* (intelligence officer) and the block seniors.

Employment Section. (*Arbeitseinsatzführer*) Section IIIa.

The head of this Section attended to all matters connected with the prisoners' work, with the exploitation of their work power, with work hours, etc. He also formed the work squads. He was assisted by an N.C.O, called *Arbeitsdienst*, and during work hours the prisoners belonging to the work squads were under the surveillance of guards, members of the *SS* garrison. The Employment Section computed the wages of the prisoners who were employed by various firms.

Administration (*Verwaltung*) Section IV.

This section administered the entire estate of the camp. It was divided into several sub-sections, e.g. dealing with currency, with the prisoners' property, etc. All magazines, also those with the property looted from murdered persons, were in its care, as well as the motor transportation.

Garrison Surgeon (*Standortarzt*) Section V.

Health matters, checking on sanitary and hygienic conditions, etc. were the domain of that section. The Garrison Surgeon had subaltern garrison doctors and camp doctors to assist him in his activities, as well as *SS* sanitary orderlies.

Agricultural Section (*Landwirtschaft*) Section VI.

Since a considerable area of land at Auschwitz was used for cultivating purposes a special Section had to attend to these matters. They included the growing of useful plants, the raising of cattle, etc., conducting experiments and investigations connected with various cultures, among others those connected with growing the plant "*kok sagiz*", indispensable for obtaining caoutchouc.

An Educational Section (*Truppenbetreung*) was taking care of the instruction of the *SS*.

VI. THE MAGNITUDE OF CRIMES PERPETRATED.

Within the framework of the above described spheres of their activity the *SS* officers and *SS* N.C.O's, employed in the particular sections of the camp administration, perpetrated mass crimes, both individually, on their own, and jointly. Certain facts, cited here as examples, can attest to the magnitude of their crimes.

A comparison of the "Concentration Camps Regulations", as reproduced by commandant Höss (*Lagerordnung für die Konzentrationslager*)[32] with the practice of everyday life shows that the *SS* had one main aim in view, namely the extermination of the prisoners committed to the camp.

Depositions of witnesses in numerous trials of the *SS*, as well as the original documents, throw a clear light upon the housing conditions of the prisoners, their clothing, food, the diseases they were afflicted with, the care (or rather the lack of care) which was taken of them. The blocks were overcrowded with inmates to an incredible extent. 700—1,000, or even 1,200 prisoners often occupied an area of approximately 400 square metres. Under the circumstances there was no possibility of resting at night after 11—12 hours of hard work. The blocks were rarely heated (Auschwitz) or could not be heated at all (Birkenau). The lack of running water at Birkenau made it impossible to keep oneself clean. Too few latrines made it difficult to use them. There were periods of time when prisoners were not allowed to remain in the latrine longer than 10 seconds. As diarrhoea was rampant, the prisoners who had to stay in the latrine longer were beaten or thrown into the cloacal hole.

The clothing issued to the prisoners was insufficient to protect them against atmospheric changes, particularly against the cold and dampness. The prisoners contracted pneumonia and arthritis, and as there was no room in the hospital and no drugs, they died. The death rate was especially high among prisoners coming from the West and South of Europe, since they were not used to the bad climate of Auschwitz, where temperature drops in winter down to 25—30°C below the zero.

---

[32] Trial of Höss, vol. 21, card 54.

The clothes issued to the prisoners were not changed for months and in result the camp was infested by all kinds of vermin. This fact, as well as the blankets, with which the prisoners covered themselves in the bunks and which were never changed, caused epidemics of scabies and typhus. The epidemics made the high death rate soar even higher.

In 1940 the prisoners got no shoes until December and so they had to go to work barefoot and to stand barefoot at the roll-calls. This caused almost universal kidney troubles and ended with the deaths of many prisoners. Later on Dutch clogs (wooden shoes) were issued and they again caused blisters on the feet which after getting infected resulted in widespread phlegmons. The high percentage of surgical cases was due to phlegmons.

We learn from the camp documents and particularly from the records of the Hygiene Institute of the *SS* and Police in Auschwitz that the food which the prisoners were getting was below the standards of most primitive requirements, both as regards its quality and quantity. The meat in the camp kitchen was very often tainted, rotten, frequently with stamps denoting that it was not fit for use.

These facts, together with the regular pilfering from the prisoners' rations by the *SS*, resulted in a decrease of the value of the daily rations to approximately 1,150 calories. Such calorie norms were completely insufficient; no wonder then that prisoners succumbed to starvation sickness after a three months' stay in the camp. The *SS*-men had an ironical saying: "A decent prisoner should not live longer than 3 months."

The camp hospital could not cope with the vast quantities of the sick. Several patients lay on one mattress, regardless of the kind of their disease. Since the patients were no longer working, their food rations became smaller still. The amount of medical remedies in the hospital did not correspond to the demand for them, although there were great quantities of all kinds of remedies, taken from the murdered persons and kept in the *SS* magazines. The *SS* ordered the prisoners to sort them and then they were sent for the use of the German soldiers at the front or to the Third *Reich*. The prisoners managed to abstract certain quantities of remedies and surgical instruments from the magazines and handed them over to the prisoners-doctors to save the patients in the camp hospital.

To reduce the number of the patients the SS doctors and SS orderlies made selections among the sick. In the camp hospital they were helped by block leaders and work squad leaders. Such selections were not based on the results of medical examination, rather were they influenced by the whim of those who performed them.

In case of a patient's demise the doctors wrote the death certificate. When reporting the death of a prisoner the name of the fatal disease was fictitious, while in the case of prisoners who were shot or killed during work hours a fictitious case history would be appended.

The cause of death could be only one of the diseases figuring in a list concocted by the SS doctors. Heart failure, pneumonia, myocarditis, enteritis, were the most frequent. But prisoners also perished during work hours, killed by the SS supervisors. The prisoners committed to penal companies worked in particularly unfavourable conditions and over ten, sometimes even scores of them would be killed by the SS each day.

The SS pursued their criminal activities also when a fresh transport was arriving. SS-men (officers of various sections) were on duty at the railway ramp according to a fixed schedule. Many of them took part in the selections described in the foregoing pages. Selections were conducted not only by the SS doctors and SS orderlies but also by SS-men from the Camp Administration (Section III), from the Camp Management (Section IV) Employment (IIIa) and the Political Section (II).[33] The fact that work squad leader Emmerich was wounded and *Rapportführer* Schillinger was shot by a Jewish woman while leading a transport to the gas chamber proves that not only doctors had taken part in the process of extermination. The above mentioned SS-men belonged to other sections in the camp, nevertheless had taken part in the extermination.

---

[33] Vide footnote [25])

The extraction of gold teeth of the corpses was done by the SS dentists. Section IV took over the looted property of the victims and forwarded it to the Bank of the *Reich* or to SS posts. According to Höss, the quantities of loot were stupendous: [34])

"Although new huts and sheds were constantly being added... and although the number of persons employed was constantly stepped up and several trucks (often as many as twenty) were loaded daily, the piles of unsorted luggage went on mounting... Thirty newly-built huts were crammed to capacity inmediately after completion, while mountains of unsorted effects piled up between them. In spite of the augmented labour gangs, it was out of the question to complete the job..."

When the Soviet Army was approaching the Nazis hurriedly emptied the storehouses with the seized property of the murdered persons. The only objects to be left there were those which in the opinion of the SS were of no value. A few days before the liberation of the camp the remainder of the retreating SS troups set fire to all magazines. In the six barracks which were not burnt down the following items, among other things, were found:

348,820 suits of men's clothes
836,525 women's dresses
5,255 pairs of women's shoes
38,000 pairs of mens's shoes

together with thousands of tooth-brushes, shaving-brushes, artificial limbs, spectacles, etc.

The hair shorn from the heads of the victims was dried in the garrets of the crematoria, then packed into bags and sent to factories in the *Reich*. After the liberation of the camp a remainder of human hair was found, packed in suitably labelled bags (*KL-Au*) and weighing 7,000 kilogrammes. Among the preserved camp documents we find a letter of the SS Economic Administration Head Office of January 4,1943, requesting the commandants of concentration camps to forward human hair for further processing to the firm *Alex Zink, Filzfabrik A.G. Roth b/Nürnberg*, at the price of 0,50 mark for 1 kilogramme.

---

[34]) Vide footnote [25]), pp. 219—220

This is an illustration of the fact that all sections of the camp administration had taken a direct part in the process of extermination.

It is difficult to determine the number of victims killed at Auschwitz mainly because the Nazis, when retreating before the advancing Soviet Army, had attempted to obliterate all traces of their crimes. Not only were the gas chambers and crematoria blasted and the storehouses with some of the looted property were burnt down, but also all kinds of documents, files, letters, reports, registers, etc. were burnt and destroyed. The prisoners' personal documents were destroyed on their arrival at the camp.

These facts make it difficult to determine today the exact number of the killed. The autopsy performed in the period from May 10, 1945 to September 26, 1946, by the members of the High Commission for Investigating Nazi Crimes in Poland, Judge Jan Sehn and Assistant Prosecutor Edward Pęchalski, assisted by the sworn court expert, Prof. Ing. Roman Dawidowski, has given the following data: [35])

"On the basis of the average efficiency of the crematoria, arrived at by means of technical computations and confirmed by depositions of witnesses, taking into consideration the number of days when the crematoria and auxiliary installations (pits) were active, further allowing for periods of inactivity during discontinuation of cremating and during necessary repairs, the expert is of the opinion that the number of persons gassed and cremated in the extermination installations of the concentration camp Auschwitz-Birkenau amounted to, roughly, no less than 4 million persons. This total corresponds to the depositions of all witnesses testifying before the District Commission for Investigating Nazi Crimes in Cracow, the witnesses being able, owing to their functions in camp, to estimate the quantities of transports which had come directly to the crematoria without entering the camp, particularly the so-called *Reich* Security Head Office transports (*RSHA* transports)."

---

[35]) Trial of Höss, vol. 11, card 52.

For an estimate of the number of persons killed in Auschwitz the list [36]) of shipments of Cyclon B sent to Auschwitz by the firm *Degesch* is very helpful. It shows that 7,478.6 kilogrammes of Cyclon B were sent to Auschwitz in 1942, as much as 12,174.09 kilogrammes in 1943, that is all together 19,652.69 kilogrammes in 2 years only. This amount should be kept in mind reading the statement of Höss; [37]) that 6 to 7 kilogrammes of Cyclon B were needed to kill approximately 1,500 persons. The SS-men had shown exceptional cruelty during the process of extermination. Entries in the diary of the SS physician Dr Kremer [38]) testify to the magnitude and intensity of their cruelty, e.g.:

"2.9. At 3 o'clock was for the first time present at a "special operation". Compared with it Dante's Inferno seems almost a comedy. No wonder Auschwitz is called an extermination camp..."

"5.9. At noon was present at "special operation" having to do with "moslems" from the women's camp. Most horrible of all horrors. *SS-Hauptsturmführer* Dr Thilo was right when he said today that we were here in the world's anus (anus mundi). At about 8 in the evening attended another special operation with a draft from Holland. The extra issue of 1/5 litre of vodka, 5 cigarettes, 100 grammes of sausage and bread induces SS-men to compete for participating in such actions..."

"12.10. At night attended a "special operation" of 1,600 persons from Holland. Appaling scenes at the last bunker (Hoessler). This was the tenth special operation."

All documents concerning the extermination bear the words: "Secret", "*Reich's* Secret", and in many cases various cryptonyms are used, as mentioned above (*SB*, etc.). These crimes were committed in an underhand manner, as we clearly see from some passages in the Autobiography of Höss: [39])

"In the spring of 1942 the first transports of Jews, all earmarked for extermination, arrived from Upper Silesia. They were taken

---

[36]) Nuremberg document NI — 11937.
[37]) Trial of Gerhard Maurer, vol. 6, card 36.
[38]) Archive of Państwowe Muzeum w Oświęcimiu. The entries are from the year 1942.
[39]) Reminiscences of Rudolf Hoess (Polish edition — Warsaw 1960), fragments selected from pp. 147—149.

from the detraining platform to the "Cottage" — to Bunker I — across the meadows where later Building Site II was located. The transport was conducted by Aumeier and Palitzsch and some of the block leaders. They talked with the Jews about general topics, enquiring concerning their qualifications and trades, with a view to misleading them.

On arrival at the "Cottage", they were told to undress. At first they went calmly into the rooms, where they were supposed to be disinfected. But some of them showed signs of alarm and spoke of death by suffocation... A sort of panic set in... Immediately all the Jews still outside were pushed into the chambers and the doors were screwed shut.

With subsequent transports the difficult individuals were picked out at once and most carefully supervised. At the first signs of unrest, those responsible were inobtrusively led behind the building and killed with a small-calibre gun, which was inaudible to others."

"The smaller children... entered the gas chambers, playing or joking with one another and carrying their toys. I noticed that women who either guessed or knew what awaited them nevertheless found courage to joke with the children, to encourage them, despite the mortal terror visible in their own eyes... One old man, as he passed by me, hissed: "Germany will pay a heavy penance for this mass murder of the Jews."... From time to time women would suddenly give the most terrible shrieks while undressing or tear their hair or scream like maniacs. They were immediately led behind the building and shot in the back of the neck with a small calibre weapon."

The SS attempted to obliterate the traces of their crimes and their magnitude by burning the bodies of the victims, scattering human ashes over adjoining fields or throwing the ashes into ponds and rivers, the Vistula and the Soła, further, by destroying personal documents of the victims. The utter and limitless arbitrariness of the camp authorities threatened the lives of all prisoners at all times during their stay in the camp. In spite of these most difficult and dangerous conditions of the life in the camp there existed in all camps a form of self-help among prisoners which consisted in sharing one's scanty bread ration with others and also in mutually bearing up against hardships. Such was the case in the initial stages of life in every camp.

It is understandable (the camp being located on Polish soil and its inmates being mainly Poles at first) that contacts with the civilian population were established at quite an early date..Thanks to them considerable quantities of food and medical remedies, even more needed than food, were smuggled into the camp. Such steps led to the saving of the lives of numerous prisoners and so hindered, partly a t l e a s t, the Nazis from their attaining their designs. But everybody knows that the prisoners themselves could n o t s t o p this machinery of extermination, they could only i m p a i r i t. The Camp Resistance Movement was also busy collecting documents concerning Nazi crimes. Such documents were sent outside the camp or handed to escapees who again transmitted them to the centres of Resistance Movements existing within the country or abroad. It is hardly possible to enumerate all these documents, but mention should be made of a thorough report on gassing which had reached the Allies as early as 1942. Of great importance was also the so-called list of Auschwitz executioners, transmitted while the war was still in progress, making public the names of well-known war criminals. Many of them are now in the docks of the court in Frankfort.

The third important task of the Resistance Movement was to prepare the prisoners for armed action in the case of a possible attempt at liquidating the camp. The plan of such an attempt, called Moll's plan from the name of its author (supervisor of the gas chambers), foresaw the bombing of the camp area by German aircraft, painted over and bearing the signs of Allied airplanes. After the bombing the area of the camp was to have been subjected to artillery fire. Special detachments of the *SS* were to liquidate the remainder of the prisoners. The camp inmates got informed about this plan and the Resistance Movement conveyed the information to its centre in the country. When the Allies made the plan public, the garrison was dumbfounded. This, together with the inevitably approaching downfall, was the reason why the plan was abandoned.

The whole of the presented materials makes a completely objective and decisive statement possible, namely that all *SS*-men, members of the armed concentration camp garrison, had committed crimes, acting with full consciousness and deliberation. The materials further show that they acted jointly and that each member of that criminal group had actively participated in the mass murders. The final conclusion, to which a survey of the presented materials leads, is that the crime of extermination and its course were planned beforehand by the Nazis, with a great deal of help from various firms and concerns.

DANUTA CZECH, M.A.

THE AUSCHWITZ SUB-CAMPS.

While the *Reichsführer SS* Himmler was visiting *KL* Auschwitz, March 1. 1941, it was decided upon to extend the camp further so that it would accommodate 30,000 prisoners and would supply the *IG-Farbenindustrie* concern with 10,000 prisoners in order to build industrial plants in the village Dwory near Oświęcim. Further big armaments works were to be established in the vicinity of the camp.

As a result of this decision the commandant of *KL* Auschwitz R. Höss supervised a systematic extension of the camp. In the villages, the inhabitants of which had been deported, agricultural estates were established in the interest zone of the camp (*Interessengebiet*) and prisoners were used as workers on them.

Since the industry of the Third *Reich* was in increasing need of having slave labour at its disposal the management of *KL* Auschwitz began selling the camp inmates as workers to the various *SS* cartels, state enterprises and private concerns.[1]

According to commandant Höss's explanations "so-called sub-camps had been built for such prisoners, at some distance from the centre of the camp. They were denominated in German: *Arbeitslager* (Work Camp). *Nebenlager* (Sub-Camp), *Aussenlager* (External Camp), *Zweiglager* (Branch Camp), *Arbeitskommando* (Work Squad), *Aussenkommando* (External Work Squad). These names do not indicate that the organisational structure of a given sub-camp differed from that of the camp proper. All names meant the same thing and were used simultaneously."[2]

The sub-camps would be established in various places, both in the vicinity of *KL* Auschwitz and in places several scores or even several hundreds of kilometres distant from Auschwitz (e.g. the sub-camps in Czechoslovakia: Brünn, Freudenthal, Lichtewerden). The majority of them was located near industrial works — foundries, coal mines, refining works, power stations, armaments factories, chemical plants, etc. or on the lands belonging to *KL* Auschwitz. Some sub-camps were connected with the experimenting stations, such as the plant-growing station (*Pflanzenzuchtstation*) at Rajsko and the fowl farm (*Geflügelzucht*) at Harmęże.

The sub-camps did not possess the rights and privileges of the base concentration camps since they were component parts of them. Only those of them which possessed the Political Section (*Politische Abteilung*) with a *Reich* Security Head Office functionary at its head could enjoy the full rights of a concentration camp. Such camps could also accept prisoners (*Anweisungslager*), sent to them by the *Reich* Security Head Office and its posts,

---

[1] In the case of any enterprise or firm making use of the man-power of the prisoners placed in a sub-camp, the *SS* still retained their ownership of the slave workers and the prisoners' names remained in the registers of the base camp.
[2] Trial of Höss, vol. 21, card 36.

they could release camp prisoners on the basis of a *Reich* Security Head Office decision or transfer them to other camps.

According to the statement of R. Höss, towards the end of the year 1944 thirteen camps existed in Nazi Germany to which circa 900 sub-camps were joined. The main or base concentration camps supplied the sub-camps with inmates who, though living in the sub-camps, were registered in the files of the base camp. Each base camp was to serve a certain region in its vicinity. *KL* Auschwitz had the region of Silesia and of the Sudeten in Czechoslovakia as its sphere of influence.

The regulations of the concentration camp were valid in all the sub-camps.[3]) A camp manager, an N.C.O. mostly, stood at the head of a sub-camp, while the managers of the base camp always had to be officers. The *SS* constituted the garrison of the sub-camps, in some cases however, soldiers of the German army did the guard duty. The soldiers belonged to those units of the army for which the factory employing prisoners was working. Sometimes factory guards, called *Werkschutz*, had the guard duties. This was caused by a scarcity of the *SS* guard formations.

Capos, recruited mostly from among German criminal offenders, supervised the prisoners at work, but the supervision of the industrial process was mostly in the hands of specialists, that is civilian foremen, etc.

The food varied in the sub-camps, depending on the importance of the production of a given factory in which the prisoners were employed.

The industrial works of the Third *Reich* were divided into 3 categories:
  I those important for life in general (*Lebenswichtige Betriebe*).
  II those important for maintaining the war (*Kriegswichtige Betriebe*).
  III those important for gaining the victory (*Siegesentscheidende Betriebe*).

---

[3]) Prisoners located in sub-camps were not made familiar with the regulations, neither were those in the base camp.

The prisoners who worked in enterprises belonging to the first category got basically the same food as those working in enterprises of the second and third category, but the prisoners in the works of the second category received additional rations for hard workers (*Schwerarbeiter Zulage*), while those working in plants of the third category had additional rations for those who worked hardest (*Schwerstarbeiter Zulage*).

Prisoners employed by private concerns (e.g. *IG-Farbenindustrie*) were fed by the concerns in question.

The daily food rations in the sub-camps did not greatly difffer from the starvation rations in the base camp.

The final objective of *KL* Auschwitz and its sub-camps had been the indirect and direct extermination of the prisoners committed to the camps. The whole of the conditions of life and of the camp regime were to serve that objective. Before losing his life a prisoner had to be exploited to the utmost by the Nazi state. The basic form of exploting the prisoners was to use them as slaves who had to be worked to death. Those unfit for further work and utterly exhausted were sent back to the base camp after a so-called selection and killed there.

The commandant's office at *KL* Auschwitz sold the prisoners' man-power to various concerns and enterprises of the Third *Reich*, but particularly to firms doing armament work connected with the war. They got 4 mark daily wages for a skilled worker and 3 mark for an unskilled labourer's work.

The following concerns and enterprises made use of the manpower of prisoners from *KL* Auschwitz: *IG-Farbenindustrie, Berghütte (Berg- und Hüttenwerksgesellschaft), Vereinigte Oberschlesische Hüttenwerke A. G., Hermann Göringwerke, Siemens — Schuckert Werke A.G., Energie-Versorgung- Oberschlesien A.G. (EVO), Oberschlesische Hydrierwerke, Oberschlesische Gerätebau G.m.b.H., Deutsche Gas -und Russgesellchaft, Deutsche Reichsbahn, Heeresbauverwaltung, Schlesische Feinweberei, Union-Werke, Golleschauer Portland-Zement A.G.* and others.

The *SS* reaped considerable profits by trading the slave manpower of the prisoners, with the assistance of the commandant's office of *KL* Auschwitz. Among the few preserved camp documents found after the liberation of *KL* Auschwitz we find proof that the bills demanding payment for 7 months' work of men prisoners and 3 months' work of women prisoners, employed by various enterprises, amounted to a total of 12,753,526 mark.

The profits of the enterprises naturally must have been much higher. Exploiting the prisoners to the utmost such concerns as: *IG-Farbenindustrie, Berghütte A.G., Hermann Göringwerke* and others got rich.

As far as the administration was concerned the Auschwitz sub-camps were dependent on the base camp. All the then existing sub-camps had been, up to Nov. 22, 1943,[4]) that is to the division of *KL* Auschwitz, subordinated to the commandant's office of the base camp. After the division of *KL* Auschwitz into three camps, i.e. *KL* Auschwitz I, *KL* Auschwitz II and *KL* Auschwitz III, the sub-camps connected with lands and experimenting stations were subordinated to the commandant's office of *KL* Auschwitz II (Birkenau), while the sub-camps established to serve the enterprises and concerns were subordinated to the commandant's office of *KL* Auschwitz III (Monowitz). After a further reorganization which had taken place on Nov. 25, 1944,[5]) following a partial evacuation of the prisoners to concentration camps within the *Reich*, the sub-camps connected with farming belonged to *KL* Auschwitz but the remaining ones were subordinated to the commandant's office of *KL* Monowitz (formerly *KL* Auschwitz III).

In the course of the years 1942—1944 the commandant's office of *KL* Auschwitz had organized 39 sub-camps.

31 sub-camps were established for prisoners who were forced to work for concerns and enterprises. The following sub-camps were among them:

1. *"Althammer"* at Stara Kuźnia near Halemba (District Katowice). Established in the middle of 1944 and liquidated in January 1945. Circa 500 Auschwitz prisoners, mainly Jews, were located

---

[4]) Vide p. 205.
[5]) Vide p. 214.

in it. They were employed building a power station. The firm Godula was supervising the work.

2. *"Bismarckhütte"* at Chorzów-Batory (District Katowice). Established in the second half of 1944 and liquidated in January 1945. 200 Auschwitz prisoners were located in it, mainly Jews. They were employed in the mechanical section, producing parts of cannons and armoured cars. They also did unskilled work like unloading. transportation, digging, etc. *"Bismarckhütte"*, which went under the name of *"Huta Batory"* before the outbreak of World War II, was in 1942 incorporated with the *"Königs- und Bismarckhütte A.G."* and belonged to the concern *"Berghütte"*.

3. *"Blechhammer"* at Sławięcice near Blachownia Śląska (District Opole), for men and women. Was established on April 1, 1944, by incorporating a Jewish forced labour camp — called *Judenlager* — at Sławięcice to the commandant's office of KL Auschwitz III. On the day of taking over the strength of the camp amounted to 3,056 men prisoners and circa 200 women prisoners. Later on the strength of the camp, both men and women, exceeded 4,000. The prisoners were employed building chemical plants belonging to the firm *Oberschlesische Hydrierwerke*. The women worked inside the camp in the *SS* and prisoners' kitchens and laundries. The camp was liquidated on January 21, 1945 by evacuating the prisoners on foot to KL Gross-Rosen where they arrived on February 2. Only few of them had, however, reached their destination. The sick and weak prisoners were shot by the SS during the march.

4. *"Bobrek"* near Oświęcim (District Cracow) was destined for men and women. It was established in the first half of 1944 on the terrain of a factory taken over by the firm *Siemens-Schuckertwerke A.G.* Circa 200 men prisoners and 50 women prisoners from Auschwitz were located there. Both men and women were employed producing various parts of electrical apparatuses for airplanes, rockets, etc. The factory formed part of the *Siemens* concern. The prisoners vere evacuated in January 1945 to a sub-camp at Gliwice and hence to KL Gross-Rosen.

5. *"Brünn"* in the city of Brno in Czechoslovakia was established on October 1, 1943, 250 Auschwitz prisoners were located there. They were employed building and fitting out the Technological Academy of the *SS* and Police.

On December 1, 1943 100 prisoners were transferred to the sub-camp *"Jawischowitz"*, and on May 1, 1944, 118 prisoners were transferred to the sub-camp *"Monowitz"*. Several scores of skilled workers-prisoners, such as locksmiths, electricians, radio-technicians, were left in the *"Brünn"* sub-camp and they were evacuated to *KL* Bergen-Belsen in January 1945.

6. *"Charlottengrube"* at Rydułtowy (District Katowice) was established in September 1944 and liquidated in January 1945. It contained circa 900 Auschwitz prisoners, Jews from various European countries. They were employed mining coal and extending the mine *"Charlottengrube"* (at present the mine Rydułtowy) which then belonged to the concern *Hermann Göringwerke*.

7. *"Chełmek"* at Chełmek-Paprotnik (District Cracow) was known as *"Aussenkommando Chełmek"*. It was established in October 1942 and liquidated in December 1942. Circa 150 Auschwitz prisoners, mainly Jews were its inmates. They worked in the stone quarry and also cleaned and dredged the ponds which formed water reservoirs for the *"Bata"* shoe factory.

8. *"Eintrachthütte"* at Świętochłowice (District Katowice) was established on June 7, 1943 and liquidated in January 1945. 500 Auschwitz prisoners, Poles, Russians and Jews, were located there. In 1944 the strength of the sub-camp never amounted to less than circa 1,300 prisoners. They worked in the *"Eintrachthütte"* (at present *Huta Zgoda*), producing parts of anti aircraft guns and fitting them. *"Eintrachthütte"* belonged to the company *"Ost-Maschinenbau G. m. b. H."*, formed by the *"Oberschlesische Maschinen u. Waggonenfabrik A. G."* (*OSMAG*) and the concern *"Berghütte"*.

9. *"Freudenthal"* in Bruntal, Czechoslovakia, was established in 1944, 301 Auschwitz women prisoners were located there. They were employed in the factory of Emmerich Machold which belonged to armament works (*"Rüstungsbetriebe"*).

According to the statement of Höss the prisoners of that sub-camp were employed building the manufactory of vitaminized drinks to be supplied to the troops stationed in Norway. The manufactory was supposed to be managed by the *SS* on their own account.[6])

10. *"Fürstengrube"* at Ławki (District Katowice), established in September 1943, was liquidated in January 1945. It contained circa 1,300 Auschwitz prisoners, mainly Jews. They were employed in the coal mine extracting coal and building a new mine. *"Fürstengrube"* (at present the mines Wesoła and Lenin) belonged to the *IG-Farbenindustrie* (51 % of shares) and to *Fürstlich Plessische Bergwerke A.G.* (49 % of shares). The extracted coal was supplied to the works *"Buna Werke"* (*IG-Farbenindustrie*), at Dwory near Oświęcim, where it was processed into synthetic petrol. In January 1945 the prisoners were evacuated on foot, while circa 250 prisoners, sick and unable to march, were left in the sub-camp. On January 27 an SS detachment set fire to the barracks housing the sick prisoners and those of them who tried to crawl out of the burning barracks were shot. Only about 24 prisoners had managed to survive the massacre.

11. *"Gleiwitz I"* in Gliwice (District Katowice), established in the first half of 1944, contained circa 1,300 Auschwitz prisoners. They were employed repairing the railway stock in the *Reichsbahnausbesserungswerkstätten*, workshops belonging to the *Deutsche Reichsbahn*. In the time from January 18 to January 20, 1945 the sub-camp *"Gleiwitz I"* was filled with Auschwitz prisoners who were evacuated from the sub-camps situated east of Gliwice. The evacuation of the sub-camp *"Gleiwitz I"* was begun on January 21, 1945. Transports of prisoners were directed to the concentration camps Buchenwald, Gross Rosen and Sachsenhausen.

12. *"Gleiwitz II"* in Gliwice was established in the first half of 1944. Circa 800 men prisoners and circa 400 women prisoners, mainly Jews, were its inmates. All were employed in the gas soot works where synthetic rubber was produced. The factory belonged

---

[6]) Trial of R. Höss, vol. 21, card 41.

to *"Deutsche Gas- und Russgesellschaft"*. Transports of prisoners evacuated on foot from the Auschwitz sub-camps were arriving at the sub-camp *"Gleiwitz II"* from January 18 to January 20, 1945. The sub-camp was liquidated on January 21, 1945. The prisoners were taken in open freight vans to the concentration camps Buchenwald and Mauthausen.

13. *"Gleiwitz III"* in Gliwice, established in the second half of 1944 on the terrain of the so-called *"Alte Hütte"*, was liquidated in January 1945. Its inmates were circa 500 Auschwitz prisoners. They were initially employed outside the foundry, at earth works and sewage, then they put into activity the *Zieleniewski* Factory which had been evacuated from Cracow to *Alte Hütte*.

14. *"Gleiwitz IV"* in Gliwice was established in the first half of 1944. It was liquidated in January 1945. Its inmates were circa 600 Auschwitz prisoners who were employed at the building and extension of army barracks, under the auspices of the Building Section of the Land Army (*Heeresbauverwaltung*).

15. *"Golleschau"* at Goleszów (District Katowice), established in the middle of the year 1942, was liquidated on January 21, 1945. It was located in one of the factory buildings on the terrain of the cement works bearing the name *"Golleschauer Portland-Zement Aktiengesellschaft Oberschlesien"*. The cement works was one of the SS enterprises. The sub-camp contained Auschwitz prisoners, mainly Jews. They were employed in the cement works and in the adjoining quarries. The number of the prisoners amounted to 1,059 in October 1944. As a result of the hard work, bad living and hygienic conditions epidemics used to break out, particularly typus epidemics. The state of the prisoners' health was disastrous. Seriously sick prisoners were sent to *KL* Auschwitz II where they died in the camp hospital or were taken to the gas chambers after a selection.

16. *"Günthergrube"* at Lędziny (District Katowice) was established February 1. 1944 and liquidated January 19, 1945. It contained circa 600 Auschwitz prisoners, mainly Jews, who were employed building *"Günthergrube"* and mining coal from the mine *Piast*.

The coal was sent to *"Buna-Werke"* at Dwory near Oświęcim to be processed into synthetic petrol. *"Günthergrube"* (at present mine *Ziemowit*) belonged to *"Fürstlich Plessische Bergwerke A.G."*

17. *"Hindenburg"* at Zabrze (District Katowice) was established in August 1944 on the terrain of *"Donnersmarckhütte"* and was liquidated in January 1945. Circa 400 women prisoners from Auschwitz, mainly Jewish, were its inmates. In the autumn of 1944 several scores of Jews were brought to this sub-camp, coming from Auschwitz, too. The women were employed in the foundries II, III and IV, producing parts of machinery, munitions, forming shells, parts of armaments for the *Luftwaffe*. They also worked in the mechanical section tending drills, lathes, milling machines, etc. The men worked in the coking plant and in the mine *"Concordia"*. Besides their food rations the women prisoners got 2 cigarettes and a cake of soap per week. *"Donnersmarckhütte"* belonged to the concern *"Vereinigte Oberschlesische Hüttenwerke" A.G. (Oberhütten)*. On January 19, 1945 the women prisoners were taken to the sub-camp "Gleiwitz II" and thence evacuated to *KL* Gross-Rosen, later to *KL* Nordhausen and finally to *KL* Bergen-Belsen.

18. *"Hubertushütte"*, also called *"Hohenlinde"* at Łagiewniki Śląskie (District Katowice) was established in the second half of 1944 and liquidated in January 1945. Circa 200 Auschwitz prisoners, chiefly Jews, were committed to this sub-camp. They were employed in the *"Hubertushütte"* (at present *Huta Zygmunt*) which belonged to the company *"Königs- und Bismarckhütte" A.G.* at Chorzów.

19. *"Janinagrube"*, later called *"Gute Hoffnung"*, at Libiąż Mały near Chrzanów (District Cracow) was established September 4, 1943 and liquidated January 18, 1945. This sub-camp was established in a former camp for British prisoners of war, designated by No. 562. The British prisoners of war, all together about 150 men, were transferred to a camp for prisoners of war VII B at Lamsdorf (Łambinowice) and their place was taken by circa 300 Auschwitz prisoners, chiefly Jews. After an extension of the sub-camp circa 900 prisoners were located there. They were employed

in *"Janinagrube"* which was under the receivership of *"Fürstengrube"*. *IG-Farbenindustrie* wanted to buy *"Janinagrube"*.

20. *"Jawischowitz"* near Oświęcim (District Cracow) was established August 15, 1942 and liquidated January 19, 1945. This sub-camp was built at the expense of the coal mine at Brzeszcze and Jawiszowice. On August 15, 1942 circa 150 prisoners were located there, on October 24, 1942 the number of prisoners amounted to 622. It rose to about 1,500 on October 19, 1944 and reached its highest point in July 1944, i. e. circa 2,500 prisoners. They were employed extending the mine, extracting coal, building a power station and working in the transportation department. The mines Brzeszcze and Jawiszowice had an official name *"Kohlengruben Brzeszcze"*. They belonged to the concern *Hermann Göringwerke* and were directly subordinated to the Upper Silesian management of the concern (*Hauptverwaltung — Bergwerksverwaltung Oberschlesien G.m.b.H. der Reichswerke "Hermann Göring"*). On January 19, 1945 the prisoners were evacuated marching on foot to Wodzisław Śląski, together with the prisoners from *KL* Auschwitz. Then they were taken by rail to *KL* Buchenwald and *KL* Mauthausen.

21. *"Lagischa"* at Łagisza (District Katowice) was established June 15, 1943 and liquidated September 6, 1944. The inmates of this sub-camp were Auschwitz prisoners, mainly Jews, Poles and Russians. They were employed building the power station *"Walter"* at Łagisza.

The building was financed by the industrial association *"Energie Versorgung Oberschlesien"* (*EVO*) [7]. There were 477 prisoners in the subcamp on January 20, 1944, while in February 22, 1944 their number had already risen to 499. The sub-camp *"Lagischa"* was liquidated because work at building the power station had been stopped. The inmates were transferred to other camps and the *SS* garrison was sent to the recently established sub-camp *"Neustadt"*.

---

[7] *Energie Versorgung Oberschlesien* was established by the General Inspector of the *Reich* for Water and Energy (*Generalinspektor für Wasser und Energie*) Albert Speer. Its shares were in the possession of the Third *Reich*.

22. *"Laurahütte"* at Siemianowice (District Katowice) was established in April 1944 and liquidated in January 1945. About 1,000 Auschwitz prisoners stayed in it. They were mostly Jews, together with a smallish group of Poles. They worked in *"Laurahütte"* producing parts of anti-aircraft guns and fitting them. *"Laurahütte"* belonged to the company *"Oberschlesische Gerätebau"* G.m.b.H. The technical staff, supervising the production of *"Laurahütte"* came from the concern *Rheinmetall Borsig A.G.*

23. *"Lichtewerden"* at Svetla near Bruntal in Czechoslovakia was taken over by the commandant's office of *KL* Auschwitz III in November 1944. On November 11, 1944 300 women prisoners from Auschwitz, Jewesses, were committed to this sub-camp. The women worked in the textile factory which went under the name of *G.A. Buhl — Flachsspinnerei*. The women were employed in the cotton mill. The factory belonged to the so-called *"Rüstungsbetriebe"*, which meant that its production was to serve the needs of the army. The women prisoners worked there for 11 hours daily and were brought to the factory and taken from it at a run. Starvation was rampant in the sub-camp. The daily food ration consisted of soup made of mangel-wurzels. Soldiers of the Soviet Army entered the camp on May 6. 1945 and liberated the women prisoners.

24 *"Monowitz"* at Monowice near Oświęcim (District Cracow) was established on October 1942, It was at first called *"Nebenlager Buna"* and since December 1, 1943 — *"Arbeitslager Monowitz"*. It was destined for the Auschwitz prisoners who had been employed by the concern *IG-Farbenindustrie* as early as April 1941 to build chemical plants (producing synthetic petrol and synthetic rubber) *"Buna-Werke"* at Dwory near Oświęcim. Up to March 1942 the prisoners were daily brought to work from *KL* Auschwitz on foot, a distance of 7 kilometres. Then they were brought by train. In October 1942 they became inmates of the sub-camp at Monowice, near the *Buna-Werke*. The sub-camp consisted of over ten barracks which had also been built by the prisoners. In 1944 there already were 60 barracks and army tents in the sub-camp. In October 1942 circa 1,000 prisoners were sent to the sub-camp. In April 1943 the strength of the sub-camp amounted to 3,301

prisoners, in January 1944 — 6, 571 prisoners, in August 1944—10,000 prisoners and 95% of them were Jews. Due to very hard work and bad living and hygienic conditions the prisoners were decimated by diseases and the death rate in the sub-camp was very high. The sick and those unable to work were selected and sent to *KL* Auschwitz II (Birkenau) where they died in the camp hospital or were killed in gas chambers. And so for instance, on October 17, 1944, 2,000 prisoners selected in the sub-camp *"Monowitz"* (*Buna*)[8]) were killed in the gas chamber of crematorium II. In November 1943 a commandant's office *KL* Auschwitz III was established in the sub-camp. It was renamed *KL* Monowitz in November 1944. On January 18, 1945 the sub-camp was evacuated and over 9,000 prisoners were driven on foot to the sub-camps in Gleiwitz. Thence they were taken by train to concentration camps in the interior of the Third *Reich*. About 850 sick prisoners, unable to walk, remained in the sub-camp. On January 27, 1945 there were 650 prisoners, still alive, left unguarded by the SS in the sub-camp. They were liberated by the Soviet Army, just then entering Oświęcim.

25. *"Neu Dachs"* at Jaworzno (District Cracow) originated owing to the initiative of the industrial association *"Energie Versorgung Oberschlesien"*, whose task it was to expand the Silesian power stations so that the produced current should supply the armament works established near Vienna. Members of that association were: the power stations at Będzin, Jaworzno and Łagisza, further the coal mines at Jaworzno, armament works at Sosnowiec and Świętochłowice, which belonged to the concern *"Berghütte"*, In 1943 they started building a thermo-electricity station *"Kraftwerk Wilhelm"* at Jaworzno, possessing the power of 300 thousand kilowatts and they expanded the power station connected with the *"Friedrich-Augustgrube"* (at present *Bolesław Bierut* Mine). The source of power for the power stations in process of building was the coal from the Jaworzno mines and therefore the output of the latter had to be stepped up considerably. This was the

---

[8]) Vide photostat of the notebook of one member of the *Sonderkommando* (squad working in the crematorium).

objective of establishing, on June 15. 1943, the sub-camp at Jaworzno, known as *"Arbeitslage Neu Dachs"*.[9] 100 prisoners were located in it and they were employed building and enlarging the camp. In August 1943 there already were 1,600 prisoners in the sub-camp, in January 1944 their number amounted to 2,00, while a year later, that is in January 1945, it rose to over 3,600. The prisoners were employed building the power station *"Wilhelm"* and extractiong coal from the coal mines *"Dachsgrube"* (*"Komuna Paryska"*), *"Rudolfgrube"* (*"Tadeusz Kościuszko"*) *"Friedrich-Augustgrube"* (*"Bolesław Bierut"*). They also built the mine shafts *"Richard"* and *"Leopold"* and laid railway tracks. Prisoners constituted about 60% of the mining crews. They worked in three shifts, in very hard conditions, often immersed in water and without any protective clothing. As a result of insufficient food, lack of any clothing and work surpassing their possibilities, they fell ill and the death rate was high. In summer there occurred 10 deaths a day, in winter as many as 30. The less seriously sick were admitted to the hospital barrack in the sub-camp. Those who were seriously ill and unfit for work were taken to KL Auschwitz II (Birkenau), where they died in the camp hospital or were killed in the gas chamber. And so, for instance, 256 prisoners were selected in *"Neu Dachs"* on January 18, 1844, 4 prisoners had died up to February 3, 1944, 3 had been crossed out of the list and the rest — 247 Jewish prisoners perished in the gas chamber of KL Auschwitz II.[10] The prisoners were evacuated marching on foot on January 17, 1945. They went to the sub-camp *"Blechhammer"* and thence, after a few hours' rest, to KL Gross-Rosen. Several hundreds of them perished on the way, shot by SS-men.

Several hundreds of sick prisoners were left in the sub-camp *"Neu Dachs"*. The detachments of the Soviet Army who had entered Jaworzno on January 19, 1945 liberated the prisoners in the sub-camp.

---

[9] It was also called *Aussenlager Jaworzno, Arbeitslager EVO Jaworzno, SS-Lager Dachsgrube, Zweiglager Neu Dachs.*
[10] The list of names of the persons selected on Jan. 18, 1944 bears the cryptonym *SB* (*Sonderbehandlung*) meaning death by gassing. A cross was put at each prisoner's name.

26. *"Neustadt"* at Prudnik (District Opole) was established in September 1944 and liquidated in January 1945. About 400 Auschwitz women prisoners, Jewesses, were put into it. The sub-camp was located on the terrain of the textile factory *"Schlesische Feinweberei"*. The women worked in the weaving-mill. The work hours amounted to 12 hours a day. *"Schlesische Feinweberei"* belonged to the *"Rüstungsbetriebe"*. In January 1945 the women prisoners were evacuated on foot to KL Gross-Rosen and later to KL Bergen-Belsen.

27. *"Sosnowitz"* at Sosnowiec (District Katowice) was established in September 1943 and liquidated in January 1945. It was located near the former "Rolling Mill Count Renard" (at present Huta of E. Cedler) which was taken over during the war by *"Oberschlesische Maschinen u. Waggonenfabrik A.G."* (*OSMAG*).[11]

In 1942 the concern *"Berghütte"* and *OSMAG* established a new limited liability company under the name *"Ost- Maschinenbau G.m.b.H."* which took over from *OSMAG Neuwerk Sosnowitz*, that is the former Rolling Mill *"Count Renard"*, adapted to be a munitions factory. The new sub-camp, called *"Arbeitslager Sosnowitz"*, was established through the care of *Ost-Maschinenbau G.m.b.H.* Circa 900 Auschwitz prisoners, chiefly Jews, were located in it. They were employed producing gun barrels for anti-aircraft guns and shells. The prisoners worked in the pressing department, treating the barrels. They were employed as turners, locksmiths, welders or their help. They had to transport the raw materials or ready elements. to work in the concrete mixing plant, servicing the machines, etc. The prisoners were evacuated on foot on January 17, 1945 by way of Gliwice, Racibórz to Opawa. The march lasted 12 days. Many of them perished during the march shot by *SS* men. The few survivors were transported from Opawa to *KL* Mauthausen by train.

28. *"Sosnowitz* II*"* at Sosnowiec was established in the autumn of 1943 after the liquidation of the Jewish ghetto.[12] Circa 100 Auschwitz prisoners were housed in the rabbinate building, 12,

---

[11] *OSMAG* was the *"Tochtergesellschaft"* (Affiliated company) of the concern *"Berghütte"*
[12] The ghetto at Sosnowiec was liquidated in the time from August 1 to August 6, 1943 Thousands of Jews were taken to *KL* Auschwitz to be gassed in gas chambers.

Targowa Street, in which the Jewish Communities' Central Office was located. The prisoners were by profession stove fitters, bricklayers, joiners, glaziers, painters, etc. and they were employed renovating the said building. After 4 months, towards the end of January and the beginning of February 1944 the renovation of the building was finished and the sub-camp was liquidated. The prisoners were transferred to the sub-camp *"Lagischa"*.

29. *"Trzebinia"* (*"Trzebionka"*) at Trzebinia (District Cracow) was established in the second half of 1944 and liquidated in January 1945. Circa 650 Auschwitz prisoners became its inmates. They were mostly Jews. They worked in the petroleum refining plant.

30. *"Tschechowitz"* at Czechowice (District Katowice) was called *"Bombensucherkommando"* (squad of bomb searchers). It was organized in August 1944 and accommodated circa 100 prisoners employed at the demolition of buildings destroyed by the bombing of the Allies. They also searched for bombs and blind bombs. After these tasks had been performed the sub-camp was liquidated and the *"Bombensucherkommando"* was transferred to KL Auschwitz in the autumn of 1944. Its members were still used for similar tasks in different places in Silesia.

31. *"Tschechowitz-Dziedzitz"* at Czechowice was established in August 1944 and liquidated in January 1945. More than 500 prisoners were its inmates. Some of them were employed in the petroleum refining plant, others were demolishing bombed buildings and making secure the refining plant in case of bombing. During the liquidation of the sub-camp in January 1945 the SS men killed circa 100 prisoners, several had managed to escape and the rest were evacuated.

Besides the above mentioned sub-camps established in connection with industrial works, KL Auschwitz also maintained many sub-camps which were established in order to make the prisoners work on agricultural or cattle breeding farms.

A group of W Offices [13] (*Wirtschaftsbetriebe*) existed in the SS Economic Administration Head Office (*SS-WVHA*). They supervised and controlled all enterprises belonging to the SS.

---
[13] *Amtsgruppe* W consisted of 8 Offices.

The Office WV [14]) (*Landwirtschaftsbetriebe*) controlled agriculture, forestry and fishing on the estates which had been taken from their owners or had been established by the SS.

The agricultural enterprises connected with KL Auschwitz were in 1942 under the care of *SS-Obersturmbannführer* Joachim Caesar.[15]) The SS Economic Administration Head Office had given him full power. Caesar, being interested in investigating several fields of plant growing, tried to get the prisoners employed on farms of KL Auschwitz under his exclusive control and got the permission of the *SS-WVHA* to accommodate such prisoners in separate quarters. In 1943 the commandant's office of KL Auschwitz organized 5 sub-camps with separate quarters for men and women prisoners. The sub-camps were connected with the adjoining agricultural estates, established in the years 1941—1942.

They were:

32. A sub-camp for men and women at Babice, connected with *"Wirtschaftshof Babice"*. Circa 180 women and over 150 men were employed breeding cows, horses and tilling the soil.

33. A sub-camp for men and women, connected with *"Wirtschaftshof" Budy*. Circa 450 women and over 300 men prisoners were employed breeding cattle, pigs, cultivating the soil and taking care of tree nurseries.

34. A sub-camp for men and women at Harmęże, connected with *"Geflügelzucht Harmęże"*. The prisoners were employed establishing a fowl raising farm, they worked in the fish ponds and in the experimental station connected with fish breeding. In 1942 the fowl raising and rabbit breeding farm was changed into an experimental station employing about 50 women prisoners.

35. A sub-camp for men and women at Pławy, connected with *"Wirtschaftshof Pławy"*. Men and women prisoners were employed there breeding cattle and cultivating the soil.

36. A sub-camp for women at Rajsko, connected with the plant growing station *"Pflanzenzuchtstation Rajsko"*. Circa 150 women

---

[14]) *Amt V* — the fifth office in *Amtsgruppe W*.
[15]) Dr J. Caesar had an agricultural diploma.

prisoners worked there doing experimental work connected with the caoutchouc supplying plant *kok-sagiz*, while 150 women prisoners did gardening work.

In the autumn of 1942 the cremating of human corpses of the victims gassed with Cyclon B in the bunkers No. 1 and 2 had begun in the branch camp of *KL* Auschwitz — Birkenau. The mass graves, in which more than 100,000 murdered persons had been buried in the time between October 1941 and September 1942, had to be liquidated. The corpses were removed from the graves and burnt in the open. A great deal of wood was needed for the purpose. Therefore the commandant's office of *KL* Auschwitz organized two sub-camps connected with the forest district administration of the Pszczyna forests, and namely:

37. *"Altdorf"*, called *"Waldkommando Altdorf"* at Stara Wieś near Pszczyna (District Katowice). It was established in October 1942 and liquidated in the autumn of 1943. About 150 Auschwitz prisoners, mostly Jews, were its inmates. They were employed as timbermen, felling the trees and working them into wood. After the liquidation of the sub-camp the prisoners were transferred to *KL* Auschwitz. The management of the Pszczyna district forest administration sent sound timber to the Silesian mines and also to be used by the railways. Timber which could not be sold, such as boughs, branches, brushwood and other refuse, was taken by the commandant's office of *KL* Auschwitz. It was conveyed to Birkenau by lorries.[16]

38. *"Kobiór"*, called *"Waldkommando Kobior"* at Kobiór near Pszczyna (District Katowice) was established in October 1942 and liquidated in September 1943. Its inmates were over 150 Auschwitz prisoners, mostly Jews. They were employed felling trees and working them into wood, making thinneries and draining meadows. The treatment of the prisoners was inhuman, many of them were shot, all suffered starvation. After the liquidation of the sub-camp the prisoners were taken back to *KL* Auschwitz.

The management of the Forest Administration supplied the

---

[16]) It has not been so far ascertained what sort of settlements there existed between *KL* Auschwitz and the management of the Pszczyna Forests.

timber to Silesian mines and the railway. The refuse was taken by the commandant's office of *KL* Auschwitz.

In 1944 the commandant's office of *KL* Auschwitz organized a mobile sub-camp, called *"Bauzug"*. Its objective was to supply the Third *Reich* with man-power to repair electric traction destroyed by the bombing of the Allies, likewise railway tracks. Bombed sites in towns railway stations, etc. had to be cleared of rubble. This kind of work meant constant preparedness and instant transferring of the prisoners to important transportation centres which had been bombed. The problem was solved by organizing a mobile sub-camp located in a train which consisted of several scores of freight vans. The regime was similar to that of a concentration camp.

39. *"Bauzug"*, officially called *"2 SS-Eisenbahnbaubrigade"*, established in September 1944. Its members were 505 Auschwitz prisoners, among whom there were 100 specialists in various fields. On September 18, 1944 the *"Bauzug"* left *KL* Auschwitz for Karlsruhe in the *Reich*. It reached its destination on September 26. There, the prisoners worked clearing the rubble in the town which was being constantly bombed. On October, 12, 1944 the prisoners were committed to *KL* Buchenwald. The strength of the brigade amounted to 490 prisoners on that day, as 10 prisoners had escaped, 2 had perished and 3 had been sent back to *KL* Auschwitz.

In January 1945 32 sub-camps still existed out of the number of 39 sub-camps organized by the commandant's office of *KL* Auschwitz. 27 out of them had been established to serve the enterprises and concerns, that is the sub-camps: *Althammer, Bismarckhütte, Blechhammer, Bobrek, Brünn, Charlottengrube, Eintrachthütte, Freudenthal, Fürstengrube, Gleiwitz I, Gleiwitz II, Gleiwitz III, Gleiwitz IV, Golleschau, Günthergrube, Hindenburg, Hubertushütte, Janinagrube, Jawischowitz, Laurahütte, Lichtewerden, Monowitz, Neu Dachs, Neustadt, Sosnowitz, Trzebinia, Tschechowitz-Dziedzitz* and 5 sub-camps established on estates, farms and experimenting stations, that is: *Babice, Budy, Harmęże, Pławy and Rajsko*. On the day of the liquidation of *KL* Auschwitz and its sub-camps, that is on the day before the evacuation of the prisoners (January 17, 1945) over 36 thousand prisoners, men and women, were still in the sub-camps according to the last roll-call. They were driven on foot along several evacuation routes. The escorting *SS*-men shot those who were ill, weak or unable to march. The evacuation routes were marked by mass graves in which the local population had buried the dead.

The survivors were loaded into vans at those railway stations which were rallying points upon the evacuation routes and from there they were conveyed to concentration camps in the interior of the Third *Reich*. Thousands of them froze to death in the open coal waggons before reaching their destination, others died on their arrival at *KL* Bergen-Belsen, *KL* Buchenwald, *KL* Flossenburg, *KL* Gross-Rosen, *KL* Mauthausen or *KL* Sachsenhausen. Only a small percentage of the inmates of the Auschwitz sub-camps lived to regain their freedom.

KAZIMIERZ SMOLEŃ, M. A.

THE SYSTEM OF PUNISHMENTS USED BY THE *SS* IN THE CONCENTRATION CAMP AT AUSCHWITZ-BIRKENAU

I

The scientist, who investigates the history of World War II, constantly comes face to face with documents pertaining to Nazi crimes, the victims of which were citizens of the occupied states. The number of the crimes is as difficult to assess as the number of the victims. If we were even sometimes able to ascertain the number of victims in a certain area under Nazi occupation, we still could not help knowing that these are only small fragmentary data compared with the whole chain of crimes. But even such fragmentary data are appalling in their numbers. The trial in Nuremberg confirmed at full length the guilt of the defendants who had taken part in murdering circa one million persons.[1])

The magnitude of the crimes caused the scientists to look for a new legal term for them, namely "genocide". This term comprises the mass murders, perpetrated by the Nazis, of members of various groups, persecuted because of political, racial and religious reasons. Whole nations became the victims of such murders. In order to realize the crime of genocide there had to exist corresponding premises, namely the inhuman Nazi ideology, which had to be made popular among suitable numbers of fanatic followers. The SS organization, among many others, had the most important part in realizing the criminal plans of the Nazis. This elite was recognizable by its death's head with cross-bones. It was the SS together with the Secret State Police (or „*Gestapo*" for short) that had as its aim to break down and to liquidate all opposition to the Nazis, In order to achieve this aim special places of isolation, that is, concentration camps, were being established ever since Hitler took over in Germany. Anti-fascists and Jews were, first of all, committed to concentration camps.

No legal proceedings were necessary to commit a person to a concentration camp. It was done on the basis of a warrant (*Schutzhaftbefehl*), issued by the *Gestapo*, with the stereotype formula that the person in question "was hostile to the state". The duration of the stay in a concentration camp was never defined. This procedure, inhuman and illegal in itself, was meant to terrorize the entire society. The person, thus illegally committed to a concentration camp, became the prey of everyone. Ever since he went through the gate of the camp, the warders, who were *SS*-men, pounced upon him, beating and abusing him. This was done to show the victim at once that there one could not expect any favours, any justice even, that one was bereft of all rights.

The first moment, ironically called "the welcome", often ended with the death of the detainee. If the victim had managed to survive

---

[1]) The American Military Tribunal in Nuremberg stressed this fact in the trial of the members of the so-called "*Einsatzgruppen*" (Special Action Groups). American Military Tribunal in Nuremberg, case No. 9. shorthand report in German, p. 6877.

it, in spite of more or less serious bodily injuries, his fate continued to be critical. The prisoner was constantly subjected to all kinds of abuse and to the excesses of the SS-men. The lawlessness of the SS-men was always sanctioned by their right to self-defence (*Notwehr*), which excused all acts of brutality, even the killing of the defenceless prisoner.

To create some semblance of legal procedure the SS-men called certain crimes, which they too frequently perpetrated, punishments. The punishments here described should not be regarded as punishments according to universally accepted criteria or prison regulations. There is therefore no need to present a legal analysis of the punishments inflicted by the SS upon the inmates of concentration camps. The chief aim of this article is to present the various chicaneries, called punishments, as derived from preserved camp documents and from depositions of witnesses in the trials against ex-commandant Rudolf Höss and the criminal garrison of the Auschwitz concentration camp. The punishments in that sense of the word and appearing under several captions are often mentioned in authentic documents which offer proof that they were in fact inflicted upon prisoners. The dialogue between the public prosecutor and Gustav Sorge, the *Rapportführer* of the Sachsenhausen concentration camp, illustrates the arbitrariness in punishing the prisoners:

Prosecutor: Are your depositions true that you had used to flog prisoners every day?
Sorge: Yes, it is true.
Prosecutor: Did you flog a man because he was coughing?
Sorge: Yes, I did, whenever a man coughed or looked gloomy.
Prosecutor: And when he was gay and looked contented, did you flog him, too?
Sorge: In that case I also managed to find some reason for flogging him.
Prosecutor: So you flogged people when they looked discontented and were gloomy and you also flogged them when they looked contented?

Sorge: Yes, that was so. I had never any trouble in finding some reason for flogging people.

Rapportführer Sorge was not an exception. The warders in all concentration camps, including Auschwitz, did the same. Certain regulations issued by the *SS* were the cause of their treatment of the prisoners.

II

Among the first regulations for concentration camps there is one specimen under the title *"Disziplinar und Strafordnung für das Gefangenenlager"* (Disciplinary and Penal Regulations for a Prisoners' Camp). The regulations were signed by the commandant of the concentration camp at Dachau, Theodor Eicke, on October 1, 1933. They were also valid in the camp at Esterwegen. The original text of the regulations of the concentration camp at Auschwitz was not found. The first commandant of long standing of that camp, Rudolf Höss, reproduced from memory an elaboration of many pages which he called *"Lagerordnung für das Konzentrationslager"* (Regulations for the concentration camp). Höss noted also that "the regulations were drawn up in 1936 and were valid as a temporary project. On the basis of acquired experience uniform and fundamental camp regulations were to have been elaborated later on." [2] One part of the manuscript dealt with camp punishments (*Lagerstrafen*) which were meted out to prisoners who transgressed against "the order and discipline of the camp" (*die Ordnung und Zucht des Lagers*). Höss mentions the following punishments:

    a) reprimand
    b) penal work
    c) committing to a penal company for a fixed period of time, up to one year
    d) detention
    e) rigorous detention with partial depriving of food
    f) detention in a dark cell up to 42 days
    g) flogging (up to 25 strokes).

---

[2] *Todeslager Sachsenhausen. Ein Dokumentarbericht von Sachsenhausen Prozess. Zusammengestellt vom Sonderkorrespondenten der "Tägliche Rundschau".* Berlin 1948, *SWA-Verlag.*

PUNISHMENTS

We learn from the manuscript that Höss differentiated between "offences" (*Verfehlung*) and "misdemeanours" (*Vorstoss*), without, however, explaining the difference. Neither does he explain the meaning of "behaviour opposed to camp regulations".

Such essential lacunae in the regulations hardly seem to have been accidental, as then "any kind of behaviour" of a prisoner could have been regarded by an *SS*-man as an "offence" or a "misdemeanour", opposed to camp regulations and therefore punishable. The above quoted deposition of *Rapportführer* Gustav Sorge confirms this fact.

A penal report (*Meldung*) was the basis of punishing the prisoner. The camp leader (*Schutzhaftlagerführer*) would note on the report the kind of punishment to be meted out. In some cases (e.g. when flogging was proposed) the report was forwarded by the camp commandant to the *SS* Economic Administration Head Office (*WVHA — SS-Wirtschafts und Verwaltungshauptamt*) with his motion to apply flogging to be confirmed.

275 reports (covering the period from Sept. 3, 1942 to Dec. 15, 1944) and 110 penal orders (covering the period from May 3, 1943 to Dec. 7, 1944) were found within the terrain of the Auschwitz camp. The materials are therefore fragmentary. The following reasons for punishing occur most frequently:

1) failing to uncover one's head when meeting an *SS*-man,
2) smoking cigarettes at times when smoking was not allowed,
3) making beds negligently,
4) keeping up contacts with civilian workers,
5) giving assistance to escapees from the camp,
6) shirking work,
7) arbitrary absence from the place of work,
8) sending letters not censored by the camp censor,
9) relieving one's needs at times and in places prohibited.

The kinds and severity of the punishments inflicted were as follows: [3])

1) 6 months of work in the road building squad
   in the case of ..... 1 prisoner,

---

[3]) *Hefte von Auschwitz.* No. 3, p. 8.

2) from 2 to 15 Sundays of penal work
in the case of ..... 90 prisoners,
3) 2 or 3 months of stay in the penal company
in the case of ..... 8 prisoners,
4) 3 Sundays of penal drill
in the case of ..... 4 prisoners,
5) committal to standing-cell (*Stehzelle*) 3 to 10 times
in the case of ..... 24 prisoners,
6) 6 weeks in the standing-cell in the case of 1 prisoner,
7) 3 times in the standing-cell plus 5 times penal work
in the case of ..... 2 prisoners,
8) 2 times in the standing-cell plus 10 times penal work
in the case of..... 1 prisoner,
9) 5 to 25 strokes (flogging) in the case of ..... 99 prisoners,

10) 25 strokes plus 14 days of detention
in the case of ..... 1 prisoner,
11) 4 weeks in the penal company plus 8 days of standing
in the case of ..... 1 prisoner,
12) no mention of inflicted punishment
in the case of ..... 43 prisoners.

All together: 275 prisoners.

Besides the above mentioned sources, entries in the original book of the penal company had also been used. This book was in charge of the clerk of the penal company's block. The first entry is of May 9, 1942, the last of November 24, 1944.

The book was partly damaged and so does not present the history of the penal company in its entirety. There are 2,470 entries in it but only 1,107 can be used for a compilation of names and statistical data.

The statistics of the duration of punishments inflicted are as follows: [4])

---

[4]) Ibid. p. 9.

1) 1 month to 6 months in the case of 226 prisoners
2) 7 to 12 months   ,, ,, ,, ,,   23 ,,
3) permanent stay   ,, ,, ,, ,,   8 ,,
4) stay till recalled   ,, ,, ,, ,, 705 ,,
5) no data   ,, ,, ,, ,, 145 ,,
                         Total   1,107 ,,

The fate of the prisoners while they were serving their sentence was as follows: [5])

1) cases of death   94 prisoners
2) release from penal company   266 ,,
3) served the sentence   69 ,,
4) shot while escaping   3 ,,
5) transferred to other camps or squads   529 ,,
6) subjected to procedure *SB* [6])   1 prisoner
7) no data   145 prisoners
                         Total   1,107 ,,

The effects of the punishments administered were various, depending on such secondary, as it would seem, factors, as e.g. weather conditions. The penal roll-calls may be cited as an example of that fact. They lasted for several hours and the prisoners were obliged to attend them standing at attention in the roll-call square. Should the day be frosty many prisoners would die right there at the roll-call, while others contracted some illness and died soon after. On sunny days prisoners died of sunstroke after being exposed to the sun for a longer period of time. Such symptoms of a sunstroke as burning of the epidermis, swellings of the face, could easily become serious through lack of medical remedies, medical care and the atrocious hygienic and sanitary conditions, which caused the festering of wounds, gangrene, and finally the death of a prisoner.

PUNISHMENTS.

The above mentioned penal order takes into account three basic groups of punishments administered in concentration camps, namely: I — punishments for transgressing the order and disci-

---
[5]) Ibid.
[6]) Abbreviation of the word *"Sonderbehandlung"* meaning the liquidating of a prisoner by means of gas or phenol.

pline of the camp, II — detention, III — flogging. Each group contains several kinds and degrees of punishments. Their amount by far exceeds the punishments mentioned by commandant Höss, but even so it does not deal with all the punishments which were in fact meted out by the SS in the Auschwitz camp. After analysing existing sources, among them also depositions and reports of former prisoners of the Auschwitz concentration camp, we are able to state that the following punishments were being administered in this camp:

A. Ban on sending and receiving letters.

All prisoners, with the exception of Jews [7]) and Russians, were entitled to write or receive letters twice monthly. The letters could be sent to one address only, specified by the prisoners. This address could be changed only by permission of the camp leader. It was usually the address of the nearest relatives. Such correspondence was "privileged" (*bevorzugte Post*).

From the wording of the penal order it follows that a prisoner was liable to be punished by the ban on sending letters or on receiving letters or both, for the duration of several weeks even. Incoming letters were then added to the prisoner's dossier.

This punishment resulted in the psychic break-down of the prisoner who was thus deprived of his only means of keeping in touch with his family.

The ban on sending and receiving letters was sometimes decreed by the *Gestapo* office which had committed the prisoner to the concentration camp. It was particularly done in the cases of prisoners denoted by various cryptonyms (e.g. "sea foam" — *Meeresschaum*) which meant that all trace of the prisoner's existence was to disappear. We learn about such facts from the letter of the Chief Office Group *DI* (Economic Administration Head Office) of August, 18, 1942, signed by *SS-Brigadeführer* Glücks and pertaining to prisoners included in the so-called *Keitel-Erlass*. Among others, the Austrian general-major Stochmal belonged to this group of prisoners.

---

[7]) Sporadically, according to the recommendation of the Reich Security Head Office (*Reichssicherheitshauptamt*, abbr. — *RSHA*). The Jewish prisoners wrote letters which were taken from Auschwitz to Berlin by a special representative of the *RSHA*.

B. Penal Drill.

Penal drill, called in the SS jargon penal exercises (*Strafexerzieren*) or "sport", consisted of being subjected to particularly onerous drilling under the supervision of an SS-man. A whole group of prisoners was frequently subjected to it in cases when it was not possible to ascertain the camp number of a prisoner guilty of a transgression or when the whole group was found guilty (e.g. the singing during the march was not loud enough, beds were not properly made or there was a lack of efficiency at work).

The drilling had different names and comprised rolling on the ground (*rollen*), crawling (*kriechen*), jumping or walking with a deep kneebend (*hüpfen, Entegang*), whirling in circles while standing on one leg, the other being raised (*tanzen*), finally falling down and getting up (*hinlegenaufstehen*), or squatting for some time (*kniebeugen*) and then running (*Laufschritt*).

The SS-men, who were supervising the drilling, beat and maltreated the prisoners. If older or crippled persons were in the group subjected to drilling, the SS-men vented their brutality particularly on them. The prisoners who were unable to endure the drilling and had fainted were brought to by sousing water over them and then had to go on with the drill. Penal drill would last up to one hour. When it was over many prisoners were taken straight to the hospital. They developed many complaints, chiefly caused by internal injuries.

C. Penal work in off hours.

A prisoner's day was filled with work from day-break till nightfall. Less than an hour was allowed for washing, dressing and eating. But the prisoners sentenced to penal work (*Strafarbeit*) were not allowed to make use of even that short break. Under the supervision of the SS they were forced to cart earth in wheelbarrows, to carry bricks, etc. This punishment was most frequent in the period of the camp's extension. The route which the prisoners thus punished had to follow pushing the wheelbarrows was picketed by supervising SS-men armed with sticks or bludgeons.

This punishment should have lasted for a strictly defined period of time (stated in hours) but the penal reports often bear notes "10 Sundays of penal work". The transgressions thus punished were of a trifling nature, e.g. smoking cigarettes while at work, having tobacco on oneself while at work, nodding off, etc.

The penal work was to be done at a run.

D. Starving.

The inadequate food rations which were issued to the prisoners were liable to be completely withdrawn as punishment. Starving (*Kostenzug*) was inflicted upon men and women prisoners, both individually and also in the case of entire work squads or in the case of the inhabitants of a whole block. On July 6, 1940 all the camp inmates were thus punished. The prisoners attending the roll-call were given neither supper nor breakfast. Dinner was issued as late as 4 p.m. on July 7, 1940.

Starving led to a further weakening of the prisoners.

E. Flogging.

Flogging was supposed to be the most drastic punishment, inflicted when all other punishments had failed and the prisoner's conduct was considered to be particularly obnoxious. According to one penal report prisoner Fiszel Szpiro, camp number 157291, was punished with flogging because he had told his foreman he would not work, as he was anyhow certain of perishing in the crematorium.

Flogging was administered upon a specially constructed whipping-block. The prisoner had to put his legs into a special chest and to lie down on the whipping-block with his arms extended forward. One of the *SS*-men would grab his hands and draw him towards himself, thus tautening the prisoner's body. The strokes fell not only on the buttocks, covered or uncovered, but also, and most often, upon the region of the kidneys. Bludgeons were used, or even poles, more rarely horsewhips. The victim was forced to count the strokes in German. Should he (or she) make a mistake in counting, the flogging would begin anew.

Flogging being the most severe punishment it should have been but rarely used, but in fact it was used very often and the official number of 25 strokes was as a rule increased. After the escape of prisoner Wiejowski (July 6, 1940) several civilian workers had been arrested under the suspicion of having helped the escapees. The camp commandant Höss demanded a death sentence for them. As an act of grace the death sentence was changed to five years' committal to the camp and to a flogging of three times 25 strokes.

One of the victims, Bolesław Bicz, thus related the procedure: [8]

"During the flogging we lay on the whipping-block... the SS-men took turns flogging us with a thick electricity flex covered with leather. 25 strokes upon bare buttocks were administered to me and my four companions. After getting down from the whipping-block each one of us had to stand at attention in front of Höss and report to him that the punishment had been administered. Then we were led to a bunker in Block No. 11, where we spent 21 days without food or water. Induced by hunger and thirst we drank the water dripping from the walls of the bunker and from the bucket with excrements. We were deprived of medical care during that period, although the wounds caused by the flogging festered and suppurated... After 21 days stretcher-bearers carried us in the evening to the square in front of Block No. 16, where we got 50 strokes. I lost consciousness and was taken to the camp hospital. I regained consciousness only after two weeks; I came to in a room where there were 36 corpses. On my request the prisoner-doctor Tadeusz G. had me transferred to another room; he took me under his care, performed an operation on me and after 7 months of constant treatment my wounds had healed... One buttock had been festering, I had had phlegmons and necrosis. I lost the greater part of muscles in the right buttock..."

From among the other prisoners who were flogged, one of them (Stanisław Mrzygłód) died. Three others were deported to the concentration camp at Gusen and were killed there. Bolesław Bicz, though seriously mutilated, was the only one to survive.

---

[8] Records of the trial of the former camp commandant Rudolf Höss, vol. III. Card 34.

5 — From the History of KL-Auschwitz

Flogging was administered in the seclusion of the yard of Block N. 11 (the Block of Death) or in the presence of all the camp inmates. Women prisoners were also subjected to flogging. During his stay at Auschwitz, Himmler ordered to be shown the flogging of a woman prisoner. He reserved for himself the right of deciding whether women prisoners were to be punished by flogging.[9]

F. Hanging from the stake.

Hanging from the stake was used, according to Höss, instead of detention, so as not to let the prisoners miss their work. It consisted in tying a prisoner to a stake, with his arms bound at his back, so that he could barely touch the ground with the tips of his toes. This form of punishment had been used ever since the establishment of the camp.

G. Committal to the so-called *Stehzelle* (Standing-Cell).

Four cells were built in the cellars of Block No. 11, each with an area of 90 by 90 centimetres.

One could crawl into the cells through an opening near the floor level (just like in a dog's kennel), the opening being closed with an iron grating and a wooden door. The only means of ventilation in the cells, which were in complete darkness, was a small vent of 5 by 5 centimetres. 4 prisoners were squeezed into each cell. People could not sit down in the cell (they could only stand close to one another) and they were liable to suffocate through lack of air.

The camp commandant Höss admitted to inflicting this punishment, but he maintained that its duration did not exceed 3 days. The reports that had been preserved tell another story, however. We learn from them that prisoners were committed to standing-cells mostly for 10 days.

A prisoner with the camp number 60970 was sentenced to stay in the standing-cell because he had tried to get his soup twice and another prisoner with the camp number 55216 was punished

---

[9] Reminiscences of Rudolf Höss (Polish edition — Warsaw 1960), p. 235.

with 6 weeks in the standing-cell because he had accidentally broken a cement pipe. Another report tells us that a woman prisoner with the camp number 47295 was punished for picking apples by having to remain in the standing-cell for 5 days.

H. Committal to an ordinary cell.

Besides the standing-cells, the cellars of Block No. 11 also contained ordinary cells. Men and women prisoners who were suspected e.g. of having contacts with the civilian population were committed to them. During their stay in the cells they used to be interrogated and tortured.

Prisoners who had been flogged were also put into the ordinary cells in order (according to Höss) to separate them from other prisoners who thus would not see the effects of flogging and the resulting wounds.

The cells were constantly overcrowded and so the *SS* frequently "cleaned them out". The camp leader and the head of the Political Section (which was called the camp *Gestapo*), together with other *SS*-men, inspected the cells. After the inspection many prisoners committed to the cells were led into the yard of Block No. 11 and shot there.

I. Committal to an ordinary cell with deprival of food.

The committal to an ordinary cell could be made more drastic by depriving the prisoner of food. The aim of such measures was to make the prisoner break down and offer the *SS* the information they were after.

In 1940 this form of punishment was inflicted on the prisoners of the penal companies for their alleged inefficiency at work. Such prisoners got no dinners during their three days' stay in the cell.

J. Committal to a dark cell.

Penal orders mentioned the possibility of committing prisoners to dark cells. In his manuscript commandant Höss confirmed the use of this kind of punishment at Auschwitz, calling it *"Dunkel-*

arrest", and adding that it was possible to sentence someone to a stay of up to 42 days in a dark cell.[10])

The dark cell had a tiny opening secured from the outside by a sheet of iron with holes (18 by 18 centimetres). Ventilation was just as insufficient as in the standing-cells. Prisoners were put into the dark cells for the night and in the morning they were driven to work. Prisoner Bogdan Gliński (camp number 11958) remained in a dark cell from November 3,1942 till March 9, 1943.

Over ten prisoners would be consigned to a dark cell. The disastrous results of a stay there were described by ex-prisoner Maximilian Kubiak in his report of what had happened there in March 1942:

"...At 9 o'clock, after supper, I went towards Block No. 11... I reported to the block senior, together with my 38 companions... The block senior reported the actual number of prisoners to the *Blockführer* on duty and they both led us to the cellars where we were locked in cell No. 20... There was less and less air in the cell. The temperature rose higher and higher, so that we took off our coats and trousers, finally our underwear, too... Around 0^{30} it became impossible to continue standing. Men began knocking into one another, fidgeting and swearing; they tried to break in the door but id did not give in. The lack of air was unbearable, the odours emitted by gasping men were uncanny, those physically weak collapsed, those who were stronger fought to get nearer to the door where there was some air. After some time all the prisoners became unconscious and in the morning, when the door was opened at 5 o'clock, we had to be dragged into the corridor and were laid there. We were stark naked. From among the 39 persons, locked into cell No. 20 only 19 had survived. Six persons out of the 19 had to be immediately taken to the hospital where 4 of them died..."

K. Penal company. Reeducative copany.

A penal company was a work squad. The prisoners, consigned to it, had to do the hardest kinds of work (often at a run) and were

---
[10]) Ibid. p. 294.

isolated from other prisoners as they slept in a separate block or barrack which they were not allowed to leave.

The first prisoners were consigned to the penal company at Auschwitz as early as 1940. Later, the men's penal company was transferred to Birkenau. Women prisoners, committed to the penal company, were at first located in the sub-camp at Budy, next, they, too, were transferred to Birkenau.

The typical tasks of a penal company were: digging foundations, erecting earth walls, constructing draining ditches, cleaning ponds by removing rushes, etc. The conditions of work were particularly hard and, on the top of it, the *SS* guards used to beat and torture the prisoners to death.

The prisoners of a penal company were not allowed to write or receive letters, to smoke cigarettes or to go to the hospital.

Those prisoners, among others, who were suspected of planning an escape would be committed to the penal company.

People were committed to a penal company for a definite or indefinite period of time (bis auf weiteres). Prisoners were sent to penal companies either by the camp authorities or by the *Gestapo* post which had made their arrest. The *Gestapo* recommended a prisoner to be put in a penal company if his release from the camp was undesirable. The committal to a penal company was tantamount to a death sentence. Only very few prisoners had managed to survive their stay in a penal company and had returned to their blocks.

Besides the penal company there existed for a short time in 1942 a reeducative company (*Erziehungskompanie*). Its members were obliged to continue working in off hours under the surveillance of *SS*-men who cruelly maltreated them. The reeducative company was liquidated in December 1942 by transferring some prisoners to a penal company and shooting the others.

L. Penal roll-calls.

The aim of a roll-call was to ascertain the strength of the camp. During the roll-calls the prisoners had to stand in ranks near the block or barrack where they lived. The roll-calls were at first held three times daily, later — when the *SS* wished to exploit the work of the prisoners to the utmost — only in the evening. The duration of the roll-call would be protracted on purpose by the *SS*. A pretext to do so was, for instance, the fact that the prisoners had not uncovered their heads simultaneously while the strength of the camp had been reported to the commandant. Or the fact that there was a discrepancy between the strength of the prisoners present at the roll-call and the numerical data in the camp files. In such cases the roll-call would last for 1 to 2 hours as punishment and the prisoners had to stand at attention all the time.

The *SS* had commanded to hold one of the longest roll-calls on July, 6,1940, after the escape of prisoner T. Wiejowski. It lasted till 2 p.m. July 7, 1940. For about 20 hours the prisoners had to maintain a squatting position, with their arms behind their necks or they had to stand at attention. The *SS*-men and the capos walked along the ranks beating the prisoners.

The effects of the penal roll-calls held in the autumn and winter of 1940 were tragic, as the prisoners had then neither caps nor shoes. Hundreds of prisoners succumbed to various diseases, which often ended with death after a few days of illness.

One of the prisoners had made notes in his diary concerning the penal roll-call, held in October 1940:

"On cold days the roll-calls are without doubt the cause of a soaring death rate. Such was the roll-call in the first months of my stay in the camp. The day, October 24,1940, was exceptionally cold and windy, and had caused the deaths of 80 prisoners. Some of them died the same night, others twenty-four hours later or in the course of the next few days. We still wore our summer drill clothes. On returning from work at noon we were ordered to attend a penal roll-call. It was said that one of the prisoners was missing. Perspiring after our work and hungry we stood motionless for 6 hours. Motionless, that meant that nobody was allowed to budge, standing at attention as soldiers do. Every movement, even the least, resulted in beating, beating, beating, of the most brutal and inhuman kind..."

Penal roll-calls occurred more frequently in the women's camp than in the camp for men. The women were often forced to kneel with their arms raised during the roll-calls.

The most inhuman penal roll-calls were those held in the hospital for men at Birkenau where all the sick were driven into the square in front of the barracks. Prisoners who were unable to stand would be laid on the ground. All were in underclothes only. They were often doused with water regardless of the weather. The Soviet prisoners of war were treated in a similar way at the turn of 1941/42.

M. Penal transfer.

To transfer a prisoner to another concentration camp was considered either as a punishment in itself or as an additional punishment. And so, for instance, Bolesław Bicz was sent with his companions to the camp at Mauthausen-Gusen, after having been flogged at Auschwitz. The prisoners in the penal companies were frequently transferred to other camps as punishment. After their arrival in the new camp such prisoners were assigned the hardest tasks (e.g. work in the stone quarries at Mauthausen) under particularly strict surveillance of the *SS*.

N. The death penalty.

Commandant Höss did not mention the death penalty in the camp regulations which he had reproduced from memory. But the death penalty figures in the regulations of the Dachau concentration camp (of October 1, 1933). The depositions of witnesses, former prisoners of the Auschwitz camp, distinctly confirm the fact that executions had occurred in the camp and namely:

1) By shooting.

Prisoners were executed by shooting during nearly the entire period of the camp's existence. The executions took place in the yard of Block. No. 11 at Auschwitz, under the wall of death. This form of punishment was particularly used when dealing with prisoners who were suspected of being members of the Camp Resistance Movement.

One execution, during which the prisoners: Col. Dziama, Col. Gilewicz, Major Bończa and Capt. Lisowski-Paolone had perished, was described by ex-prisoner Ludwik Rajewski:

"...on October 11, between 10^{20} and 11 a.m., while some of us were waiting in the Political Section, where we had been brought from the bunker, and while our fate still hung in the balance, they dealt in a bloody way with people not yet interrogated, whose only guilt was the fact that they were Poles. The other interrogated men: Gilewicz, Woźniakowski, Szumański, Lisowski-Paolone used in their defence the same arguments as we did — that they did not belong to any military conspiracy, but their statements and explanations did not matter — their fate had been decided upon beforehand. Death sentences upon several scores of men "guaranteed quiet in the camp". The first to go under the "screen"[11]) were Col. Dziama and Capt. Lisowski-Paolone. They behaved as soldiers should. When they reached the "screen", Dziama turned to his executioners, Stiewitz and Clausen, with the request not to be shot in the back of the head but with pistols straight in the face, like soldiers. The executioners seemed to have respected their courage, the request was granted. Lisowski cried out, "Long live free and indep...", this was his last word. They died like soldiers, like faithful sons of their Country "which will not perish".

Prisoners were also shot in the pits from which gravel was raised (*Kiessgrube*). A firing squad performed the executions. Later on the prisoners were shot in the back of the head (*Genickschuss*), with small-calibre weapons.

In 1942 20 prisoners of the penal company at Birkenau were shot because they had not disclosed the names of the organizers of a mass escape. All together several thousands of prisoners were shot at Auschwitz.

2) By hanging.

Prisoners caught while escaping or suspected of maintaining contacts with the civilian population were usually hanged during the evening roll-calls. The same punishment was meted out to prisoners suspected of sabotage.

---

[11]) The prisoners called the wall of death "screen".

The Head of the Office Group of the *SS* Economic Administration Head office issued an order (of April 11, 1944) to the commandants of concentration camps, which said:

"It frequently happens that the camp commandants demand the punishment of flogging for those prisoners who had committed acts of sabotage in the armaments industry plants.

In the future they are requested to propose executions by hanging in the cases of sabotage which had been proven (a report of the management of the plant must be added).

The executions should take place in the presence of all the prisoners belonging to the work squad in question. Signed: by proxy, Maurer, *SS-Obersturmbannführer*."

Prisoners sentenced to death had the sentence read to them in German by the camp commandant. Then the sentence was translated into the language of the condemned man. On July 19, 1943, on a specially erected joint gallows 12 prisoners were simultaneously hanged. The execution took place in the following manner:

"...The roll-call formalities having been exceptionally quickly fininished with on that day, the prisoners: Woźniak, Sikorski, Skrzetuski, Majcisz, Sławiński, Wojtyga, Kulikowski, Garncarz, Ohrt, Foltański, Rajcer and Rapacz were brought to the gallows and placed facing the roll-call square near the kitchen, so that they had a full view of the gallows, together with the ropes. They all were dressed in drill prison clothes with no underwear, their wrists were bound behind their backs. Then they were told to mount the stools standing each under each noose, and, as far as I remember, two prisoners brought for this purpose from the bunker put the nooses round the necks of the condemned men. All the camp sentries had been reinforced. When the condemned men had the nooses round their necks, Höss stepped forward from the group surrounding him, together with the interpreter... and began reading the sentence... But he had not finished reading because Skrzetuski, the first in the line, kicked out the stool from under him and hung down. When they saw this, the *SS* officers in Höss's group hurried towards the other victims and pushed away the stools on which they had been leaning. After the execution

Höss and his SS-men left and we were ordered to return to our blocks. After some time the doctor came to certify the deaths of the executed. The corpses were removed the same evening."

The last execution by hanging took place in the women's camp in the first days of January 1945. Women prisoners working in the *"Union-Werke"* factory perished then. They were accused of stealing explosives from the factory and handing them over to the prisoners employed at burning corpses. The prisoners of that special squad (*Sonderkommando*) raised a mutiny which was cruelly quelled by the SS. All mutineers had perished.

The arrested women did not give away anyone, in spite of being tortured. Ex-prisoner Raja Kagan had witnessed the execution:

"A few days after the New Year a gallows was erected in the camp for women. It was designated for the four girls from the *"Union-Werke"*. The execution was to be carried out during the evening roll-call. Our work squad, which worked till eight p.m., thought they would be spared the "spectacle"; but unfortunately the supervising SS-man told us to stop working half an hour earlier and to return to the camp... We were trembling as we marched into the camp. We were told that two had already been hanged during the roll-call and now the remaining two were awaiting their end. The women prisoners had to gather close to the cellar of Block No. 4. A sign was given and we were led to the blocks where the *"Union-Werke"* squad lived. The gallows stood there... Hössler's voice was heard, "all traitors will perish like that.." I was standing between Ela and Lola and thought, "I must see and remember everything."

3) By starvation.

Death by starvation was inflicted as punishment for the first time after the escape of one of the prisoners had been ascertained on April 23, 1941. Since the escapee had been the inmate of Block No. 2, the camp commandant Höss, together with some officers and N.C.O.'s, selected 10 prisoners of this block and had them committed to a cell in the cellars of Block No. 11. According to Höss the selected prisoners were to stay in the cell without food or water till the recapture of the escapee.

Since that time this punishment was often used, but instead of 10, as many as 20 prisoners would be selected.

The selected prisoners were usually put into the above described dark cell. The cell was as a rule opened only when the deaths of all its inmates had been ascertained.

Prisoners caught while escaping were also doomed to death by starving. The death penalty by starving was a consequence of the collective responsibility of prisoners, which was a rule in the camp. There were cases when the prisoners selected to die by starvation were already dead and the escapee was recaptured a few days later. Then he, too, was doomed to die by starving.

O. Other punishments.

Besides the above mentioned punishments there were many others inflicted upon the inmates of Auschwitz. It is not possible now to give an exact report af all of them. An example of some of them would be, for instance, kneeling a whole day long at the camp gate, which was frequent in the camp for women. In the camp for men, prisoners were again ordered to stand between the rows of the wire fences. This was the punishment of those who had been caught stealing food or food offal. The prisoners in question had then to stand at attention or to remain in a squatting position all day long until the evening roll-call. After a prisoner's escape the nearest relatives of the escapee would be brought to the camp (parents, fiancees). They were put at the entrance to the camp and when prisoners were returning from work they were forced to look at them. The aim of that procedure was to keep others from running away.

The punishments described above fail to illustrate all the criminal devices of the *SS*. Quite frequent were, for instance, cases of sending a prisoner outside the sentry chain around the place of work in order to make him retrieve an object thrown there on purpose (e.g. a prisoner's cap). When the prisoner crossed the sentry line the *SS*-men shot him and then officially, though quite untruthfully, reported the fact, using the stereotype formula: "shot while attempting to escape". An *SS*-man was not punished for this act, what is more, he was rewarded by a few days' leave and an official acknowledgement "for having frustrated an attempt at escaping".

The preserved documents which had been the basis of this work show that the Nazis had tried to create some semblance of legal procedure when punishing the prisoners. But the seemingly legal character of the punishments plainly brings out their criminality when confronted with the reality of a prisoner's life in camp.

The main objective of the *SS* was the extermination of the prisoners who had been put behind the wires of a concentration camp. The system of punishments, used by the *SS* and described above, was one of the means which served to achieve this objective.

TADEUSZ IWASZKO, M. A.

ESCAPES OF PRISONERS FROM THE CONCENTRATION CAMP AUSCHWITZ-BIRKENAU.

THE SYSTEM OF SECURING THE CAMP.

The Nazi concentration camps differed from prisons by the fact, among other things, that the prisoners were not housed in one basic building. The camps consisted of a complex of buildings and barracks, usually situated in an isolated spot. This was the situation when the new Nazi concentration camp Auschwitz was established in 1940.

Since the autumn of 1942 three separate parts of the camp had existed: the camp at Auschwitz, the camp at Birkenau and the camp at Monowitz.

Beginning from November 1943, when the camps had been separated from one another, they had acquired some sort of independence, but they were still subjected to the authority of the SS garrison commandant in the person of the commandant of the Auschwitz camp. In all the three camps (and also in the sub-camps, subordinated to the commandant of the Monowitz camp) the essential security of each camp depended on three factors:

barbed wire fences
posts of the small sentry chain
posts of the big sentry chain.

At Auschwitz the fencing consisted of a double row of barbed wires, whereas in the remaining camps (Birkenau and Monowitz) there was only one row of barbed wires, supported by concrete pillars. At night the zone of the wires was lighted by lamps hanging from the pillars and the wires were connected with the electric power grid (triphaser current of 220 voltage). The electric current would be disconnected during the day, as the majority of prisoners were then outside the fences. In the evening, when the prisoners' work squads had returned from work and on Sundays, the wires were again charged with electricity.

The posts of the small and big sentry chain were located in wooden watch towers. Those of the small sentry chain (near the fences) were manned day and night, without intermission, while the posts of the big sentry chain left the watch towers immediately after the evening roll-call. But if it was found that a prisoner was missing, either in the course of the day or at the evening roll-call, then the posts of the big sentry chain were reinforced and kept at the watch towers for the next 72 hours. This was done to make it impossible for the escapee to get through the line of posts, should he be hidden somewhere within the guarded camp.

The zone around the camp and surrounded by the watch towers of the big sentry chain was called the "closed area" (*Sperrgebiet*). SS families, who lived within this zone, or other persons, received special identification cards, stamped in the office of the commandant of the Auschwitz concentration camp. Entrance into the above mentioned zone was possible only at several points of entry, manned by *SS* posts (*Schlagbaumposten*). The duty of each post was to verify the identity of each person entering or leaving the "closed area", regardless of their rank or their being members of the *SS* or the German army. All vehicles had to stop at these points of entry and their drivers were obliged to show a travel order (*Fahrbefehl*). These regulations were intended to make a prisoner's escape from the area around the camp impracticable. If any negligence on the side of the *SS* guards was made known, they would be reminded of the regulations in special orders issued by the commandant's office. Such orders were usually made public after the escapes of prisoners who had taken advantage of an *SS* guard's carelessness.

Since civilian workers were employed by private firms which were commissioned by the camp authorities to do all kinds of jobs within the area around the camp, these workers were also subjected to the same restrictions. Each civilian worker received a special pass stamped in the commandant's office and signed by him. When moving about in the closed zone the civilian workers had to wear a green arm-band on their left arms with the words *"Zivil Arbeiter"* stamped on it. When entering the area of the big sentry chain the civilian workers were obliged to show their passes to the *SS* guards and to uncover their heads. As the prisoners had their hair shorn, they would be easily recognized with their heads bare and so their escape would be prevented.

Both during the day and at night additional *SS* patrols checked the area around the camp, inspected the particular posts and stopped suspected persons.

When discussing the prisoners' escapes from the concentration camp at Auschwitz one should bear in mind the attitude and morale of the *SS* garrison, consisting of the so-called „Death's Heads" troops (*SS Totenkopf Verbände*). As soon as the concentration camps had been established, specially trained *SS* detachments of the "Death's Heads" were formed and their task was to watch the prisoners. The training to which they were subjected consisted, first of all, in inculcating in them a deep hatred for prisoners and Jews, the enemies of the state, in teaching them to behave brutally and to perform all commands of their superiors in a rigorous way. Specially trained Alsatian shepherd dogs were also used to guard the prisoners. There was a detachment with dogs at the Auschwitz camp. They were always used when chasing the escapees.

Most of the SS garrison at the Auschwitz camp had been trained on such lines and so the period from 1940 to 1943 was characterized by an exceptional brutality of the SS towards the prisoners. In the following years new detachments of the *"Volksdeutschen"* were detailed in great numbers to guard duty and as their training had been rather brief, they did not show exceptional zeal in the performance of their duties. The attitude of the SS guards was also influenced by the mass extermination of the Jewish population and the resulting looting of the effects of the gassed persons. The SS-men, who were pilfering the Jewish property on their own, in spite of strict prohibition, were also open to bribery and themselves sought contacts with the prisoners. This resulted in a kind of interdependence which the prisoners made use of when organizing escapes (military uniforms and even weapons were bought from the SS-men). The camp authorities were conscious of the state of things and proceeded to punish transgressing SS-men, but no orders issued could change the fact that discipline was becoming lax.

The steady development of the camps and the increasing numbers of prisoners had also changed the numerical ratio of prisoners guarded by 1 SS-man. In August 1944 one SS-man had on the average 64 prisoners under his surveillance at Birkenau, 14 at Auschwitz and 23 at Monowitz.

An SS guard company in the camp stood in readiness without intermission and it would immediately proceed with the chase of a prisoner as soon as the camp siren sounded, a sign that an escape had taken place. Should it prove to be necessary additional companies would be mobilized, thoroughly searching all possible hide-outs of the escapee. The search was organized not only in the area around the camp but also in the entire zone of the concentration camp's interests (*Interessengebiet*) or even beyond its boundaries. SS motor patrols used to block all adjoining roads and exits. Information about the escape was immediately wired to police posts and frontier stations and the name of the escapee was entered into the wanted persons register (*Fahndungsbuch für das G.G.*).

The success of an escape depended to a large extent upon the help shown by the local Polish civilian population. As early as 1940 the *Gestapo* spies had reported that the local population was "fanatically Polish" and hostile to the occupational authorities, therefore every escapee could count upon their immediate help.

Since that attitude of the Polish population was well-known to them, the *SS* authorities of the Auschwitz camps started deporting the population of the neighbourhood almost immediately after establishing the camp.

Together with the uprooting of the Polish inhabitants the local authorities originated the action of germanizing the neighbourhood by bringing German settlers (*Volksdeutsche*) e.g. from Rumania, who were expected to guarantee a "proper" attitude towards the administration by the occupants. But the deportation action had not yet been totally finished by 1944, as the demand for man-power was considerable. The escapee could therefore still count on the help of the Polish inhabitants who were living in the settlements and villages situated in the distance of a few kilometres from the camp.

Not only Poles escaping from the Auschwitz camp were helped by the Polish civilians, but also scores of other escapees, Russian prisoners of war or Englishmen. The Polish population gave them shelter and food at the risk of their own lives, showed them what routes to follow in their escapes. When the *Gestapo* or the police discovered any instance of help, they dealt mercilessly with the family in question, which would be arrested and committed to the camp or the prison.

ESCAPES.

The prisoners committed to the Nazi concentration camps mostly failed to realize, in the beginning of the camp's existence at any rate, what conditions of life they would find there.

Each newcomer, after passing the gate of the camp, became a camp number only and his life depended on the whims of almost every *SS*-man. The prisoner acquired his camp experience day after day in a hard struggle for his survival. The confinement, the work which surpassed one's possibilities, the starvation, executions and the bestiality of the *SS* guards caused many prisoners to dream of escaping. This idea became an obsession with many prisoners and made them undertake the most risky attempts.

But it should be quite definitely stressed that to attempt an escape and to prepare it a prisoner had to believe in its success and to be physically fit to surmount all hardships connected with it.

The work of putting the camp in order and developing it was the cause that the prisoners of the Auschwitz camp were mainly employed outside the camp proper. Thanks to this fact there existed (in spite of prohibition) the possibility of illegal contacts with civilian workers. Such conditions were, without doubt, favourable to potential escapees.

The first escape was organized by prisoner Tadeusz Wiejowski on July 6, 1940, that is only a few weeks after the establishment of the camp. His escape became quite legendary. It is most probable that Wiejowski, his striped prison clothes very dirty, had mixed with a group of civilian workers and so had managed to leave the camp. After many days of wandering he succeeded in getting to his home where his wife hid him for a longer period of time. This was the type of escape called a "wild" escape, when the escapee made use of the first possible opportunity, counting on his luck and on the help of the local inhabitants. Such escapes happened throughout the whole period of the camp's existence, but were most frequent in the years 1941—1943.

On September 1, 1941, there was a great deal of excitement in the Auschwitz camp in connection with the escape of prisoner Jan Nowaczyk, who ran away disguised as an *SS*-man. He had abstracted the *SS* uniform, arms and a bicycle from the living quarters of one of the *SS*-men and thus left the area around the camp. Some time before noon he came to the village Poręba Wielka, several kilometres from the camp. He was not refused help when he entered the first encountered house asking for a hide-out and food. The family, by name of Kulig, took pity on the starved escapee. By a lucky chance the chase did not reach Poręba Wielka and nobody seemed to have noticed the escapee when he had arrived on his bicycle in front of the Kulig home.

Nowaczyk, after having been fed and supplied with civilian clothes and some provisions, left Poręba Wielka that same night.

Among the many escapes some only were universally acclaimed as feats of exceptional courage and gallantry. Such undoubtedly was the collective escape of four prisoners: Eugeniusz Bendera, Stanisław Jaster, Józef Lempart and Kazimierz Piechowicz. These prisoners were working in a military magazine (*T.W.L.* — *Truppen Wirtschaftslager*), situated within the big sentry chain. They decided to make use of the SS uniforms and weapons which were stored in that magazine.

To get impressions of the several keys of doors which led to the premises they wanted to enter and counterfeit them presented no difficulty as two of them were working in a garage. This fact was most important in their plan as the prisoners had decided to take one of the motor-cars, "*Steyer 220*", standing in the garage, which was situated next to the *T.W.L.* magazine.

On Saturday, June 20, 1942, the group of prisoners working in the *T.W.L.* as usual returned earlier to the camp. This was the day in the week when they used to work less hours, because the SS-men finished their work earlier and the prisoners were not allowed to stay in the vicinity of the magazine without supervision.

According to their plan, they reported at the main gate and Kazimierz Piechowski, who spoke German well, reported to the *Blockführer* on duty that 3 prisoners, pushing a cart with refuse, were leaving. Piechowski had an arm-band with the words "Foreman" on his arm, which arm-band he got hold of before. The prisoners were allowed to pass the gate without any difficulty, the more so as the guards of the big sentry chain had not yet left their posts. The escapees reached the magazine of the *T.W.L.* without being stopped and got inside by way of the chute through which coke was shovelled into the boiler-room. There, using the counterfeit keys, they could enter the other rooms. They dressed in the *SS* uniforms, took also weapons and munitions and then left the magazine going away by car. The greatest danger awaited them when passing the post at the border of the big sentry chain. If they had been stopped there everything could have had a tragic end. Coming to the barrier at which the *SS* post was standing, one of the escapees leaned out of the car and pointed to it with a decided gesture. The guard did not stop the car (though he should have done so) and the prisoners proceeded without hindrance. In the distance of several scores of kilometres from the camp they abandoned the car near the mountain settlement Sucha and illegally crossed the frontier of the *General Gouvernement*.

But not all escapees were so lucky. There were cases when prisoners decided on escape because this seemed to be the only possible means of avoiding imminent death. Such a situation had existed in the penal company (*SK*) in June, 1942. Polish prisoners were at that time in the majority in the penal company to which they were committed without any apparent reason. Everything was pointing to the fact that the prisoners had been doomed to inevitable extermination. One of the escapees thus told their story:

"We went to work digging a big draining ditch, draining the waters of Birkenau into the old Vistula river bed.

It may have been on June 8, 1942, that one of my companions said, while we were going to work: "Look, there are so many of us and only 8 *SS*-men." I would not, perhaps, have paid any attention to his words if it had not been for the fact that at that time some of our fellows were told to go to the Political Section from which they failed to return. Our situation seemed hopeless. We had learned from the block clerk that 50 of us were to go the next day to the Political Section, so it seemed highly probable that we should be shot, all of us, with time... I must stress the fact that the penal company was only responsible for itself, we all were under suspicion and doomed to die, so we thought it would be better to risk. Some might be saved, after all. But the escape would have to be a mass affair, so that as many as possible could be saved and so as to sonfuse the guards." [1])

Several scores of the prisoners from the penal squad, knowing the secret, were awaiting the signal to start running away. The whistle, blown at the end of the work hours, was to be the signal. When hearing the whistle the prisoners were supposed to stand to and to leave the place where they had worked.

On the day in question work was over earlier because it was raining. The whistle, which was to signal the escape, was blown earlier and surprised the majority of those initiated into the plan. They had not yet managed to get into positions favourable for escaping. In the ensuing confusion only less than twenty prisoners started running away in the direction of the adjoining groves. The chase was immediate, but not quite successful because night was falling. Several escapees had managed to leave the area around the camp.

One of them (August Kowalczyk) was found in a completely exhausted condition by a woman inhabiting the nearby village Bajszowy. Thanks to the help of the local inhabitants he managed to get through to the *General Gouvernement* [2]) after some time. The other escapee to be saved was Tadeusz Chróścicki.

The camp authorities were undoubtedly most alarmed, not by any accidental escapes, but by those undertaken by prisoners employed as clerks in the various offices of the camp administration. Such prisoners had access to numerous documents, were well informed about the extermination system in the camp and so could disclose many secrets, which the SS wanted to keep hidden. This was the case with the escape of 4 prisoners organized towards the end of December 1942. Their names were: Jan Baraś (Komski), Mieczysław Januszewski, Bolesław Kuczbara and Otto Küsel. Their escape is also noteworthy because it had been one of the first to be organized in agreement with the illegal organization and with the help of the local population. The escapees maintained their contacts with the world outside the camp by means of secret

---
[1]) Related by ex-prisoner Tadeusz Chróścicki.
[2]) Two women were the helpers in this case — Lucja Szklarz from the village Bajszowy and Helena Stópkowa from the town of Oświęcim.

letters, taken from, and brought to, the camp by prisoners from the surveyors' squad. The surveyors were moving about in the area around the camp and in the nearby fields and so could get into touch with the Polish inhabitants in spite of the severe ban on such contacts, imposed by the camp authorities.

Two women, living at the town of Oświęcim, Janina Kajtoch and Helena Stópkowa, promised their help in the escape. In one of the letters, concerning this matter, the prisoners wrote as follows: "Dear Miss Janina, Jadzia has left, so I want to ask you to help us to escape. Four of us are planning to run away. Three men have civilian trousers and jackets, but I have nothing as I can't put on three layers of clothing. I shall be leaving disguised as a guard and shall wear my striped clothes, which I shall discard outside the camp, on top of the uniform. So I should need one suit of clothes and two caps... I'd like to leave on the 28, 29, or 30 of this month which means that we should be waited for on these three days from 10 a.m. to 2 p.m.... Dear Miss Janka, I'll bring lists of names of all those who had died in the camp in 1942. The road leading to Brzeszcze would be the most convenient for us..."

The author of the letter quoted above was Kuczbara [3]), who was working in the camp hospital (dental clinic), the other escapees were working in the Employment Section.

On December 29, 1942, a dray drawn by two horses passed the gate at Auschwitz in the forenoon. In one of the wardrobes, placed upon the dray, Kuczbara was hidden, dressed in the *SS* uniform. The passing of the dray with three prisoners aroused no suspicion, particularly as Otto Küsel was well-known to all *Blockführers*. When they were passing the checking post at the border of the big sentry chain, Kuczbara in his *SS* uniform was sitting in the back of the dray and he showed the necessary pass which they had cleverly forged. The dray proceeded towards the village Broszkowice and stopped at the appointed place in front of a house formerly inhabited by Poles who had been deported. Here the dray and horses were abandoned and the escapees changed into the civilian clothes, supplied by helpful people. Then they pre-

---

[3]) He was said to be the nephew of Gen. Sikorski.

tended to be navvies repairing the road and passed the bridge across the Vistula pushing wheelbarrows which they left there. This make-believe was necessary as nearby, in the fields of Broszkowice, groups of prisoners were working under the supervision of *SS* guards who looked on without suspecting anything.

The escapees were accompanied by liaison men Adam Fortuna, Stanisław Wójcik, Ludwik Denda and Tadeusz Szopa. Marching rapidly they got to the village Libiąż, a distance of over ten kilometres. The organizer of the whole action, Andrzej Harat, was obserwing the escape closely. He gave shelter to the escapees at Libiąż putting them up in the church tower. After three hours the search party reached Libiąż but failed to find the escapees. In a hiding-place in the house of Andrzej Harat, Kuczbara wrote down his reminiscences from the camp and left one copy with his host, taking the other copies to Warsaw together with some other documents. His report and the documents were transmitted to the High Command of the Country's Army and to the Delegate of the London Regime. All the escapees had reached Warsaw without meeting with any obstacles since they had been supplied with the requisite identification cards.

The frequency rate of the escapes, particularly those arranged with the help of the illegally active group of the Resistance Movement (*Kampf-Gruppe Auschwitz*), rose in 1944. It is true that as early as the spring of 1943 the escape of prisoner Kazimierz Hałoń (he went under the name of Wrona in the camp) had been organized, but the situation in the camp just then and the reprisals made, deterred the organizers from a more lively activity. In 1944 the organization mentioned above had arranged the escapes of about 30 prisoners of the Auschwitz camp, cooperating with partisan groups operating in the vicinity of the camp. The escapees were of Polish and Austrian nationality, but there also were Jews (e.g. Szymon Zajdow-Wojnarek). Of great importance in arranging the escapes was a proper functioning of the liaison, preparing hideouts in villages near the camp terrain and being familiar with camp conditions.

The prisoner Konstanty Jagiełło rendered most notable services in arranging escapes. Following the recommendation of the camp organization he had organized, jointly with Tomasz Sobański, a successful escape from Birkenau. Their escape was, among others, a fine example of good conspiratorial work. Both escapees, living at Birkenau, moved about in the area around the camp as they were working in the roofers' squad (*Dachdeckerkommando*). Making use of that advantage the escapees hid in a concrete cellar near the building of the *DAW*, located in the closed terrain belonging to the Auschwitz camp. This was very important since the search after them, when they had been missed on June 27, 1944, was led towards the Birkenau camp, omitting the place where they had hidden. They had intended to spend the rest of the day in their hide-out and to continue their escape at night. But their companions, who knew the secret, were unable to move in time the motor placed on top of the cellar entrance (put there to mislead the searchers), so they left the hiding-place only the next night and proceeded to Wilczkowice, where they had been waited for the night before. Since their escape both ex-prisoners continued to operate in the adjoining villages and to help the next escapees.

In the case of the following escapes which were organized for the successive groups, liaison men familiar with the terrain were waiting for the escapees in appointed places where they took the runaways over, recognizing them by tokens agreed upon beforehand. Hide-outs were prepared for the escapees where they could rest and where they were supplied with forged identification cards and arms. When their hair had sufficiently grown, some escapees proceeded to Cracow and there their tattooed camp numbers would be removed.

One of the escapees, Lucjan Motyka, who escaped on July 19, 1944, hid in the *SS*-men's kitchen which proved a safe hide-out while the search for him was going on in other directions, particularly since he had never worked in the kitchen squad. His escape had been planned in cooperation with the Camp Resistance Movement and proved a success. But Lucjan Motyka had met with some unexpected difficulties, namely the river Soła was at flood and he was obliged to swim across it, renewing his attempt several times. Such surprises often were the lot of escapees, even if the whole operation had been prepared down to the most minute details. One could arrive too late at the appointed place or lose one's way when escaping, which was quite possible considering the fact that the prisoner moved at night in an unfamiliar terrain.

There were greater possibilities of organizing a successful escape if such things were smuggled into the camp as wigs, forged documents or arm-bands, worn by civilian workers. But even they were of no avail if the prisoner in question was not allowed to pass outside the wire fences. (Certain prisoners were obliged to stay within the wire enclosures). This was the case with prisoner Józef Cyrankiewicz who had been supplied with all the necessary paraphernalia in order to escape disguised as a civilian worker, but could not do so, though the above mentioned escapee, Kazimierz Hałoń (Wrona) had managed to leave the camp as such.

The organized escapes, though made easier by careful planning, were still full of risks.

And so the escape of a group of prisoners from Birkenau, with Lucjan Nowakowski, Tadeusz Uszyński, Jerzy Sadczykow and Rudolf Szymański, ended tragically. Their hide-out, where they expected to spend three days and three nights, was a tunnel under an unfinished barrack in the sector situated to the north of the camp (the so-called *"Mexico"*).

On August 3, 1944, the above mentioned prisoners assembled in the hide-out. The following night they tried to cross the line of posts of the big sentry chain but were discovered at a most unexpected moment. Three of them were shot dead, the fourth, though seriously wounded, had managed to crawl back into the hide-out unobserved. This was Tadeusz Uszyński who had spent more than a week in the solitary hiding-place, which was situated within the camp area and could have been discovered at any moment. Secret letters, informing about his fate and giving successive dates of his probable appearance at the appointed place, were almost daily sent out from the Auschwitz camp.[4]) The stubborn and almost

---
[4]) A detailed report of that correspondence appeared in *"Hefte von Auschwitz"*, No. 7, (T. Iwaszko — *"Höftlingsfluchten aus dem Konzentrationslager Auschwitz"*, pp. 35—36).

hopeless struggle ended with a success. The escapee, having sufficiently recovered, was able to get out from the camp area and to reach his appointed destination.

One of the last escapes, which occurred on October 27, 1944, proved to be equally tragic. Everything pointed to its success, as it was particularly carefully planned by the Camp Resistance Movement Organization. The members of the management of the Camp Resistance Movement Organization (*Kampfgruppe Auschwitz*), who were to participate in the escape, were: Ernst Burger and Rudi Friemel (Austrians), Bernard Świerczyna, Czesław Duzel, Zbigniew Raynoch and Edward Pyś. The entire group was to leave the camp in a big chest inside a truck which used to take to Bielsko the prisoners' clothes and underwear. Two SS-men shared the secret. On the day of the escape only five out of the above mentioned prisoners hid in the chest. One of the group, Edward Pyś, was prevented to come to the appointed place at the proper time and thus saved his life. The driver of the truck, *SS-Rottenführer* Roth (of Rumanian descent) had turned traitor and had informed the Political Section about the planned escape. The escapees were dragged out from the truck and were led to Block No. 11. SS-men proceeded to the appointed place where the truck was being awaited. Konstanty Jagiełło, who was to take over the escapees, was shot dead that day at the village of Łęki.

Besides the above described organized escapes, others had taken place, too, initiated by groups of prisoners who did all the preparations by themselves. And so 4 Jewish prisoners escaped from the camp at Birkenau on March 2, 1944, making use of a hiding-place in the area of "*Mexico*". They were: Abraham Gecel, Mendel Eisenbach, Kuba Bałaban and Stefan Majewski. After spending three nights in the hiding-place the prisoners heard German commands. This meant that the posts of the big sentry chain were withdrawn. They could then leave the area around the camp without the risk of meeting the SS guards. The escapees tried to cross the river Soła, but were impeded by its depth and its whirlpools. So they continued running away and put off the crossing till the next time. They spent the day in hiding and when the night fell they approached a solitary house. This is the report of one of them, Kuba Bałaban.

"When it grew dark I went to the village alone. I stopped in front of the first house. I heard people talking inside it, so at first I listened to make sure what language they were speaking. When I heard them speaking Polish I opened the door without hesitating. A woman with three small children was sitting in the house. They were frightened very much when they saw me and I was unable to say a word. When I came to, I explained that I was an escapee from a labour camp in Germany and wanted to get to Porąbka, that is the village across the river Soła, but I did not know my way. First of all the woman gave me some food and she also supplied me with some flour-cakes..." [5]) Besides giving the food the woman directed him how to proceed further. In another place the escapees were again given information by a young Polish girl who led them to the spot where they could ford the river Soła. But in the vicinity of Porąbka the prisoners were surrounded by the military police who instantly recognized them as escapees from the camp, when they noticed their camp numbers. They were taken back to the camp.

Another group of Jewish prisoners had started from the same place, using the same hiding-place, namely Alfred Wetzler and Walter Rosenberg (his name is at present Rudolf Vrba). This escape was organized on April 7, 1944. When planning their escape the prisoners wanted not only to save their lives, but first of all they intended to get to Slovakia and to bring news that the concentration camp at Auschwitz was being prepared for the next phase of the extermination of the Hungarian Jews. Such rumours were heard in the camp and they were confirmed by the fact that work at the inside railway ramp at Birkenau was nearly finished. The escapees took with them notes made in the camp (both were employed as block clerks). They left their hiding-place at night and while continuing their flight they only by the merest chance escaped death or arrest, nearly colliding with Nazi soldiers in a wood near Porąbka. Though exhausted and footsore they proceeded towards the Slovakian frontier. They met a Polish woman who

[5]) Report of ex-prisoner Kuba Bałaban.

contacted them with a partisan. He led them towards the frontier, showed them where to cross it and gave them addresses of people on the other side who could be relied on to help them. He also gave them a pistol. This escape was completely successful. The escapees got into touch with a conspiratorial Jewish organization in Slovakia. They wrote a report of all they had seen and experienced in the camp and after copying and translating it, the report was sent to Hungary and to other countries. As early as 1944 the same report appeared in the United States as a pamphlet, in English translation. But their efforts and sacrifice did not bring the expected results, just as the efforts of two other Jewish escapees — Czesław Mordowicz and Arnold Rosin. Transports of Hungarian Jews began arriving at the Auschwitz concentration camp ever since the middle of May, 1944.

Besides the escapes from the camps at Auschwitz, Birkenau and Monowitz, one should not forget the escapes from the sub-camps. The inmates of the sub-camps often prepared an escape by digging tunnels. The digging of a tunnel meant concerted work of several prisoners at least and lasted for weeks. Meanwhile any kind of carelessness on the side of one of the prisoners or the accidental discovery of traces of earth work might destroy all hope of escaping and meant death to those planning to run away. We had such unsuccessful attempts at escaping in the sub-camps *Neu Dachs Janinagrube, Fürstengrube*. Whenever the prisoners had managed to finish digging their tunnel undisturbed, more than ten prisoners would escape at the same time.

Not all documents concerning the escapes of the Auschwitz concentration camp prisoners have been preserved. On the basis of such fragmentary data as telegrams sent to pursue the escapees, documents of the Camp Resistance Movement, reports of the participants of escapes or of persons, who had given them assistance, we can determine 667 names or camp numbers of prisoners who had organized escapes. 270 persons who had, for a certainty, been recaptured, should be deducted from that total. But there are no exact data as to the fates of the remaining 397 persons and so it is not possible to state how many of them were in fact successful in their escapes. While investigating this matter, the addresses of about 100 ex-prisoners-escapees were found.

One third (232) of the total of 667 escapees comprises prisoners of Polish nationality. Then there were 95 Russians and 76 Jews among the prisoners who had escaped from the camp.

REPRISALS AFTER ESCAPES.

All measures taken to make the camp secure had in view not only the isolation of the prisoners and keeping them from contacts with the civilian population but also, and above all, preventing them from escaping. But the various measures, together with the alarm system, had proved to be insufficient. Almost since the very first days of the camp's existence the prisoners had managed to make use of the weakest spots in the existing system of making the camp secure and so they attempted escapes. The camp authorities were helpless which aroused their fury to such an extent that they began making the most cruel reprisals directed both against the escapees themselves, if recaptured, and against all persons who gave assistance or were suspected of giving assistance to the escapee. Even the families of the escapees became victims of the reprisals.

To terrorize the prisoners collective responsibility for escapes was introduced, particularly in the first phase of the camp's existence. The fear of death by starvation or by shooting, imminent if a fellow-prisoner had escaped, was to induce the prisoners to spy on one another and to checkmate any attempts at escaping.

Selections of prisoners, doomed to die by starving, were not preceded by any form of inquiry. It was accident that made people go to the bunkers of Block No. 11. Mostly they were prisoners from the same work squad or block as the escapee. Thus 10 or even 20 guiltless prisoners would be doomed to starve to death.

The camp authorities did not hesitate to perform public executions of several, sometimes even a score or so, of persons, in order to terrorize the prisoners. The executions by hanging were performed in the roll-call squares in the camps of Auschwitz, Birkenau, Monowitz and in the sub-camps. The effect of such executions was often quite opposite to that intended, as the doomed persons openly manifested their attitude of contempt for, and hatred of, the SS.

In 1943 the families of the escapees were brought to the camp at Auschwitz after several successful escapes. The members of the escapee's family were dressed in the striped camp clothes and put on a platform facing the street in the camp along which the prisoners used to march when returning from work. A signboard with a suitable inscription informed everybody that the parents of the escapees were committed to the camp as retaliation for their son's escape. After the escape of prisoner Stefan Kubiczek (on March 29, 1943) his mother, aged 60, and his fiancee, Helena Handzlik, were committed to the camp.

Such reprisals had undoubtedly some effect in holding prisoners back from escaping but they could hardly prevent escapes in general.

The SS-men from the camp Political Section used to conduct investigations connected with the escapes. They made use of the so-called "sharp interrogations" in such cases, which meant that people were subjected to the worst tortures that could have been devised. The recaptured escapees were sometimes unable to bear the tortures. If they mentioned some persons who had given them help, the latter would immediately be arrested and committed to the bunkers of Block No. 11. An example of that kind was the case of the escapee Nowaczyk (mentioned above) who having been recaptured and interrogated, had mentioned the name of the Kulig family of Poręba Wielka. Wawrzyniec Kulig perished in the camp and the same fate befell the miner from Brzeszcze, Władysław Markiel who had given assistance to an escaping prisoner.

The entire Dusik family was arrested for helping escapees on November 27, 1944, namely the father, Julian, the daughter, Wanda, and the nephew, Franciszek Dusik. This family had put its house in the nearby village Łęki-Zasole at the disposal of escapees who found there a hiding place, and so the Dusik family had rendered invaluable services to the runaways. They were arrested in consequence of the betrayal of one of the SS-men, who knew about the escape of the group of 5 leaders of the Camp Resistance Movement Organization.

The above mentioned names were picked out from among the many names of those living in the vicinity of Auschwitz, who laid down their lives helping the escapees.

The escapees, if recaptured, could expect nothing but death. Some of them, dressed as circus clowns, were forced to march along the camp streets shouting, "Hurray, here I am again!" The bodies of the escapees, who were shot dead while escaping, were brought back to the camp and publicly displayed. Suitable inscriptions informed all and sundry who the victims were.

Before they died, the recaptured escapees were subjected to interrogations in the Political Section. To get information as to the routes of the escapees, their possibilities of getting into touch with the outside, was important in view of elaborating more efficient ways and means of making the camp secure. After the interrogation the majority of the runaways or of those suspected of organizing the escape were shot or publicly hanged, sometimes they were detailed to the penal company which was tantamount to a death sentence.

The entries in the so-called book of the bunker of Block No. 11 are the best illustration of the fate of those who were suspected to plan an escape. Out of 390 prisoners, committed to this bunker because of the above mentioned reasons, 196 were executed by shooting under the wall of death.

Professor Dr WŁADYSŁAW FEJKIEL.[*]

ETHICAL AND LEGAL LIMITS OF EXPERIMENTATION IN MEDICINE — IN CONNECTION WITH PROFESSOR CLAUBERG'S AFFAIR.

The spectre of Auschwitz made its unexpected appearance once more after 11 years had passed since the downfall of Nazi Germany when the public opinion of the world was alarmed by the press informing the readers that Professor D. C. Clauberg had been identified and arrested after his return to the German Federal Republic with a transport of German prisoners of war repatriated by the Soviet Union. As we know, Professor Clauberg died in prison in 1957 before his trial had started.

---

[*] Former prisoner of KL Auschwitz, at present Professor of the Academy of Medicine in Cracow.

Clauberg's affair is at present not only one more contribution to the characteristic of fascism. It is also a warning against a regime which by breaking all legal and ethical norms was unavoidably using scientific achievements of men of genius for its own criminal aims. We are again faced with the problem of medical experiments, their importance and the conditions in which they should be conducted.

As a biological science medicine must have recourse to experimentation for the sake of its development. Experimenting not only helps to verify proposed hypotheses and to demolish erroneous theories but also to construct new ones.

The word experiment means investigating a phenomenon, not as it occurs in nature (this would be observation) but under optional conditions, specially chosen and changed. In other words the nature of an experiment consists in modifying and selecting conditions of the appearance of the investigated phenomenon. Experimentation is chiefly used when we want to ascertain the interdependence of cause and effect in the origins of a phenomenon by stating its repetitiveness and correctness. Observation alone is mostly unable to do this for us.

In the seemingly uniform or homogenous chain of cause and effect relationships among phenomena we can find main and secondary ("accidental") causes. This differentiation is very essential; Wł. Biegański[1] speaks about it, calling it a circumstance which makes the process of cognition difficult. He particularly stresses the fact that some single phenomena, appearing within the whole of an observed occurrence and not connected by causal dependence with the main trend, but only resulting from, or being part of, other ("secondary") occurrences, tend to make the subject of inquiry obscure. In connection with this fact the aim of a scientific experiment would be to separate within the investigated occurrence the essential phenomena from the accidental ones, then to distinguish between the main causal relations and those that are their consequent.

---

[1] Wł. Biegański – *Logika medycyny* (The Logic of Medicine), Warsaw, 1908, p. 146.

Experiments were first conducted when investigating inorganic nature. In mechanics, physics and chemistry the experimental method was initially used "intuitively", later on (since Galileo's times) with full consciousness. In natural science experiments were introduced much later. It was only in the 17th and 18th century that biologists and physicians were able to use experimentation with increasing success.

Medical experiments can be divided into three main groups:
1) Experiments conducted outside the living organism (*in vitro*).
2) Experiments conducted within the living organism (*in vivo*).
3) Experiments upon corpses.

The first group embraces physico-chemical investigations of the phenomena taking place in the tissue and organic fluids, in blood, in secretions and excrements, together with biochemical investigations of resected tissues and investigations within the field of serology and bacteriology. Such experiments have been widely used in medicine and it is thanks to them that medical practice has gained the means to diagnose many diseases, has learned to prevent and to cure them. But this method enables us to investigate only those biological phenomena which can be completely isolated from the living organism without losing any of their essentials. It often fails, however, whenever there is need to connect the subject of investigation and the results of investigations *in vitro* with the living organism.

Experiments on corpses are a particular form of experimenting outside the living organism. They are mostly of a limited nature. Only some experiments can be conducted here; it is also possible to observe parts of clinical experiments conducted while the patient was alive, that is to observe the results of the action of drugs taken upon some organs or to observe the consequences of surgical operations, etc.

I have already stated that experimenting outside the living organism is not sufficient to promote the development of science and so we are obliged to experiment upon living organisms (*in vivo*), upon animals and men. Experiments upon animals have been conducted since a considerable time on a successively growing scale In many cases the results of experimenting upon animals are quite satisfactory and can easily be transferred by analogy upon the physiology and pathology of man. But it is not so in every case, therefore experimenting upon man becomes unavoidable. The human organism is more highly organized than the organisms of animals, even of those most similar to man. Practice shows that *homo sapiens* reacts to the same stimuli in many cases differently than animals do. Claude Bernard[2]) therefore stresses the fact that in the phenomena of life two separate elements are to be strictly differentiated:

1) qualities of tissues, common to all living beings,
2) an organizing mechanism, different in particular species and entailing differences in anatomic and physiological forms.

And so, when dealing with the general characteristics of living tissues, the results of an experiment can in all cases be transferred with an almost complete certainty to all species of living beings, man included. But experiments dealing with the organizing mechanism must be treated in a different way. Here the results may be transferred with a maximum of probability only to members of the same species or to those of a very similar species. The more distant the genealogical relationship between any two species the less founded is a mechanical transference of results obtained from one species upon the other. The results of experimental investigations conducted upon animals will therefore have only some degree of probability when applied to the physiology and pathology of man, which means that they would have to be additionally and finally verified on man himself.

The health and life of man being of the utmost value and protected by laws and a system of ethics, all interventions beyond the normal medical treatment (that means experiments) must be strictly regulated by legal and deontological norms. This fact

---

[2]) Cl. Bernard — *Introduction à l'etude de la medicine experimentale*, (Introduction to Experimental Medicine), 1865, p. 191, quoted after Wł. Biegański.

clearly pertains to experiments outside the living organism (*in vitro*).

When experimenting upon corpses we cannot disregard certain aspects of the matter. This kind of experimenting might be called experimenting outside the living organism, too. But due to many aspects of our civilized customs and religious beliefs, experiments conducted upon corpses must be subordinated to certain norms, too. With many religious denominations the human corpse is protected by a certain awe and is considered untouchable. The nearest relatives are legally empowered to dispose of a corpse or to protect it from outside interference which indubitably is a result both of the ancient cult of one's ancestors and of the circumstances connected with the development of our civilization. External interference into the realm of the family's privileges can only be excused by the necessity of guarding the public interests (e.g. autopsies ordered by law courts or health boards) or by the necessity of serving mankind in promoting the development of science. In the latter case we have to do both with anatomo-pathological autopsies and with experiments upon corpses. We know that dissections of, and experimenting upon, corpses are differently regulated in different countries by administrative norms. But the surgeon is always obliged to maintain a strict decorum and to protect the corpse from being profaned.

When experimenting upon animals *in vivo* general norms of civilization and humaneness should be observed which enjoin us to spare them unnecessary suffering and to avoid ill-advised or aimless operations. The tendency to protect animals from suffering sometimes becomes exaggerated. There are cases when the members of the societies for the prevention of cruelty to animals radically oppose experimenting on animals or hinder them. Our consciences dictate to be as humane as possible when experimenting on animals, but we can hardly pay attention to the exaggerated demands of such societies. Szumowski [3]) is right when drawing our attention to the fact that legal limitations of experiments upon animals might

---

[3]) Wł. Szumowski — *Polska Gazeta Lekarska* (The Polish Physicians' Journal) 1933, No. 48. pp. 3—4.

lead the experimenters to experiment on man, which would be against all feelings of humaneness.

While experiments on corpses or animals need no particular legal rulings, experiments conducted upon the living organism of man should be strictly limited by definite rules. All civilized countries possess a system of basic ethical norms and laws accepted by universal custom and sanctioned by agelong tradition. This system deals with the relationship between the doctor and the patient. It chiefly contains rules to be observed in medical practice and general rules of deontology, but it lacks definite legal norms regulating the relation of the experimenter to the person experimented upon. And so, for instance, in many countries the experimenter according to existing laws is only responsible for bodily injuries of man as the physician pursuing his profession (mistakes in medical art, unintentional bodily injuries, unintentional causing of the death of the patient, etc.). Polish legislation also lacks definite rules of that kind. But we know that we cannot identify experimentation on the living organism with the medical practice and we need definite legal norms, guaranteeing the rights of man and protecting the scientist from possible conflicts.

Medical experiments conducted on man can be divided into two main groups:

1) experiments on the sick,
2) experiments on the healthy.

Very essential is also the division of experiments into risky experiments and those that are not risky. This division is connected with the one above.

We shall first consider the experiments conducted on the sick, with their division into safe and risky interventions. Safe experiments are widely used in hospitals and centres of scientific research and their objective is either diagnosis or therapy. Here belong all pioneering attempts at diagnosis, examination of secretions of organs, of the marrow, all — scopies and — graphies, sections of tissues. For the sake of therapy pioneering attempts are undertaken, such as special kinds of diet, administration of new drugs, different dosage of traditional drugs, the use of new sera and vaccines, etc.

Risky experiments are those which are undertaken for the first time in order to save a sick person, but they might cause bodily injury or even the demise of the patient. Their aim is also to try out new methods of curing the given ailment. We can mention here such operations as the excision of the stomach (Rydygier, later Billroth), surgical operations on the heart and vessels (Blalock, Bailey, Crafford), operations on the brain (Horsley, Cushing and others). Thanks to them not only lives of patients had been saved (when the traditional methods of treatment had failed) but they had also helped to create new methods of operating to be applied on a large scale.

In many cases the need arises to experiment on the healthy man normally reacting to stimuli (which is not to be expected in the case of a sick man). It is not the benefit of a given individual but the common good that lies at the root of such experiments. Generally speaking they do not meet with any considerable opposition as long as the experimenter feels that, according to his best knowledge and his conscience, they are not risky. But the situation is quite different if the interventions are risky, if they threaten the health or life of the subject of the experiment, a healthy person, after all, who therefore would not benefit in any way, even should the experiment prove wholly successful.

The distinction between risky and safe experiments, introduced here, may cause considerable difficulties in practice. An intervention which to the best knowledge of the experimenter seems trifling may sometimes cause dangerous complications under specific circumstances. Unforeseen complications (at an operation for instance), reactions of the organism which are far from the average, finally mistakes in the technique of the experiments do happen. When a physician decides upon the experiment he must, therefore, carefully consider whether in the given case there is any risk (permanent injury of the body or even death) or not, and whether the possible risk would be justified by the personal benefit of the patient.

A special case are those experiments, even risky ones, which the experimenter conducts upon his own person. It is a frequent occurrence in medical practice to experiment upon one's own self by trying out new drugs, sera, vaccines, applying special kinds of diet, etc. The history of medicine is full of heroic examples of the self-sacrifice of outstanding researchworkers for the good of mankind and for the advancement of science. They did not hesitate to sacrifice themselves by undertaking dangerous experiments. It is sufficient to mention the names of scientists like Moczutkowski [4]) who injected into his body the blood of a patient ill with typhus, caught the disease and thereby proved that the disease carrying factor was in the blood of the patient. Or Hunter [5]) who introduced the secretion of the urethra of a patient ill with gonorrhea into his prepuce and became infected not only with this disease but also with syphilis which the patient had had too. There was Koino [6]) who swallowed 2,000 eggs of the ascarid, then got pneumonia and coughing violently expectorated the larvae of the ascarides thereby proving that they directly penetrated from the digestive tract to the circulatory system and to the lungs. Pettenkofer [7]) swallowed 1 million of fresh cholera culture in broth but did not fall ill in spite of his advanced years (he was 74) and so proved that the presence of the bacillii, even in such a huge quantity, would not by itself cause infection without the action of other factors. Finally Nitsch [8]) of Cracow endeavoured to prove his hypothesis by injecting under his skin a considerable quantity of fresh laboratory virus of hydrophobia, not to mention many other scientists who had similarly risked their lives. Such experiments, even the most dangerous ones, when voluntarily conducted on one's own self, can arouse only our admiration and sincere approbation. But even in such cases the experimenter's activities should be most carefully checked by his environment as there exists the possibility that he might decide upon an experiment while mentally disturbed or without having properly assessed its risk.

---

[4]) J. K. Kostrzewski — *O kilku ostrych chorobach zakaźnych* (Some Acute Infectious Diseases, PAU, 1947, p. 175.
[5]) *Traité de la Syphilis* (Treatise on Syphilis), 175, Vol. I. 1931 p. 328.
[6]) *Neue Deutsche Klinik* (New German Clinic), Vol. I. 1928 pp. 606, 607.
[7]) Wł. Szumowski — *Historia Medycyny* (The History of Medicine), 1935, p. 622.
[8]) R. Nitsch — *Doświadczenia z jadem laboratoryjnym (virus fixe) wścieklizny* (Experiments wisth the Laboratory Virus of Rabies), PAU, 1904, p. 244.

Three essential premises lie at the root of medical experimenting upon the living organisms (of the healthy and of the sick). They also form the most general and necessary condition of it being ethically admissible, namely that its objective should be:
1) either the individual benefit of the patient,
2) or the more general benefit of man (advancement of science),
3) or both.

An experiment whose subject is an individual may be subordinated to the personal good of the individual in question (and simultaneously to the benefit of mankind and the advancement of science) only when the person in question is ill. The same experiment conducted upon a healthy person (with that person's consent, of course,) or upon the healthy experimenter himself, has solely the benefit of mankind and of science in view.

Besides this basic condition which is the moral affirmation of the aim of the experiment, other particular conditions are also necessary. As was mentioned above, these conditions have never and nowhere entered into a system of definite, coordinated norms. In spite of this fact every experimenting physician should be conscious of them, deducing them from the basic tenets of universal ethics, from legal norms accepted in civilized countries and from the prevalent customs, if the former and the latter agree with the tenets of ethics and deontology.

Particular attention should therefore be paid to the substantiation given by the American Military Tribunal in Nuremberg in its verdict of August 20, 1947 in the case No. 1 against Dr Karl Brandt and other Nazi physicians, as it is the first, I believe, attempt to specify in detail the admissibility, conditions and limits, of experimenting upon living human organism.

But as this substantiation (some parts of which form the subject matter for my reflections), while basically sound, contains yet several instances of inexactitude and some lacunae, I should like to polemize with certain of its formulations before attempting to define the circumstances when medical experiments are admissible.

The Nuremberg substantiation justly stresses the fact that to conduct experiments on living men it is, first of all, necessary to have their legally valid consent to do so. In consequence the persons in question must be fully entitled to transact legal business. This formulation, however, omits many exceptional cases to be found in practice, namely it restricts experimenting to adults who are of age, mentally sound and therefore able to express their personal consent. To such exceptional cases belong medical experiments dealing with the sick and undertaken solely in their own interest, when the patients are minors or certified adults, and such cases need a different kind of formulation. Their own consent should then be replaced by a corresponding declaration of their legal curators. It might also happen that a group of physicians would be obliged to be endowed with legal power to decide upon a novel experiment while undertaking a hazardous operation upon the victim of a casualty, when no time is to be lost and life is in danger, the patient is unconscious or a minor or mentally ill. In such cases it would be impossible to obtain the consent of the patient in question or of his curators as a delay might prove fatal and the experimental operation might be the only chance to save the patient. It is a matter of course that the person giving the order to undertake an experimental operation of this kind should shoulder the entire responsibility for a proper evaluation of the consent given. It is a most subtle and difficult matter to define the limits within which the legal curators of persons, unable to give their own consent to the experiment, can go. So is the stating of "an urgent need" which motivates action in emergency without the consent. In such cases the group of physicians and their superiors must be particularly careful and must act with the utmost circumspection.

All experiments, however, to which physically and mentally healthy persons are subjected (risky or safe experiments which lack the character of a cure) can be undertaken only with the full consent of the person in question (if the person is of age), after duly informing him or her about all the possible consequences and dangers of the operation.

The statement of the Nuremberg Tribunal unjustly excludes the possibility of undertaking curative experiments upon sick persons, as we learn from Par. 2 of the quoted document, "The experiment must be of the kind to promise results useful to the common good, which results would not be attainable by any other means or methods of scientific research." As we see, the document does not mention the possibility of undertaking experiments by which the patient would profit directly and the community only indirectly. Par. 3 connects, it is true, experiments with a state of disease, "An experiment should be planned in such a manner, be based on results obtained with animals, on the knowledge of the disease and of other problems, so that its probable results would justify undertaking it." But the categorical passage in Par. 5 confirms our thesis that the statement of the Nuremberg Tribunal regulates only one section of the problem of experimenting on man, namely experimenting on the healthy, subordinated to the profit of mankind (science). Par. 5 is as follows, "It is not permissible to undertake any experiments if a priori there exists the possibility of resulting permanent bodily injury, with the exception perhaps(?) of those experiments to which the experimenters subject themselves." And yet it is universally accepted that a physician is morally entitled to decide upon a risky experimental curative treatment of the patient (naturally keeping within bounds of all the above mentioned stipulations and exercising the utmost care), should all traditionally used methods fail and if there is a chance of saving the patient's life, even at the cost of permanent bodily injury. Naturally, the experimental treatment of the patient cannot involve a greater risk than the disease itself when treated in a traditional way. The risk connected with the curative experiment must "pay", not only from the point of view of the abstract notion of "mankind", but also from the concrete point of view of the patient's good.

The motivation of medical experiments by "results useful to the whole human community" (Par. 2.) seems to be rather regrettably worded. The trouble namely is that nearly all the experiments conducted by Nazi doctors in camps and prisons (just like all the Nazi crimes in occupied countries) had as their objective "the be-

befit of the human (i.e. German) community", thus peculiarly interpreted by Hitler's dictatorship. History, even in the most recent days, has often shown that cliques of dictators will commit the most atrocious crimes under the guise of serving "the common weal". Therefore the only proper motivation of experiments on living men should be (besides other motives) the good of mankind (or science) as that concept is wholly unequivocal.

It hardly seems just, too, to dispute the research worker's right to undertake an experiment on himself, even if it involves permanent bodily injury (Par. 5 — "...with the exception of, perhaps, those experiments to which experimenters subject themselves"). Outstanding scientists (among them those mentioned in the introduction) subjected themselves to the most hazardous experiments which involved not only bodily injuries but also death, we can, however, have no doubts as to the high moral incentives of their action and can only respect and admire their heroic courage in the face of such great risks.

Coming to the end of my critical discussion of the norms concerning experimentation as formulated in the statement of the Nuremberg Tribunal, I should like to stress the enigmatic redaction of its Par. 6, which might lead to arbitrary interpretations and abuses ("the degree of danger must never overstep the bounds set by the significance, common to humanity, of the problem to be solved").

It is evident from the above quotation that the statement of the Nuremberg Tribunal was negatively influenced by the lack of distinction between operations performed on the sick and on the healthy, and also by the absence of a division into risky and safe experiments. According to my opinion this distinction is essential from the point of view of methodology.

Before passing on to an attempt at systematizing the conditions and norms of experimenting on the living man I shall briefly survey the ethically inadmissible operations, with particular stress laid upon the experimental practices of Dr C. Clauberg.

The history of medicine tells us about numerous examples of experiments on men which were, without doubt, of great significance for the development of science, but which in a civilized community have aroused or should arouse a decided moral condemnation. All of them were connected with a violation of the rights of the individual for the sake of the so-called common good. But even the noblest end cannot justify the means. And so, e.g. in the Alexandrine School (IV century B.C.) men condemned to death were dissected alive. This was done in order "...to see in a living organism the colour, shape, size, organization, hardness, softness and smoothness of each organ; what it is joined to, where it is convex and where concave, where it is attached to and what it covers." [9] In modern times Philip Ricord [10] conducted mass experiments on prisoners infecting several hundred men with syphilis. During World War II a certain Turkish physician [11] infected several hundred healthy prisoners of war with typhus. Physicians, heedless of ethics, were known to experiment in the field of bacteriology. It must be admitted that such proceedings were, in modern times, always decidedly disapproved of by medical circles and by the progressive part of society. But the moral disapprobation of these deeds was probably not sufficiently strong since during World War II many physicians and scientists in Germany and Japan had found it right and proper to serve their Fascist regime by experimenting on a scale, more vast than ever before, upon the population of occupied countries. The Fascist ideology which had undermined all moral and legal norms of human co-existence in the occupied countries became a source of inspiration for these experimenters. The doctrine, teaching about "superior" and "inferior" races, doomed whole nations to be exterminated and thereby justified all crimes, giving German and Japanese doctors a free hand in experimenting, provided they served the ruling nation.

There were thousands of experiments conducted upon prisoners but among them those effected in the Buchenwald Camp [12] excelled

---

[9] Wł. Szumowski — *Historia Medycyny* (The History of Medicine), Cracow, 1935, Vol. I. p. 87.
[10] A. J. Kartamyszew — *Kožnyje wienericzeskije bolezni* (Veneral Skin Diseases), Medgiz, 1954, p. 339.
[11] J. W. Gromaszewskij and G. M. Wajndrach — *Epidemiologia szczegółowa* (Epidemiology), Warsaw, PZWL., p. 434.
[12] Wł. Fejkiel — *Przegląd Lekarski* (Medical Review), 1955, N. 4.

in ruthlessness, cruelty and their vast scale. Various sera against typhus were tried out. In the course of 2 years the doctors Mrugowsky, Genzgen, Ding and the well-known Professors Hirt and Hagen had infected circa 600 prisoners with several malignant cultures of typhus; nearly all of the victims died. Rascher [13]) experimented in Dachau with the influence of low temperatures on the human organism and caused the death in horrible agony of over 200 prisoners. Again in Dachau Rascher and Romberg [14]) experimented with the action of low atmospheric pressure upon man and as a result of these experiments many people died after most painful sufferings. There were experiments with drinking the salty sea water, experiments to clear up the toxicity of sulphonamides, and many others.

All these experiments were motivated by the circumstance that they would benefit the German community. They were criminal because they violated the welfare of the individual who was forced by terroristic measures to surrender to them. But the experiments of Dr Clauberg deserve an even stronger ethical and legal censure. They aimed at arriving at new methods and techniques of mass sterilization of the women in occupied countries, thereby being in complete disagreement with the welfare of mankind (and *ipso facto* of the individual) and they were a preparatory step towards genocide. They do not, therefore, deserve to be called medical experiments *sensu stricto*, although "technically" they had to do with experimenting. Clauberg's experiments do not stand alone in this respect. An accessory part to genocide had also the experiments of Professor Schumann [15]) in Auschwitz, dealing with the sterilization of men by means of X-rays, to be used on a mass scale later on. Similar experiments were conducted in Buchenwald. There, the poisoning action of aconitine was investigated. Aconitine was put into the bullets of guns, the idea being of using such weapons at the battle fronts. Healthy prisoners were shot at from revolvers the bullets of which were filled with the nitrate of aconitine and the poisoning of the wounded was then observed.

---

[13]) B. Grzywacz — *Eksperymenty na człowieku a eksperymenty na zwierzętach* (Experiments on Man and Experiments on Animals), Not published, Cracow, 1952.
[14]) Vide footnote [13]).
[15]) J. Olbrycht — *Przegląd Lekarski* (Medical Review), 1948, pp. 108, 109.

MEDICAL EXPERIMENTS

The experiments of Clauberg formed part of the "new science", the so-called "negative demography" [16],) which the German Fascism had created. The name itself tells us that it had to do with elaborating methods of biological extermination of whole nations then under the yoke of the Nazis.

The conception of Clauberg's experiments originated in Himmler's headquarters. The choice of the experimenter was rather accidental. Professor Clauberg, a popular gynaecologist, was known before the war to cure the sterility of women successfully. Himmler himself had requested him to treat the wife of one of the SS officers of high rank. In those days of Nazi dogmas sterility was almost tantamount to disloyalty to the regime which was preparing to people the world with the members of the "superior race". It was then that Clauberg volunteered to elaborate a method of effecting lasting sterility in women. After a time of trial the method was to have been used on a mass scale.

The necessary preparations had been quickly made. Professor Clauberg soon came to Auschwitz and the camp management placed a separate block (No. 10) at his disposal, while Himmler's headquarters took care to supply it with all the necessary equipment and demanded frequent information about the results of the experiments.

Block No. 10 was isolated from the rest of the camp forming one unit together with the well-known "Block of Death", i.e. Block No. 11. It was guarded by SS wardresses. The inmates of this block were women prisoners from about 14 countries. Clauberg had simply bought them from the camp management paying 1 Mark a week for each.[17])

Clauberg himself selected his experimental material from among candidates presented by the Chief Garrison Surgeon, Dr Wirths, a gynaecologist too.

"*Häftlinge für Versuchszwecke*" (prisoners to be used for experiments) had to fulfil the following stipulations: complete

---

[16]) Himmler's staff used the term "negative demography" for sterilization and other depopulating measures.
[17]) Statement of former prisoner. Dr Alina Brewda (Trial of R. Höss, commendant of the Auschwitz-Birkenau Concentration Camp, Vol. 17, cards 59—62.)

sexual maturity (17—40 years of age, preferably from 20 to 30), well-built, well-nourished if possible and generally in good health. Regular menstruation was stipulated as in camp amenorrhoea, the so-called "*Kriegsamenorrhoea*", induced by physical and mental hardships, was prevalent. Those who had been mothers were privileged, there being then no doubt as to their fecundity.

The experiments were conducted by Clauberg himself, assisted by the chemist Dr Gebel, *SS* N.C.O. orderly Binning and several women prisoners, nurses by profession, who were compelled to give their help. The entire proceeding was conducted strictly confidentially and the participants were treated as being in the know of state secrets (*Geheimnisträger*). The X-ray chamber on the ground-floor of Block 10, strictly isolated, was the place of the operations. After writing down general gynaecological data of the patient the victim was placed on the table used for gynaecological examinations and then Dr Clauberg, having uncovered the vaginal part of the uterus, seized it by means of a vulsellum forceps and introduced a uterine catheter into the canal of its neck. With the help of the catheter he injected under pressure the contrast medium. The movements of the contrast medium were checked by X-rays. In this way the degree of patency of the genital tract was ascertained. If the oviducts proved to be patent, the examined woman was released and was told to run about the room for some time.[18]

Meanwhile another woman, waiting her turn, was examined in a similar way. After some time the first victim was put again on the table and using the above described procedure a special liquid, mixed with the Roentgen contrast (to enable the checking of the liquid by means of X-rays) was introduced into the uterine cavity. The chemical composition of the liquid, which was of a whitish colour, was unknown. According to the records of the *SS* Institute of Hygiene at Rajsko (quoted after J. Olbrycht)[19], it probably was a certain solution of formalin. I spoke many times to Dr Samuel, prisoner-doctor in Block 10, about this matter, and he was of the

---

[18] Trial of R. Hoess, commandant of the Auschwitz-Birkenau Concentration Camp—Explanations of the defendant, Vol. 21, cards 132—137.

[19] J. Olbrycht — *Sprawy zdrowotne w obozie koncentracyjnym w Oświęcimiu* (Sanitary Matters in the Auschwitz Concentration Camp), *Przegląd Lekarski* (Medical Review), 1948, 4, 139.

opinion that besides formalin other unknown irritating liquids must have been used in these cases. After the last enema the patient was left alone, usually for a period of 6 weeks. But in the initial stage of the "researches" checking examinations were undertaken even before the lapse of that time. They were to show whether the intended closure of the oviducts had already been effected and in what stage of closure they were. The checking consisted in introducing the contrast and then X-raying. Practice had shown that the intended results were usually obtained after a period of 6 weeks. Clauberg's statement to the camp commandant R. Hoes should be quoted here; he said that the procedure caused in all cases a sealing up of the oviducts which then ceased to be patent. But as against that statement "positive results" had not been obtained in many cases. Then Clauberg would order the procedure to be repeated and liquids of a more powerful concentration would be introduced. The same patient was sometimes forced to undergo this treatment several times at intervals of 3—4 weeks.[20])

Another kind of experimenting conducted by Clauberg in Block 10 consisted in trying out new contrast media to be used in X-ray examinations. The German chemical concerns which produced various substitutes for iodine contrasts initiated the experiments. Clauberg's assistant, Dr Gebel, was his co-worker in the researches concerning these contrast media, and as a representative of the concern *Schering-Werke* he was just as interested in them as Clauberg. The contrasts were called by the prisoners "Gebel's liquids".

The experimenting procedure was the same as in the case of normal iodine contrasts. The "experiments" had systematically shown the uselessness of the new contrasts; the X-ray pictures obtained with them were indistinct. The experiments were most painful for the victims subjected to them.

What were the consequences of Clauberg's experiments? As was mentioned above they resulted in lasting barrenness due to the closure of the oviducts. The lack of patency of the oviducts was

---

[20]) Based on oral information given by Dr Samuel, then working in Block 10 and on the report of Dr Vuysje (Trial of R. Höss, commandant of the Auschwitz-Birkenau Concentration Camp, Vol. 16. cards 129 —138).

attained as a result of an inflammatory process caused by the introduction of the irritating liquid. Strong, caustic chemicals introduced into the uterine cavity, the oviducts and the peritoneum of the small pelvis resulted in an inflammatory state of the organs (*endo-myoperimetritis, salpingoophoritis et pelveoperitonitis*). More sensitive women (especially if the solution was of a higher concentration) even succumbed to gangrene of the corresponding part of the genital tract and the peritoneum.

It would be a mistake to attribute the inflammation of the genital organs solely to the irritating action of the chemicals. The great susceptibility of a woman's interior genital parts to bacteria infection is well-known and infection can easily be induced by careless operations. And so, e.g. doctors who intervene by insufflation of the oviducts (with quite an opposite aim in view to that of Clauberg) are obliged to be particularly careful. The dangers of that operation are described by eminent German physicians, such as Sellheim who was the first to use the method of insufflation in Germany, also Stoeckel, Martius and others, and with these facts Clauberg must have been wholly familiar. In connection with the danger involved a physician's duty would be, before resorting to insufflation, to examine the general state of health of the woman and to ascertain whether in the genital organs there are any foci of infection which could spread over the whole genital tract and particularly over the peritoneum. Therefore he should, among other examinations, check the temperature of the body, the reaction for blood sedimentation rate and he should ascertain the degree to which the vagina and the neck of the uterus are free from infection by examining the secretion under the microscope.

But the records and statements of the witnesses make it clear that Clauberg had completely neglected the above described preventive measures. What more, he wilfully exposed the women to infection ordering them to run about the room after the salpingography, which must have favoured the spreading of infection within the genital tract and the peritoneum, not to mention the sufferings caused thereby.

Every physician will be certain that such cases of infection must have occurred under the circumstances. They are confirmed by the statements of prisoner-doctors of Block 10, Dr Alina Brewda and Sława Klein, who deposed that besides the normal consequence of introducing caustic fluids into the genital tract, namely a searing pain during the intervention, and afterwards the chemically induced inflammation (with febrile state, shivering, uterine bleeding, a general feeling of malaise, etc.), there were, in many cases, symptoms of a widespread infection, characterized by high septic temperatures, violent shivering and painful infiltrations of the adnexa, which symptoms lasted for many months.[21])

The same applies, *mutatis mutandis*, to operations with Gebel's contrast media, but they were much more painful so that during their performance pitiful cries of the victims were heard from Block 10. Uterine bleeding and collapse were also frequent (Dr Brewda).

In recapitulation it is to be stated that Dr Clauberg's and Dr Gebel's experiments in Block 10 caused a series of somatic and psychic consequences and in particular:

1) they resulted in barrenness, 2) they induced acute and chronic inflammation of the genital organs, 3) they caused inexpressible mental sufferings. Besides being conscious of their cripplehood (barrenness, inflammatory complications,) the victims knew that as exploited "guinea pigs" they would be killed, which was the usual fate of all persons in the know of state secrets.

It is now time to sum up the foregoing considerations and to formulate the conditions and norms of experimenting upon man.

1) By medical experiments on the living man we mean a physician's pioneering intervention into the biological conditions of the human organism, aiming at solving still unknown problems of physiology, pathology and therapy. In consequence of that definition both a healthy and a sick person can be the subject of medical experiments.

2) A medical experiment on the living human organism must aim at the benefit of the given individual or of mankind (science), it may have both objectives in view. All medical interventions

---

[21]) Vide footnote [17]).

on man devoid of these objectives are outside the pale of that concept.

All interventions which have other objectives in view are ethically *a priori* to be rejected. It is of essential importance to put a sign of equality between "the good of mankind" and "the good of science". Conflicts between those two concepts should never arise. To make use of science in order to attain objectives harmful to mankind or to some groups of it (races, nations, etc.) deserves strong condemnation.

3) Experiments on man (whether risky or not) must, without question, be based upon his consent.[22] In case of therapeutic experiments on persons who are not legally able to act the consent should be given by his or her legal curators. In emergency cases, when delay is fatal to life, the decision as to the undertaking of the experiment should be left to a group of doctors or to one individual even, possessing necessary professional qualifications.

4) A risky experiment on man should be undertaken only if all other possibilities were tried, as far as laboratory experiments and experiments on animals go. It should be based on a thorough knowledge of scientific literature.

5) A therapeutic experiment must not expose the patient to incommensurable dangers or sufferings. The risk undertaken must "pay".

6) The rule should be accepted that all risky experiments be conducted only in scientific institutes by highly qualified physicians. Therapeutic experiments in emergency cases could be excepted from this rule.

7) When conducting all experiments n man (and on animals, too,) the physician should try to spare the person in question any unnecessary physical or mental sufferings. It is obvious that an experiment on man (just like all operations) should be prepared

---

[22] The consent must be given in a legally valid manner. As norm the thesis should be accepted that all experimenting on prisoners and condemned men is prohibited, because it could give rise to abuse. But the question arises whether it is admissible to give someone with a death sentence the right of choice of submitting to a risky experiment by which choice the death sentence could be quashed? It seems that legislation might allow the possibility of that kind of expiation.

having regard to the psyche of the patient and it should be conducted in a proper atmosphere.

From the above discussion the conclusion is clear that Clauberg's so-called experiments (together with those of other *SS* doctors) were not medical experiments. Clauberg's experiments cannot be classed together with ordinary crimes; they belong to the hitherto unknown category of accessaries to the crime of genocide.

Professor Dr WŁADYSŁAW FEJKIEL

STARVATION IN AUSCHWITZ.

The first symptoms of disease caused by starvation were observed among the prisoners as early as September 1940. I myself saw in October prisoners with swellings and diarrhoea. They were moving about with difficulty and they besieged Block No. 28 where the out-patient clinic was situated. Such patients, allegedly having kidney trouble and an "upset stomach", got carbon or "hexal" tablets from the prisoners-doctors and were given "learned" advice not to drink water, to use very little salt and other stimulants, and then they had to go to work. This therapy certainly helped — the disease, if not the patient.

At that time it was small wonder that the prisoners-doctors were unacquainted with the starvation sickness which they thought was diarrhoea (*Durchfall*). We knew, all of us, that acute starvation was possible and that it was a disease, but it was known rather as the result of tragic experiences of men who had lost contact with the civilized world, such as castaways, mountain climbers and so on. Acute starvation can sometimes be observed in daily life as the result of certain diseases when eating becomes difficult as e.g. in cases of stricture or obstruction of the lumen of the esophagus or the lower parts of the alimentary tract (chiefly a consequence of tumours). It sometimes happens that people refuse to eat (prisoners, mystics or mental cases) and are ill in consequence. But no one among us had expected to see people ill with starvation in the neighbourhood of Cracow, where starvation was completely unknown throughout the twentieth century.

The patients suffering from this disease were treated by the *SS*-men and capos just as if they were healthy — all had to march to work to the tune of Prussian marches early in the morning. Their feet and legs being considerably swollen they dragged them with difficulty or fell down and were beaten and kicked by the supervisors *in feldgrau* (khaki), and sometimes by the prisoners--supervisors in striped camp clothes.

It sometimes happened that many marched barefoot because their shoes had been either stolen by stronger fellow-prisoners and bartered to the civilians[1]) for bread or cigarettes, or because the swelling had been so pronounced that they were unable to squeeze their feet into the shoes. It must be stressed that *SS*-men did not punish people going barefoot to work in autumn and in winter.

Under the circumstances the only help was a kind and still strong friend who supported the sick man, dragged him on when going to work and comforted him with soothing words. Such friends were to be found quite often.

The general emaciation of prisoners could be noticed only by a newcomer to the camp, the prisoners of long standing were quite used to the sight. Only those prisoners who held some posts in

---
[1]) Working in the camp.

the camp looked well among the mass of grey, bony and sad-looking human beings. At that time the prisoners with functions in the camp were on the whole plump, red-cheeked, sometimes even smiling. After the evening roll-call they would walk about in groups, engaged in lively discussions, and still having some strength left they tried by all means to evade the moment when they would look like the rest of their fellow-prisoners.

As time was passing the number of the emaciated and sick prisoners increased, particularly when it grew colder and living conditions got worse. New transports of prisoners were steadily arriving. The living space became more and more cramped, one could not wash, the underwear was not changed for months.

Besides fasting other inseparable companions of the prisoners made their appearance — dirt, lice, fleas and scabies, and the starvation diarrhoea was spreading more and more.

During work hours someone would look faint and then diappeared in the nearest secluded place. Then many others followed his example. After work the social life of the camp inmates centred, not in front of the camp kitchen as before, but in front of the latrines or the out-patients clinic. One could but rarely see prisoners walking about. They were either so weak that they stayed in the barracks or they visited the above mentioned institutions.

The camp latrines were besieged by hundreds. The queues became longer and longer and, instead of the usual quietness, shouts and curses were heard there. The stronger men jumped the queues and the weaker ones could not reach the latrine in time or had not strength left to get there. Being afraid to enter the latrine they sometimes relieved nature near it and were then beaten up by the orderlies. The weak ones were afraid to go to the latrines because of an accident which had happened when a capo had pushed down an exhausted prisoner into the cloacal hole. This man was too weak to get cleaned and washed and so the block senior would not let him in into the barrack. The unlucky man was obliged to spend the few remaining days of his life on the cement floor of the barrack corridor while in the daytime he had to go to work.

Those with some inventiveness tried to escape further sufferings or even mishaps by reducing their visits to the latrine. They gathered old papers, rags, dry leaves or wood shavings and manufactured some kind of padding. The author did so, too. Those who were less inventive or too weak to exert themselves had to stay soiled and stinking.

The camp hospital had at that time room for a few hundred patients only (not separate beds) and could not cope with even a small fraction of the patients. Even very sick persons were treated as out-patients and were given each one tablet of carbon or tanalbin [2]) It was not easy to get the tablets. They were rationed and each was noted down in the patient's register by the *SS* authorities. Besides, in order to see the helpless prisoner-doctor the sick had to stand for hours in front of the clinic in rainy or cold weather.

Those who were more impatient or tried to force their entry into the corridor of the clinic were beaten up by the *Pförtner*[3]) on duty, a well-fed man, usually with a strong stick in his hand which enhanced his authority.

The prisoners tried to save themselves by any available means. Those who were "well-off" burnt their bread to carbon, while others, who had little bread, burnt wood and fed themselves with the carbon all day long. Quite helpless prisoners could get carbon made of beech wood from all kinds of camp caterers. But to get a sufficient amount of carbon they had to barter their last piece of bread. The sick men gave away their bread and ate wood.

They often fell victims to camp hoodlums who extorted from the gullible their last slice of bread, promising them better work indoors with facilities to get more plentiful food.

The death rate was increasing. If one was lucky or had some backing, one died in hospital. But the less lucky ones died in the barracks, with some considerable help from the block senior or his substitutes.

In their difficult physical and moral crisis the prisoners sought comfort visiting the numerous fortune-tellers in camp who foretold,

---

[2]) Anti-diarrhoea remedies which did little to help the starvation diarrhoea.
[3]) Janitor.

for a bread ration or a few potatoes, certain and speedy release from the camp.

One day, towards the end of October 1940, it grew suddenly cold and there was an unexpected snow-fall. After the evening roll-call, during which festivity two camp friends of mine had died, we were shut in the barracks. The SS-men, the block-leaders and block seniors told us this was done because of our health, we were about to receive warm clothing. Winter was approaching — thus did the prisoners justly reason — one had to have warm things.

Before we were presented with some Jaeger underwear and warm socks, the SS-men told us to squat down and sing some pretty and long German military songs. The squatting position made it difficult to believe we would get the promised gifts, but according to the old camp tradition each prisoner preferred to think he would get a warm sweater rather than a whipping.

Soon after we were ordered to lie down on the floor and sleep. At the same time several carts drawn by prisoners were passing along the main camp street. The transport conveyed about ninety corpses to the crematorium — our fellow-prisoners who had died that day.

At the beginning of that month every dead prisoner was carried out in a wooden box. There were not more of such coffins than a few daily. Nobody paid much attention to that daily occurrence. The camp had then about five thousand inmates — a few deaths daily did not seem out of the ordinary, so prisoners thought.

The next day we learned that single coffins ceased to be taken to the crematorium where several corpses were now simultaneously cremated in one oven.

Since that day the relatives of the deceased no longer received the ashes of their dear ones. Such ashes as were helter-skelter shovelled out of the ovens were sent to them. The sight of the carts with the dead bodies of our many fellows who had died in one single day was most depressing. We now knew that if things continued as they were, we should, one day, drive to the "chimney" in a cart, too.

I think it was then that for the first time in the history of Auschwitz we had noticed the fact, persisting till the end of the camp's existence, namely that the number of the crematoria ovens and their staff could not cope with the SS production of corpses.

Whole transports were dwindling away. The first and the third Warsaw transports had the highest death rate, also the second and the third transport from Tarnów. People died in the daytime while working, they died at night in the barracks, in the latrines and in front of the out-patient clinic.

The hospital took in only a fragment of the sick, the rest had to go back to work and according to the SS health service regulation they were considered to be healthy. The sick had to march to work together with the healthy. They were lucky if the SS-man or capo failed to notice them. They had a chance then to die quietly in front of the clinic.

In the living quarters the prisoners slept on the floor upon spread paper mattresses which had a rather disembowelled look. To turn at night one had to waken one's next neighbour, if not the whole row of sleepers, and to ask them to turn too. Curses or even blows followed.

Nobody wanted to sleep next to those who had diarrhoea. They were pushed and crowded all together into one corner of the room. They were obliged to leave the room often at night and, being weak, stumbled and fell upon their neighbours. Shouts, quarrels and curses followed and sometimes lasted the whole night through. If one of the sick wanted to avoid all this, he went early in the evening to the latrine and, having secured his seat there, spent the whole night in that place. One day after another passed in this way till death came and brought release.

In the winter of 1941/42 the number of patients with starvation sickness increased to such an extent that the camp authorities forbade to send them to work outside the camp area. A special squad was formed for them, the so-called light work squad (*leichte Arbeit*). There was no gassing as yet and so the work in the squad was to kill them off. The work consisted in sitting in the snow and frost and cleaning bricks and roof-tiles which were to be used for building purposes.

But it appeared that this system had not produced the expected quick results and so another method of liquidating the sick was applied. The exhausted prisoners were crowded together in the yard of Block 11, were kept there for a day or two and from time to time were showered with cold water. Naturally nearly all of them died. If someone managed to survive this treatment he would be sent to the hospital. Among those who survived this "water cure" was Jan Nowak, a pediatrist from Warsaw who afterwards convalesced in my ward at the hospital.

As far as disease symptoms are concerned the starvation process can be divided into two stages. The one was characterized by emaciation, muscular weakness and a progressive decrease of motorial energy. Deeper going lesions of the organism were not yet visible. The sick moved slowly and were weakened, but hardly showed any other symptoms. No considerable psychic changes were to be noticed, except a certain excitability and a characteristic irritability.

It was difficult to fix the border line between the first and the second stage. With some patients the border line was quickly crossed, with others it was a gradual process. On the whole one might assume that the second stage was reached when the starving individual had lost one third of his ordinary weight. Not only did the emaciation become more and more pronounced and so did the weakness, but the facial expression would change, too. The eyes were opaque, the face wore a look of indifference, apathy and sadness. The skin became greyish or livid, it was thinner and like parchment, hardened and desquamative. It was very susceptible to all infections, particularly to scabies. The hair was rough, brittle and lustreless. The head became elongated, the outlines of the zygomatic bones and the eye-sockets became distinct. The patient breathed slowly, spoke in a low voice and with great effort.

Depending on the duration of starving smaller or more extensive swellings would appear. The first to swell were the eyelids and feet. The swellings would be localized in different areas of the body at different times of the day. In the morning, after the night's rest, they would be seen best in the face, in the evening they appeared on the feet, legs and thighs. Depending on the position of the body the swelling liquid would flow down into the lower parts of the body. The swellings increased with time and with people who were obliged to stand for a longer time they would reach the legs, thighs, buttocks, scrotal pouch and even the abdomen. The swellings were accompanied by diarrhoea, but there were cases when diarrhoea came first.

At that stage the patients grew dull and indifferent to the surroundings. They no longer formed part of their milieu. If they could move they did so very slowly, without flexing their knees. As a result of their lowered body temperature which fell below 36'C, they trembled with cold.

A group of them observed from afar reminded one of praying Arabs. This was the origin of the camp expression denoting starving people — "moslems".

They were aroused from torpor only by the sight of food or when visual or auditory impressions reminded them of food.

The somatic changes produced also disturbances in the psychic sphere. In the initial stages of starvation we had only noticed signs of excitability. People became irritable, quarrelsome, hysterically groaning and complaining, asocial. Food was the cause of most quarrels and bickerings. They complained that their neighbour got a larger food ration, had less water in his soup, more meat, potatoes, etc. The feeling of hunger was most intense at that stage. The patients often experienced a flow of saliva when thinking of food and they constantly thought of food. As long as the starving had some strength they would choose a place of rest where they could at least see food or talk about it. Patients of that type flocked round the kitchen, store-rooms, refuse heaps, or they surrounded those who were eating, watching them with avidity and waiting for the rare opportunity of licking clean the mess tin or the food container.

The moslems were on the whole not capable of concerted action, but sometimes, when food was the incentive, they attacked, e.g.

the *"Kesselkommando"* (bearers of soup kettles) on their way to the barracks.

In this way the hospital was left without food one day. Strong prisoners were usually chosen to carry the food from the kitchen but even they could not resist the attackers. Several scores of moslems swarmed over them like locusts. The kettles were overturned and the soup was mixed with the mud. The starving moslems fell upon the food, mixed with mud as it was, and started to eat in a prone position. Soon the road was clean — the soup and partly the mud had disappeared.

Another time the bread carted from the bakery to the camp store-room had disappeared in a similar way. The escorting SS-man was surrounded by a crowd while others were stealing the bread. The SS-man used the butt-end of his rifle and finally began firing into the crowd but to no avail. The bread was seized and immediately consumed.

The moslems tried to obtain food in different ways. Very often they searched the refuse heaps, with small results however, as Auschwitz was not a place where food would be thrown away. But they could sometimes find there rotten vegetables, kitchen refuse, potato peelings or bones from which they tried to extract the non-existing marrow. It was exceptional luck if one could find the mouldy rind of a piece of bread.

The moslems who were in a better state tried their luck directly in front of the kitchen. They attempted to mix with the rows of the squads who got the evening's "second helping". But it was rather risky to do so. Instead of the second helping one was apt to get a blow on the head with the ladle.

The conversations of the moslems were typical for their state. They said they would be more provident when they returned home. They would consume several platefuls of thick barley soup with cracklings and several loaves of bread with butter and bacon at one sitting. They would always stay at home and help their wives to prepare the meals.

Some of them, endowed with a more liberal measure of imagination noted down what they would eat. The recipes were mostly concerned with dishes full of fat and were quite nonsensical from a culinary point of view.

I used to know a lawyer in whose mattress we found after his death two thick notebooks full of culinary recipes for various dishes of his own invention. He had used the paper from old cement bags as his writing material. He had been certain of having invented sensational dishes, unknown to culinary experts.

The day-long tortures of hunger, intensified by thinking and speaking of food, were followed at night by dreams about eating. The patients dreamed about parties in houses where good food was served, about restaurants with a good cuisine, such as Polonia, Bacchus, Poller's, or about small, cosy Jewish eating-houses in the provinces. It usually so happened in the dreams that when the well-laid table was quite ready, one had to wait for a belated guest or for another dish and so the feast was postponed. And when one was finally ready to grasp the knife and fork and attack the food, the camp gong sounded and one had to waken to one's daily work.

The dreams were so vivid that they provided the next day's topic of pleasant conversation and comments till the evening when new banquets would appear in one's dreams.

I also had my share of them. While I was in the hospital in Block 28 because of starvation diarrhoea, I dreamed one night that I was bathing in a tub full of cream. It was standing in the cellar of my mother's house and I was afraid she might come in any moment. The worst part of the dream was that I could swim in the cream, even dive into it, but could never taste it. When I awoke I saw above me the face of my "moslem" friend, Janusz Krzywicki, an officer from Warsaw.[4]) The sight of him reminded me of the fact that I was in the camp.

In the initial stage of starvation people with some strength of character were still able to use self-control and to preserve their human dignity and definite ethical norms. But in the later stage all restraints broke down. Man became like a starved animal, completely irresponsible for his deeds. To make such men behave like members of an ordered community one had to use coercion.

---

[4]) He is at present manager of the Polish Airlines LOT.

I often witnessed how a father would systematically steal the food ration of his partly unconscious, delirious son, in order to eat it himself. A stronger prisoner would strangle his neighbour at night to get at his ration. Both were surprised when I had severely rated them for their deeds. They discontinued their practices only when we had bound their hands and feet for the night.

I mention these facts because malicious people, failing perhaps to grasp the symptoms of the disease, sometimes made derogatory remarks concerning the nationality, profession or beliefs of the starvelings.

I cannot refrain from mentioning one more method to curb starvation. Some prisoners used to smoke cigarette-butts rolled into thick paper. It was a general belief that such a "cigarette" smoked after breakfast, which consisted of so-called "coffee" only, helped to feel less hungry. But only those prisoners who worked in the squads which served the *SS*-men could afford the cigarettes. Prisoners did not, as a rule, throw away cigarette-butts in Auschwitz. Those who got money from home could buy cigarettes (or butts) and sometimes also ersatz food stuffs, such as vegetable salads, no longer fresh, rotten snails, mustard and soup made of horse-chestnut flour.

Starving the prisoners was instrumental in curbing and degrading them, but above all it served as a means of extermination.

The starving prisoners were not able to offer any resistance, they turned into a passive, apathetic mass, devoid of any capability for cooperation.

Sociologists and experts in forensic medicine pointed out the fact that suicide was rather infrequent in concentration camps. Systematic starvation had been responsible for this phenomenon. A starveling is indifferent to life. The few cases of suicide which had come to my notice at Auschwitz concerned prisoners not yet wasted away by starvation.

It was hardly a coincidence that in concentration camps only people not yet underfed could still maintain an active attitude towards life and show an inclination to fight against oppression. It was they who were organizing the resistance movement, escapes from the camp, actions of sabotage. They maintained contacts with the world outside the camp and helped their fellow-prisoners.

It is worth-while to mention, by the way, the attitude of the camp authorities towards the starvelings. The *SS* authorities were fully conscious of the fact that the daily food rations would sooner or later lead to cachexy and the extermination of the prisoners. Using their propaganda slogans they argued that the cachexy of prisoners was solely based on the racial characteristics of the representatives of the "lower" nations.

I was present one day when an *SS* doctor explained to a visiting sanitary commission, consisting of members of the Third Reich's satellite states, why the physical condition of prisoners was so bad. When an Italian had asked why the patients looked so poorly, the doctor did not hesitate to answer that they were Poles and the Poles, being a barbaric nation, were used to feed mainly on plants like mangel-wurzel and to drink vodka. Transferred into better conditions they could not get used to them.

When the Italian heard this reply he in turn asked me whether I, too, had looked as poorly before coming to the camp, as I did then. Having listened to the *SS* doctor's explanation I naturally said that I had always been a weakling and was feeling better in the camp. I knew that any unguarded reply might have had sad consequences for me.

After the visit the allies were shown various diagrams and results obtained through alleged scientific researches, illustrating the success of the camp authorities in their struggle for better health conditions of the prisoners. A most helpful method to maintain the prisoners in good health was to add to soup nettles, leaves of the beet-root or some yeast. But no mention was made of the quality and quantity of a prisoner's daily ration.

The highest authorities of the *SS* held the opinion that a prisoner subsisting on the daily food ration should survive about three months. After that time he should grow cachectic and die. (*"Ein anständiger Häftling darf nich länger als drei Monate leben, sonst ist er ein Dieb"*.) [5]

---

[5]) An honest prisoner should not live live longer than three months, otherwise he is a thief.

The calculations of the *SS* were correct, but in my opinion only in the case of young or middle-aged prisoners who had arrived in camp well nourished and in good health. In other cases it was difficult to survive even three months, particularly in winter and when engaged in hard work.

There were exceptions, of course. I remember a young man from Warsaw who was quite phenomenal in this respect. Without any help from the outside, only having his "official" ration and working the whole time he had managed to live for seven months but finally got to the hospital and died there.

In the initial stage of the camp's existence a prisoner's daily ration consisted of 1,500 calories at the most. This, as we know, is not sufficient for a man to live, even if he was quietly reposing in room temperature. Besides the low calorie value the food stuffs were of poor quality. They mainly contained vegetables of low nourishing value, generally used for fodder. The daily ration contained circa 15 grammes of proteins, 20 grammes of fat and circa 300 grammes of carbohydrates. The fate of a prisoner was sealed, above all, by the acute deficiency of proteins, fats and vitamins.

Many additional factors, besides the insufficient quantity and poor quality of the food, had their influence upon the sooner or later appearing symptoms of starvation.

The age of the victim was of importance. It is generally known that young people possess a greater store of vitality and energy than the older ones. I consider people who have not yet attained 35 years of age to be young. In camp conditions people between 18 and 30 years of age had shown the greatest resistance. To the best of my knowledge prisoners below and above that age generally succumbed to starvation more quickly. It seems that in our geographical situation people below the age of eighteen are not yet physically fully developed.

The resistance and strength of the will to survive shown by some of our fellow-prisoners were sometimes astounding. Once a young prisoner, by the name of Adolf Gawalewicz, [6]), was under my care in the hospital. It was, I think, in the winter of 1941/42

---

*) L.L.D. — is at present employed in the National Municipal Council of Cracow.

that he was brought to the hospital in a state of unconsciousness, with far advanced symptoms of the second stage of starvation. I do not think his weight could have been more than 35 kilogrammes, swellings and all. At that time the most important part of a doctor's duty in prison was first of all a thorough evidence of the dead, so I knew beforehand that I had to prepare a death certificate at once. This was usually done in the case of those seriously sick. The next morning, in the short time before the morning roll-call one had to hand in the reports about the patients in the hospital and there must be no mistakes as to the identity of the person. In those days the prisoners had not yet their camp numbers tattooed, to make a mistake was an easy but a dangerous thing, as then the commandant could send the doctor to a bunker from which one seldom came back alive. After having filled in the death certificate I proceeded to try and save the patient's life. We covered him with blankets, fed him some hot soup and gave him a cardiac drug injection.

When visiting the patients in the morning I found Gawalewicz smiling and asking for food. With sincere joy I tore up the death certificate which had been prepared beforehand. The patient quickly recovered and soon left the hospital.

After some months my friend Gawalewicz returned to us in a much worse state than before. He was unconscious for twenty-four hours. The next day, after having regained consciousness he told me he must recover and get back to Cracow to his mother. I looked at him with compassion, unable to believe he would again recover, his state being so alarming. But his will to live and his appetite brought him round to health and finally to his mother in Cracow.

Of great importance in the course of many diseases, including starvation, was the length of time spent in camp. People who came to the camp for a shorter stay, were more resistant, even if the food was the same. Prisoners perished with a greater frequency after a longer stay in the camp.

It seems that prison, besides its action on the nervous system, blocks all vital processes, fosters general slackness and induces a state of apathy. Lack of fresh air, exercise and normal contacts with men are indubitably pernicious, not to mention scant food and the characteristic, constant atmosphere of terror.

The so-called individual constitution was of great importance, too. In the days of my boyhood I liked to listen to the war experiences of some peasants from the neighbourhood of Krosno. Many of them had survived the siege of the fortress of Przemyśl during World War I. They recalled that slight and thin people had borne hunger and all kinds of hardships longer than anybody else. During my stay in the camp I found their observations very apposite. Short and slight men were in fact more resistant to starvation and physical exertion. Tall individuals with a large mass of bones and muscles soon deteriorated. Obese people could not stand starvation, lack of normal conditions and hard work.

While in prison in Jasło we amused ourselves in our cell by "predicting" who would be most likely to survive the hardships which awaited us.

We were unanimous in declaring that the most likely person to survive would be a certain landowner, a tall and exceptionally hale looking fellow. We thought that our friend and fellow-prisoner Staszek Socha [7] had the smallest chance of survival. He was of the same opinion and we all were sorry for him because he was universally liked. Socha was the opposite of the landowner, being short, thin and physically rather weak.

Socha was with me in the camp for the whole time. He worked hard and endured starvation quite well while our landowner became one of the first victims of exhaustion.

The fate of a prisoner was also, to a certain extent, influenced by his previous way of life, his profession and his parentage. Workers who had been used to work in the open, often in bad weather conditions, were more proof against starvation. White collar workers and peasants succumbed to starvation most easily.

It seems that with peasants the worst hardship was the lack of a quiet atmosphere to which they were used. The decrease in food quantity was also detrimental. Polish peasants ate poor food before the war but they ate it in great quantities. Therefore the

---

[7] At present manager of the bank at Krosno.

peasants felt the scarcity of food most keenly and most frequently broke down mentally.

The percentage ratio of peasants who had perished in the camp was the highest, perhaps, among all prisoners. They were also unhappy because of other reasons. They could not get adjusted to the noisy and polyglot milieu, they were clumsy in their movements, could not understand the German language, neither could they make friendly contacts with people. They were unable to develop the cunning necessary to survive. Thoughts of their farms and families tormented them and so did their longing for open spaces.

And to survive in Auschwitz, particularly in its initial phase, one had to work as little as possible, to cheat the camp authorities, to be cunning and able to organize (which does not mean stealing from one's fellow-prisoners) and to think as little as possible of one's family and of one's return home. The best thing to do was, generally speaking, to do what one was not allowed to do.

Those who could do so had the greatest chance of survival. But youth and individual adaptability were, naturally, the greatest assets in so far as survival was concerned.

ZOFIA POSMYSZ*

"SÄNGERIN"
(THE SINGER)

"Midday break" — that means — half an hour's rest. The rays of the July sun fell vertically upon the earth. Women, who by some chance had aprons, could cover their heads with them. But I hadn't an apron. The wood nearby was full of shade, a smell of resin was wafted from it. One's body was just one big ache. The *Rottenführer*[1]), nicknamed the Wag, was bored again. So the spades had to work in a flying tempo, they cut the roots as if with knives. I felt a throbbing in the back of my skull and tried to put some

---
* Former prisener of *KL* Auschwitz, at present well-known writer.
[1]) Lower rank in the *SS* troops.

damp earth under it to cool it... *"Wilia, oh, Wilia, du Waldmägdelein..."* [2])

Luśka was lying next to me. "Bitch", she growled softly, "bitch, bitch",.... Luśka was the only one in the squad to use such words. She was Polish and yet had a black triangle. That fact gave her the right to hate, to lack the feeling of belonging with the other women prisoners. She raised her head, shouted "Quiet" in German, then cautiously lay back, pressing against the ground. The singing did not abate. Trude raised herself from where she lay in the orchard. She had thin legs covered with livid spots, a reminder of abscesses, a bowed back, a small head with yellow hair crowning her long body. But Trude was lazy that day. She did not feel equal to investigating who had been sufficiently insolent to shout "Quiet". She only said, in an undertone, "You shut your trap there, or..." Luśka was almost weeping. "I'll strangle that bitch tonight." Nobody paid any attention to her. We were lying half-dead. From under the striped skirts thin legs appeared with skinny sacks in place of calves, with livid balloon-like swellings where ankles had been.

The *"Wilia"* song had come to its end, we suddenly fell asleep and woke as suddenly. *"Leise fliehen meine Lieder"*, — Schubert's Serenade. Some fragments of pictures floated before one's eyes, a garden with the moon shining, a terrace, Paderewski's mane of hair above the piano keyboard. The "Singer" was singing in a low voice, she knew we were cursing her, she wanted to spare us, it always began like that, and then the *Rottenführer* would say, "Come on, sing properly", he liked a loud song, there was no escaping it.

Each day it began that way. The shouts of the German women supervisors, "Where is the Singer? Come to the officer!" The slight figure flitted by, followed by our angry glances, by Luśka's blind fury. "I'll strangle that tart one night. And that Jewess, her teacher, too."

One of the prone figures raised herself on her elbows and knees and crept among the lying bodies. Her eyes on Luśka, her face

---
[2]) A German song.

distorted by fear. Emma had "a Polish number", that was her only hope, and there she was being called a Jewess! Emma was scared of that word, she was more afraid of Luśka than of Lore or Trude, more even than of the *Rottenführer* himself. The backing of the Singer had so far protected her from the Germans, who knew it was she who was teaching the Singer all those songs: "It was not love", "I am dancing with you", "I am in love". The *Rottenführer* had a long time ago got tired of the Polish songs the words of which he could not understand. He kept demanding, "Sing something in German". Emma had a supply of what the *Rottenführer* demanded. Her careful education, her musical talent which she had been developing during her stay in Vienna, the Bechstain grand piano in her exquisite drawing-room in Cracow, stood her in good stead at present. She was giving lessons to the Singer who was to die and yet still lived because she could sing. And so Emma would live, too, because she was indispensable to teach the Singer as everybody knew. The lessons took place in the latrine at night. They both squatted on their heels—sitting on the stones might induce colds — Emma's fingers were imitating the movements made when playing the piano and she made sounds like the sounds of piano music... pa-ram-pam-pam-pam... "My songs slowly flee through the night to you"... The Singer then repeated the phrase so faultlessly that Emma felt weak. With admiration, she thought, though really it must have been hunger. Emma did not get paid for her lessons. Her only fee was — hope. Hope to acquire backing, needed when soup was added, when work was assigned, and in all those cases which in Budy inescapably led towards the end.

We all were destined, sooner or later, to meet death. An accident could only make this inevitability come more quickly. Such was the case of our seven companions who had been killed and such was the case of the Singer, almost, who was to have·shared their fate, though our squad did not want to remember that fact at the present moment.

In the Montelupi prison in Cracow she was just a singer and belonged with us, in spite of always repeating what no one of us would say — "It isn't possible", She said these words when they had pushed her, sobbing violently, into our cell, and later on she would repeat them when days passed and she was still not released. And also when she saw women from our cell returning after an interrogation.

She was in prison for no reason at all. She was accidentally taken from her shoemaker's with others in a round up and never doubted that the mishap would soon be cleared up. When after two months in prison the wardress, Ula, a woman from Silesia, called her name, she began kissing her for joy. But when she heard — "Transport to Auschwitz", she again and again repeated, "Not possible".

She did not fare badly in the Montelupi prison. She used to clean the offices in the daytime and sing in the evening. We had asked her to sing, then. The women's prison was located in a former convent and through the barred windows one could see the orchard, white with the blossoms of May. We looked at the orchard and asked her to sing. She mounted the window sill, grasped the bars and sang. She sang best in that position. The guard downstairs sometimes roared, "Get down, you there" but he would usually listen, too, turning his back to the window. The Singer was the diva of the Montelupi prison.

In Auschwitz, however, she immediately became a nobody. The short nights in the camp were full of shouts of people who having had a nightmare awoke to another and much more troublesome nightmare. The days were filled with the yells of the slave-drivers and the quietness of the roll-calls. There was no room for singing in that reality. But she still kept repeating, "this is not possible". She may have been right, impossible things did happen to her. Once, a guard, a Latvian, gave her some of the remaining midday soup and then offered her advice to wash her face with urine in order to keep her skin fair and to avoid sun-tan. Another time a certain *Rottenführer* asked her how old she was and why she had got to Auschwitz. She thought this interest was due to compassion. But the most important thing was what had happened while we worked in the water squad [3]).

---

[3]) A squad which cleaned the ponds.

The cleaning of the ponds had been going on for two weeks. We worked immersed in water up to our waists, up to the armpits even. Every morning, when putting on my wet clothes, I used to think, "Only today". But next morning came and one's body shook again with the fear of the cold water. The roll-call, marching out of the camp and returning to it with the knowledge that nothing would change. The stillness of the night was interrupted by shots and cries which resembled the screeching of train wheels on rails. These were not screeching wheels, however. It was the voice of a human being caught by the electric current. During the morning roll-call we saw human forms hanging in the wires. We tried not to see them, at least at first we were most anxious not to see them. The work in the water squad taught us to look at them and to think of them.

It was raining that day and it was frightfully cold in spite of its being June. The squad moved in complete silence into the pond and out of it with the weeds we had pulled out. Nobody was looking at anybody, nobody said a word to anybody. Thus one could bear it. The day before a woman was severely mauled by a dog because she did not get sufficiently quickly into the water. That day the rain was a help as the guard and the supervisor stayed on the dyke under some trees, cowering under their respective rain capes. In spite of their being away the squad did its work almost at a run. It was not necessary to drive anyone into the pond. It was warmer in the water.

I was carting a hand-barrow together with the Singer. She walked in front of me, I could see her back and when we left the pond — her legs. Blood was streaming down them, in streamlets, in clots. The burdock leaves were but poor substitutes for sanitary pads. The Singer was weeping. I raised my head to avoid looking at her legs and saw her moving shoulders. She was sobbing convulsively, in the way one did sob in freedom, but not in the camp. She sobbed just as she did when she was first pushed into the prison cell.

In the afternoon the capo drove us to the other end of the dyke. We had to pass near the guard and the supervisor. The Singer continued her sobbing. The guard and the supervisor were still under the tree and the former was the first to notice the Singer's unusual sobbing and its reason. He turned his eyes away and grumbled, "What filth". But as we were returning that way he told her to remain on the bank of the pond. The supervisor, the same who had the day before baited a woman with the dog, did not protest.

And so the Singer still kept repeating, "That's not possible". She said so when one woman from our squad ran away and we were waiting for the commandant to come and give the order to decimate us. But she was not at all afraid. She warned the weeping women to let sleeping dogs lie. And she was right, there was no decimation that time. The water squad had been exceptionally leniently treated. The heads of its members were shorn and everybody was sent to the penal company at Budy.

The name Budy meant nothing to us then. It was the name of a hamlet several kilometres from Auschwitz. Our squad was the one to start the history of Budy. During the course of two months two hundred and forty three women prisoners had perished at Budy out of the number of four hundred women.

The Singer passed through the gate of Budy with almost a smile. She did not see herself. Her face, with the rest of her hair sticking out above it, was marked with degradation and could no longer evoke comparisons with that of a wronged child. The smile on a face like hers was shocking. The Commandant of the camp at Budy, a young *Unterscharführer*[4]) with a patrician's subtle face, interrupted the counting of the women. With the handle of his horsewhip he raised the chin of the Singer so high that the veins of her thin neck visibly protruded. "There is nothing to laugh about here", he said in a soft voice, "It's a penal company", he added just as softly, turning to the squad.

We were allowed to enter the barrack. Not long ago it had been a school-house and now the class-room floors were strewn with mattresses lying close to one another. We hurried to occupy them. We could not expect a meal earlier than next day at noon and so we crouched upon our mattresses. But hunger did not allow us to

---
[4]) Rank in the SS.

go to sleep. And it grew very cold in the small hours of the night. We were not given any blankets, so we tried to get close to one another to get some warmth. Just when our stupor was passing into sleep a gong sounded and the room seniors crashed into the barrack. They ran treading upon the sleepers and hitting them with their sticks at random, "Up! Get up!"

This was the penal company.

The killing proved to be a protracted business and the squad was left alone for a time. Lore and Trude were busy in the alderwood grove. They left it from time to time, perspiring, shouted in the direction of the meadow in a perfunctory manner and again disappeared among the trees. They took turns. First the one and then the other, so as not to lose their strength. The alderwood grove resounded with blows, similar to those made by flails. The larks were singing above the meadow. There must have been lots of them, several hundred perhaps? We were as if immersed in their singing, trying to forget everything else. We said, "This is the end", when one of the killers sat down on the bench, we pretended not to hear the groans which were still audible above the singing of the birds. Humanity prodded us on to go to that alderwood grove, so we had to think of other things, had to control our impulse.

We carried the murdered woman as we had observed men do it. Like people who carry portable holy images during church processions. The rakes served as carrying poles, the corpse was placed across them. The woman, a peasant from the highlands, was not yet dead. The death rattle was still being heard and blood was streaming from her open mouth. (When some years later her children had asked me what their mother had died of, I told them it had been heart failure. They were glad to hear it, it was what they had been informed of when the death announcement had come from Auschwitz.) We hoped she would at last die before we had arrived at the camp. Lore and Trude were all the time circling round the four of us who were carrying the maltreated woman. We told them "she is dead" and kept praying for her to be really dead.

This was the first victim. The first from among us. She had come from a highland village, was strong, could tackle even the hardest work and was resistant to the cold. She had had a chance to survive the penal squad. If only she were able to exist without food... All the three potatoes she had got for lunch were rotten. First she had burst into tears and then had asked Lola, the German supervisor, to get her some other potatoes. Lola started beating her and the peasant woman gave her a push, she was strong enough to do it. And so she was the first from among us to be killed. She had started the killing.

The Singer said, "It was her own fault. To give the supervisor a push?" There was an element of her former "this is impossible" in these words. Her eyes were the eyes of an insane person. But nobody wanted to join the discussion. We wanted to believe that the Singer was right. The next victims, however, did not defend themselves when the first blow fell and were killed nevertheless. They did not even try to shield themselves against the first blow. And yet their fate was sealed according to the penal company law which decreed that one should not "attract notice". A prisoner, once hit, had to die. Not necessarily at once, but next day, perhaps, her dead body would be carried back to the camp.

Our Singer from the Montelupi prison had attracted attention. It had happened while we were busy with the hay in the course of the third week of our stay at Budy. That week was the beginning of our end. The starvation rations of Auschwitz had been drastically cut down by one half and the German women with functions in the camp were pilfering the scanty food right and left. They were on the best of terms with the *SS*-men, they spoke the same language, they shared the loot with them and rendered them services of another kind. We saw that our squad was doomed. We were driven to the fields at dawn and were kept there working long after the sun had set. The heat, the cold, the rain, all of them were exhausting. Fear only drove us on, but our spurts of energy were growing steadily weaker. The *Rottenführer* whose name was Hans, had the rosy, smiling face of a wag (hence his nickname), ears like a bat and the fists of a boxer. One blow of his fist would stun the victim who generally was unable to rise again. Trude and Lore, the latter called *"Lorelei"* because of her golden hair full of pretty locks, then proceeded to make the victim "come to". And the end was usually the same — the victim was carried back to the camp lifeless on rakes which served as carrying poles.

That day the Singer was moving more slowly, her reactions were less quick. She did not realize she had been observed. Diarrhoea was torturing her, she had stopped eating to get rid of it but the sickness would not abate. She was unlucky because she had not yet learned to relieve herself where she stood. And "to relieve nature" at Budy was circumscribed by definite rules, it could not happen without the presence of a guard who would stand close to the squatting woman, look at his watch and flick her naked buttocks with a switch. "Go on, hurry up, be done with it, you creature". The guard stood watch over the Singer for the sixth time and so he remembered her and complained to the *Rottenführer* about it. A blow on the head felled her to the ground but she managed to get up and shakily stood at attention. The *Rottenführer* looked at her critically and Trude and Lore were in readiness He said, "Pick up the rake". She stooped down quickly, felt dizzy and her knees sagged under her. But she got up. He came nearer and told her how to hold the rake, she was doing it quite wrong. She eagerly kept nodding her head. So he retreated one step and she began the raking. But she did not rise after the next blow. He kept kicking her inert body. We recognized where the blows fell owing to the typical sounds — that was the head, the back, then the hipbones. Tony, the third supervisor, said, "Now it has started" There was some compassion in her voice. Tony, the gay one, never took part in the murders.

In the evening, however, the Singer managed to get back to the camp without the help of anybody, thanks to the heat which caused Trude and Lore to seek other pleasures in the afternoon. Their orgy with the guards continued in the alderwood grove until our return and so they forgot all about the victim that should have been slaughtered. Killing women with bludgeons was not their only pleasure, after all.

Next day, however, they remembered her and wanted to find her ever since the morning. It was not so easy to find her. Her face was not marked by the blows as, by some lucky chance, she had kept it covered with her arms. The blows had left marks on her body only and it was hard to recognize her face among all the other, similar faces. Our faces were very much the same, then, swollen with starvation, coarsened and blackened like the faces of primitive roadside figures of saints. Any other woman could have been taken for her and we were fully conscious of that fact. Trude and Lore were prowling among the squad, carefully examining each face. The nightmare lasted, we were afraid to meet our eyes. There was horror in them, after some hours there was murder in them, too.

They had found her towards the evening and immediately proceeded with their work but were unable to finish it. The Singer again returned to the camp, not helped by anyone. She had just one night to live. Only one night. She knew it just as well as the whole squad did. The block senior's words, when issuing the bread, were just a confirmation. She said, "You don't need any swill any more". But the Singer demanded her bread, in a raised voice, too, as if she wanted to have it happen now, at once, before the nightfall. Trude and Lore were absent, however, and the block senior, fat and asthmatic, was taking care of herself. So the doomed woman got her bread and began eating it voraciously but then stopped just as suddenly. She gave the bread to a woman standing nearby and left the block.

She went straight towards the wires and towards the guard who was walking on the other side of the wire fence. The sky was still pinkish over the wood nearby, but the wood itself was already black. The Singer turned her face with its streaks of blood towards the western sky. Just like once in the Montelupi prison cell she had grasped the bars, here she grasped the wires. Did she forget that the wires at Budy were not charged with electricity? She began to sing. Just as she did in the cell, "Stop, gentle knights, who of you will take my heart with you, who will keep it in his hand — ay, ay, ay, ay..." The block senior catapulted from the block, followed by her helpers armed with bludgeons. She was singing and the wood was echoing her voice. The camp was filled with the "ay, ay, ay", in manifold repetition. "She is to sing", said the guard before the first bludgeon could reach her. The furies stood still as if petrified, then turned back. The Singer said to the guard, "They want to kill me". He did not appear to understand and continued making his rounds along the fence. When he returned he found her standing at the same spot. He said in broken German, "Don't go to the block. Stay here". He was a Latvian and spoke little German. She recognized him then. He was the same Latvian who once had given her advice to wash her face with urine. She wanted to tell him about it but thought better of it. She had not followed his advice, after all. She went towards the block, squatted down outside of it and so spent the night.

In the morning the squad regrouped. The haymaking was almost done, half of the squad would suffice to finish it. When leaving the camp the first ten fives were counted and were told to go and finish with the hay under the supervision of Trude, Lore and another *Rottenführer*. The remaining fifty women were to go with the Wag, Toni and another supervisor, and dig ditches in the wood. Trude immediately noticed that the Singer was not among her ranks. She began scrutinizing the ranks of Toni and found her victim there. She said, "You'll go with me". The Singer remained motionless. Trude snatched her by the striped prison dress and jerked her towards her own group. "You've got to come with me", she shrieked. "No", replied the Singer. Trude made her way right into the middle of the ranks overturning two women on her way there. And then unexpectedly Toni had her say, "She's staying with me", she announced. Trude started shouting but stopped at once. The day before Toni had taken advantage of the fact that Trude and Lore were busy chasing the rotten Pole and had been very busy with the *Rottenführer's* fly. So she had forestalled her rivals and became quite arrogant as the result of her conquest. Trude had to desist. Her yellow eyes glanced at the Singer's face, beaten black and blue. "We'll meet again. You'll have to sing for me."

But her threats came to nothing. Toni informed the *Rottenführer* in the first half of the day that there was a singer right in his squad.

At noon, when the *Rottenführer* had had his lunch in the clearing of the wood, the two supervisors called out, "Where is the singer?"

She was lying next to me, face upwards, her arms flung aside. She looked ripe to be carried on rakes. Her skin was translucent in the sun and underneath it one could see a mass of bloody flesh. Her brow was cut, a swelling the size of a fist below it. I did not notice whether the eye was still there.

She did not move when she heard the supervisors calling out. She either did not hear them or failed to connect their shouts with her person. Neither did I at first. I was thinking of the end of the day and of the fact that Trude would surely make a final reckoning with her in the camp. The Latvian would not be there and Toni? She had opposed Trude out of contradictoriness and in order to stress her new situation. But in the evening she would again accept the law of the penal company. She belonged to those others, after all. (Lore was her "intimate friend", which was a euphemism to describe Lesbianism among the German women.)

The Singer had probably similar thoughts. She was ready even since yesterday, when she had given away her bread. That was why she had said "No" to Trude. And now she did not react to their calls.

Toni turned to the squad, "Find her. A small, blonde one. She was singing in the camp yesterday". I told the Singer, "They mean you". She gave no answer. "She needn't be afraid. The *Rottenführer* wants to hear her sing", Toni was reassuring us. I spoke again, "You should go". Then she rose and walked towards the spot where the *Rottenführer* was resting. After a while we heard the song, "Ah, for the charm of your eyes which sparkle so..."

Her voice was the only possession she still had, unchanged since the Montelupi prison days. It vibrated in the air, deep, sonorous, improbable and absurd in a place like this. After the first song the *Rottenführer* demanded another and another still.

This was the beginning.

She was not yet saved. Trude and Lore had not given up yet. The squad was reunited again and they kept prowling around, waiting for a change of the *Rottenführer's* mood. But the Wag was enjoying the afternoon concerts more and more. Red with overeating (our sausages fried in our margarine had supplemented his *SS*-man's meal) he lay down in the shade, loosened his belt and listened to the singing. He sometimes raised himself up to fart more comfortably, detonations followed and the supervisors eagerly shouted, "Your health", each time. It also happened that he fell asleep. But the Singer could not stop as then he would immediately wake and ask, "What's wrong? Are you tired perhaps?".

The golden-haired Lorelei was the first to accept the situation After several days she turned to the Singer, "Do you know this?" and hummed in her deep, throaty voice, "What you had told me of love and faithfulness was a lie, just a lie"... And at the same time she looked at Toni who was openly necking with the *Rottenführer* within the sight of all of us. The Singer did not know that song. Lore was dissatisfied. "Always those Polish shit songs..." Trude at once joined forces with her, "You could sing in German just for once". The *Rottenführer* had heard the remarks. "Sure", he said, "she should sing in German".

There was no concert the next day. The *Rottenführer* did not want to listen to Polish songs. The Singer was sent away, the midday break was shortened. The squad got a special job to do in the afternoon.

Trees had been felled in the wood in spring but the trunks were not removed. They lay almost half covered by the earth. We had to raise them up, carry them to a spot several scores of metres farther and stack them into cords. And all this had to be done with our bare hands, there were no tools of any kind. At this time Luśka, the heftiest of the entire squad, the tallest and the strongest, weighed less than fifty kilograms. The trunks were five, ten, metres long, they kept slipping from our hands, women fell down. The *Rottenführer* roared, struck, kicked. So did the supervisors, Trude, Lore and another, nicknamed the Cow. (When some months later the Cow had died of typhus the women prisoners of her squad held a tranksgiving service.) The Singer was carrying trunks along with us. Her singing protected her from one thing only — beating.

But this privilege was extremely precarious. Trude was again circling round her. Hopefully relying on the *Rottenführer*'s fury she tried provocation. "Come on, come on, Singer! You ought to work, too. Or do you think you needn't?" — she kept calling, all the time looking at the SS-man not to miss that one, one only, nod of his. But she had no luck. The *Rottenführer* ran towards another group where some confusion had arisen. While the women were crossing a ditch the trunk fell upon the leg of one of them and broke it in two places. We heard the screams of the woman and we saw the supervisors dragging her into the bushes. She kept screaming and trying to elude their grasp, skipping upon one leg. (It looked from afar like some folk-dance.) Then the *Rottenführer* rushed up and shot her in the back of her head. The screaming had stopped. But there were no other victims to be carried back to camp that day. Some other casualties were led to the camp supported by us.

That evening behind the latrine only a few women performed the ritual of a very sketchy washing. One litre of water in the bowl from which one ate had to serve for everything... It was prohibited to draw water from the creaking well after nine o'clock. The women poured water on their palms and washed their private parts. The guard kept passing back and forth behind the wires. He was not disturbed by the sight of straddling women busy with that job, neither were they. The Singer possessed one large handkerchief, preserved since the days of freedom. It was an invaluable possession as it served as soap, sponge and towel at the same time. It helped in a lot of ways. In case there was a crowd in the corner between the wires and the latrine one was obliged to queue up and wait as washing was not allowed in any other place under threat of blows. The Singer was less dependent thanks to her handkerchief. She just dampened it with water and could wipe her face and neck with it wherever she stood.

I hadn't known Emma till then, neither had I known anything of her. When she squatted next to me with her bowl I noticed her legs, covered from ankles up to the knees with knobs of abscesses. I didn't raise my eyes to see who those legs belonged to, I preferred not to have any friends among people I would, perhaps, be obliged to carry to the camp on rakes in a few days' time.

(That is the reason I remember so few faces, now I am writing this. I only remember legs, hands, flabby buttocks, sagging breasts. There are no faces. My Auschwitz monument would be devoid of features, only shinbones, trunks, scaffoldings of bones.)

But she had decided otherwise. I heard her turning to the Singer, "I can teach you some German songs". The Singer did not reply. She was looking with dismay at her handkerchief which got torn while she had rinsed it. "This is your chance", Emma insisted. It was only then that the Singer looked at Emma, "I have nothing to pay lessons with", she replied. "Never mind, it's enough if they know I am your teacher", Emma reassured her feverishly. She seemed to be very anxious to be the Singer's teacher. They had spoken in whispers but the women behind the latrine must have heard them. They were convinced that the *Rottenführer* had been so furious that day because he had missed his usual entertainment. They insisted the Singer should try to learn German songs.

Diarrhoea made me a witness of that first lesson which was taking place in the latrine. They both squatted there in the darkest corner, Emma had her hands spread out in front of her. She said, as if excusing herself; "My memory is in my fingers. I couldn't recall a tune if I didn't visualize the piano keys". She tried to recall something simple, something the other could master in the course of one night. But her fingers kept remembering the songs of Schumann, Schubert, Mozart. She re-created one or two phrases and discarded them in panic. The time was so short. A beam of faint luminosity, entering through the door, was moving more and more towards the centre of the latrine. At last she found it — "It was not love, alas, because you have no heart," She sang the song to its end. "You now. Sing it with me".

They were not alone. Over ten squatting forms were there in the latrine. Half of the squad had diarrhoea. Groans, moans, sounds of torn bowels mixed with the song. "It was a fairy tale and fairy tales are not true..."

This was the song the Singer presented to the *Rottenführer* the next day.

At that time the squad felt grateful for her singing. Even the greatest sceptics among the women prisoners tried to believe that the songs might bring some alleviation of their miserable lot. They tried to catch at straws just to be able to have some hope.

One morning Toni told the Singer, "You will become a forewoman". That meant that for the first time a Pole would have a function in the camp. We all thronged to be in her group. Only ten, however, were so lucky as to get there. I was among the lucky ones, Emma and also Luśka with the black triangle, the same who later on threatened to lynch the Singer. We enjoyed a blessed interval in our lives. We spent the entire day idly standing about, and when the group with a German forewoman, which was working close to us, moved a little farther, we even permitted ourselves the luxury of sitting down. Emma stretched her knobbly legs on the bank of a ditch and groaning with pain continued to teach the Singer other German songs. It was quiet in the wood that day. Neither Trude nor Lore had appeared since the morning. We did not know what was the matter.

But towards noon we began to understand. The empty cottage at the edge of the wood was full of life and activity. Smoke rose from the chimney, there was laughter outside it, one could even hear a mouth organ. The supervisors were in the cottage. The *Rottenführer* had decided to have a thorough wash that day. Toni and Lore (who had renewed her friendship with Toni) were most busy there, while Trude stood watch and shouted encouragement through the window from time to time. The Cow played the mouth organ and cooked. The wind wafted towards us a smell of fried potatoes and sausages. We felt terribly hungry smelling the food. A midday concert added splendour to the orgy. "*Wilia, oh, Wilia, du Waldmägdelein...*" was heard from the cottage and the squad came to think of the Singer as of a heroine.

On the third day, however, the new forewomen were again demoted and Trude, Lore and the Cow again regained their absolute power. The idyll had come to an end. The whoring tricks about which these queens of the sailors' taverns had often whispered in the evenings had for the time being satiated the sexual appetite of the *Rottenführer*. And so he turned to the pleasure that would never pall — the pleasure of beating and killing. Harvest time gave him ample opportunity to indulge in both.

The penal squad was almost daily visited by officers from Auschwitz. The *Rottenführer* got hysterics and so did the supervisors. We sadly recalled the peaceful days when only one victim was carried back lifeless from the field. But it should be added that it was the victims' own fault, the trouble was they died too quickly. The killing tempo of working twelve hours a day when one subsisted on two pieces of bread and half a litre of watery soup had done its share. The *Rottenführer's* fist just crowned the work. A blow directed at the temple generally meant instantaneous death, nothing else was necessary. Thus Trude, Lore nad the Cow, having lost their employment, began to work single-handed.

And at noon songs soared over the dying squad. It had become part of a ritual which was carefully observed. The more blood-shed in the morning the louder and more insistent were the shouts of the supervisors. "Singer! Come on to the *Rottenführer!*" She would then begin her German repertoire supplemented each day by new songs. But she took needless pains over it. It was doubtful whether anyone would have noticed had she sung each day the same song. The *Rottenführer* used to converse with the supervisors about the life in brothels, a subject which always interested him and about which they were always able to speak with expertness and gusto. He cackled, rolling about on the grass, belched freely, hiccuped. Schuman's *"Traümerei"* was just as interesting to him as the woman prisoner who had lost her eye owing to his blow at lunch time. He had then wiped his hand on the grass and had gone on with his guzzling. But gypsy romances, operetta arias and song hits were nevertheless obligatory at noon.

To bear this singing became more of a nuisance to us with each day. Precious minutes of rest were lost and there was no profit in it one could notice.

Only two weeks had passed since the Singer sang for the *Rottenführer* for the first time. Nobody then thought the worse of her for it, not even Luśka who had later on grown to hate her so blindly. The squad understood that she had been struggling to save her life, to postpone the end that had seemed so imminent as to appear inevitable. The *Rottenführer's* music loving whim could not have been stronger than the rule of camp according to which a prisoner once struck would be beaten more and more often till the end came. But no one remembered the antecedents now. Everybody thought solely of her own safety, that of others no longer counted. The Singer was at the moment safer that the rest of us. She could have succumbed to diarrhoea, to the incredibly hard work, but she was safe as far as one kind of death was concerned — neither the *Rottenführer's* fist nor the bludgeons of the supervisors would kill her.

"That damned *Sängerin*", Luśka had once said. And nobody had called her by her name since then, just *"Sängerin"* in German. Thus her place had been defined. We knew, it was true, that she used to hide among the farthest ranks after the midday soup had been issued, that she tried not to hear when they called her. She was, then, just as afraid of the noon-break perhaps as of Trude's and Lore's bludgeons. She was paying a high price for the prolongation of her life-span. The squad saw her tortured face when she was sneaking among the women lying prone on the ground. But nevertheless one or two would spit in her direction. There was no compassion in us. Should the *Rottenführer* one day fell her with a blow some of us would think, "It will be quiet at noontide".

Only Emma remained staunch, consistently and stubbornly staunch. She forced the Singer to go through with their lessons in the latrine. She told her, "You are not doing anything that is wrong. This is your chance. The thing is to survive the penal company. They say there is an orchestra in the base camp and when we get back there from Budy we'll try to become its members. If we leave Auschwitz I'll make a singer of you! You'll see, you'll be a singer".

She spoke of leaving the camp! She, with her legs eaten away by abscesses. Did she believe in miracles? Her being the Singer's teacher meant much to her, that was true. Thanks to it she could belong to Toni's group which was quieter. But Emma still had fever and was in pain, no group would cure that. When marching she used to perspire so much that on cold mornings her striped dress was steaming. The Singer, on whom Emma used to lean for support, perspired, too. How long would she stand it?

Then a strange thing happened during one of the evening roll-calls. The commandant of the camp, a pale *Unterscharführer* with a low voice and aristocratic features, took the report. Then, looking at the ranks, he said, "Which one is the singer? Let her leave the ranks!" The moment between the order and her leaving the ranks seemed interminably long. "Yes", he murmured when she stood in front of him, and there was even the shadow of a smile on his lips. "Show us what you can do".

She began singing Schubert's Serenade, the result of their lessons in the latrine during the former nights. Emma leaning on my shoulder whispered, "How she sings..." The *Unterscharführer* sat down on the schoolhouse step. When she had finished the song he said, "Yes, you sing quite well". And then added, "But die you must, anyhow". Luckily he spoke in a low voice, as usual, so that neither the supervisors nor the block senior had caught his words. They had only seen his nod of approval. And that, together with the fact that the *Unterscharführer* had known of the Singer's existence, was enough for them. After the roll-call Lore came to the Singer. "You will sleep with me". Emma, taking the Singer's arm, wept quietly. "I have taught you, don't leave me. Save me". We passed her by without a word. We had already heard Luśka's vulgar comment, unequivocally suggesting why Lore wanted to have the Singer in her bed.

But Luśka was wrong. She had not foreseen an even worse contingency. Lore had wanted the Singer beside her so that she should sing for her. Only that much. "I always feel so sad in the evenings", she explained to a German woman who had seemed disturbed by the thought that Lore was looking for an "intimate friend" among the members of another nationality. And so the midday concerts were repeated at night. The garret, inhabited by Lore and the other

German women (being a strategic position in case of attack), was most acoustic. Singing, even in the softest voice, was heard throughout the whole barrack. Luśka who also lived in the garret spat the most vulgar words into her pallet. She cursed the Singer's family down to the fourth generation. Other women were silent, but they wrapped their blankets round their head as closely as possible. Luśka's psychosis was, however, infectious. The eyes of the entire squad were following the Singer. One evening, when the women were mounting the steps leading to the garret, the Singer, being in the rear of the crowd, was pushed down the steep staircase. She was not hurt but she might have been. The idea of an accident was now firmly rooted in many minds. The Singer would now be threatened not by Luśka only. Any other woman, even the weakest, was dangerous. It was so easy to drown a person in the latrine, just one push of the sitter into the cloacal hole...

The Singer could not grasp the situation and behaved as if nothing had happened. And the squad... Whenever I met her at night in the latrine I wanted to tell her, "Don't leave the barrack when it gets dark". But I did not say anything. Just like the whole squad.

The days were passing incredibly slowly, the tension was mounting. One evening, Emma after entering the room, fell upon the mattress and said, "I won't get up, let them kill me". She did not get up for supper and when the Singer had brought her the bread ration she would not touch it. She only drank the herb tea. And then she stretched out her hands and began exercising her fingers as pianists do before playing. "We'll play the Serenade now", she announced. She was delirious with fever.

The Singer decided upon an unprecedented step. She asked Lore to intercede on Emma's behalf with the block senior. The problem was to keep Emma for some days in the block without sending her to work. The camp was electrified by the news that the request had been granted. It was quite an unprecedented event. Only German women at Budy were allowed to be ill. An ambulance from Auschwitz arrived once a week and took them to the hospital in the base camp. Those who were not Germans had to go to work and nothing could absolve them of this duty. If they were unable to walk they were carried to work and if they had not died during the day or were, by some oversight, not finished off, they would be carried back to the camp in the evening. To remain in the barrack was most strictly prohibited. Emma was the first among the Poles to be so privileged and the squad's hatred of the Singer abated. The women no longer spat when she inobtrusively sneaked to her midday concert. Even Luśka stopped calling her a bitch for the time being. It almost seemed that the Singer was forgiven.

But Emma's situation was nevertheless hopeless. The block senior could any day refuse to keep her in the block. Only a surgeon's knife could be of help to her legs, a stay in the hospital, dressings. She had not even a piece of cloth to dress her abscesses with. When the first abscess had opened she tore away the leg of her panties and wrapped it round the wound. According to the camp rules this deed could be qualified as sabotage only.

I had heard the Singer's conversation with the block senior. She asked her to send Emma with the next transport to the hospital in Auschwitz. The block senior was adamant in her refusal. She had done too much, anyway, hiding Emma in the block. Others went to work with their legs in a worse state. I told the Singer, as soon as the block senior had left, "Don't insist on her going to the hospital. Emma should do all she can to avoid going there. Those with phlegmons get no treatment in the hospital. They are killed with phenol injected into the heart". The Singer looked at me, her eyes full of dismay. Her lips moved as if forming the words, "Not possible". But perhaps I had only thought so. It was a long time since she had used the words, and later on I did not hear them either... Or rather once. Once only.

The second month of our stay at Budy was coming to its end. There probably was not one among the women prisoners who did not eat raw potatoes, berries of the mountain ash, roots. Turnips and cabbages were delicacies hard to find. Some women had even managed to acquire the art of eating raw crustaceans found in the marshes. Diarrhoea was in full swing. The squad stank. Neither our striped dresses nor our underwear had been changed since we left Auschwitz. We washed our underwear ourselves during the midday break. At least we used to do so while we were in the water squad and at Budy, too, at first. The washing was done without soap, with the help of sand and stones, but still... It was a sign of an indomitable spirit, a manifestation of the will to live. But in our second month at Budy there were only sporadic spurts of individual energy and they were becoming more and more rare. We were so weak that we hardly managed to visit the latrine. Those who were sick with diarrhoea did not manage it, they relieved nature where they stood. Menstruation spots were no langer removed by washing from the striped dresses or underwear. (But luckily only one or two still menstruated.) The chemises were stiff with excrements and by rubbing the flaccid legs left red welts upon them. This led to suppurating abscesses. One or two among us sometimes tried to remove the hard crust of excremental residue from their chemises but such efforts were less and less frequent. We had no strength left to wash our faces. A queer coating had covered them like some kind of moss. We did not notice it, neither did we smell our odours. That was probably the reason why we did not resent the presence of Emma with her suppurating leg in our room, Great amounts of pus were forever flowing from her abscesses and were soaking into the stinking mattress which was full of vermin. It was only sometimes that Emma's nearest neighbour would yell at night, "You hide your damned pins or you'll drench my blanket!"

Only the Singer was looking at Emma's mattress with horror. She had reasons to be dismayed as the block senior could any time notice that rotting mattress. Emma had no fever and was no longer in pain since her abscesses had opened. The Singer had sufficient daring to want to save Emma, that was the reason why she fearfully looked both at the mattress and at us. She understood that she had been guilty of being safe and full of hope while we were not. She knew that the squad hated her but she did not grasp the extent of that hatred. So at last I told her, "They will kill you if you don't stop singing". She did not catch my meaning", I was singing so that they wouldn't... — "Not they", I interrupted. "The squad will kill you", She must have grown very pale for me to notice her pallor under the mossy coating on her face. She repeated several times, swallowing hard and choking over the words, "It isn't possible. Not possible." — "It can happen any time," I said. She did not believe it. "The Poles would do it?" she asked. „The Poles, yes. If you don't stop, they'll kill you", I answered.

The only thing that could save us from that horror and from the final extermination of the rest of the squad was our return to Auschwitz. So we at least thought. Whenever we had some news about our possible return we seemed to recall human speech. We spoke about returning to Auschwitz as if it meant returning home. But such talks were getting to be less frequent from day to day. Our numbers decreased from day to day, too. The remains of the squad seemed to be melting away.

And yet the return became a fact and quite unexpectedly, too, when nobody thought about it any more. We were recalled from the fields before it had grown dark and were told to form ranks. Guards with dogs were standing in front of the camp gate. We were not allowed to leave the ranks, neither were we given supper. The squad was frightened. And then somebody said, "To Auschwitz". We were unable to believe it. But soon an ambulance arrived to take those who were ill and unable to walk. The *Unterscharführer* announced, "Those with temperature and bad legs". A commotion ensued and as usual the German women were in the first ranks. The ambulance could not take all the sick, so the *Unterscharführer* personally began selecting those who were really unable to walk. The squad was amazed when he first of all had eliminated all the German candidates for the ride. When they complained, he said in his low voice, "But you are quite well". Somebody spoke to the Singer, "This is the first German to be just". She eagerly nodded and I saw a look in her eyes which I had noticed before. It always appeared when one of these beasts who had the authority over us betrayed some human trait.

But even so, the ambulance could not take all the sick women. Emma grew restless when the ambulance got filled before the *Unterscharführer* had managed to come round to her. Luśka was the last to squeeze into the ambulance, she had been feverish for the last two days. Emma was in despair. "You must intercede, I won't be able to get to Auschwitz with my legs," she begged the Singer. But the Singer was silent. Even the German women with some function in the camp did not dare to approach the *Unterscharführer* directly. He was known to cut with his horsewhip the face of anyone who dared to speak to him without being called to do so. Thus he was safe from any complaining. "You sang for him, he will remember you, you must save me", Emma hysterically pulled at the Singer's sleeve. But the latter was still unable to pluck up sufficient courage. "There is no room there", she said in a low voice. "But there are those who are not so ill as I am. Have mercy", sobbed Emma.

The driver was already starting up the motor. We saw the Singer step from the ranks. We waited in suspense, expecting to see what the *Rottenführer* had some weeks ago begun with his blow, to see the Singer falling to the ground. The *Unterscharführer* was looking at her steadily ever since she had left the ranks as if waiting for her to come nearer. She stood at attention in front of him. We did not hear her say anything. He regarded her for a while and then asked in his soft voice, "Well, Singer, do you want to sing for me, perhaps?" She stood with her back to us and we did not catch her answer, only his weird voice again, "Well, are you ill, too?" And after a moment, somewhat louder, "Which one? Let her leave the ranks". Emma hurriedly did so. The odour around her was dreadful, so that stinking as we ourselves were, we became conscious of it. Emma had been provident enough to remove the bandage made of her panties and pus was freely flowing from several open abscesses into her wooden clogs. One heard the pus squelching in her shoes as she walked. The *Unterscharführer* drew back.

"Aren't you stinking to heaven?" And then, turning to the Singer, "Is she your mother?" He nearly smiled when he heard the reply, "My teacher. My music teacher". He went to the ambulance opened its door with an elegant gesture, prodded Luśka with his horsewhip to make her get off the steps of the ambulance and nodded to Emma, "Get in, quick". Emma had no time to say anything, she just turned round and looked at the Singer with a smile of happiness on her lips. The *Unterscharführer* closed the door with a bang, the ambulance started. Luśka took Emma's place in the ranks, next to the Singer. For a while she looked in front of her with stupefied eyes, not seeming to understand what happened, but then, all at once, she sprang towards the Singer. "I'll die, but so will you, you bitch, you'll get it for my wrongs!" she kept mouthing. The Singer had no time to jump aside. She tried to defend herself, I saw how she tried to tear Luśka's hands from her throat, but she was too weak. Her knees sagged under her and she fell down. So did Luśka. The ranks broke, though everybody remained motionless. But the lack of motion was only apparent. We were, all of us, participants in the struggle and all of us were, maybe, on Luśka's side. Each second threatened to bring with it an outlet of the hatred, an explosion of the fury. The attitude of the *SS*-men all but encouraged us. They did not intend to interfere. The *Unterscharführer* quietly smoked his cigarette, the guards talked paying no attention to the squad, only the dogs were growling. But they always growled whenever there was some commotion. It was clear that nobody would lift a finger in the Singer's defense. That was all that mattered to us at the moment. Nobody asked what would happen next. They could have baited the dogs or begun shooting any moment. We forgot how the Germans had always made use of situations which had only a slight semblance of a riot. The instinct of self-preservation had stopped to warn us.

All at once the *Unterscharführer* began laughing. He came close to the two women rolling on the ground and slightly, jokingly kicked Luśka's behind with the point of his boot. "You silly cow", he said, "silly, old cow". and went on laughing, louder and more heartily still. The guards followed his example and so did the supervisors. We looked helplessly at him and at one another, trying to understand that merriment. Finally one of the women shouted, "Are you crazy? Do you want to drag a corpse eight kilometres?" Not waiting for permission, regardless of possible consequences, we threw ourselves upon the fighting women, drew Luśka away from the Singer and helped her to her feet. We had to support her as she could hardly stand. The *Unterscharführer* was still laughing. He hadn't stopped even when the squad was passing through the gates of Budy.

We did not return to Auschwitz. The women's camp was by that time transferred to Birkenau. The unknown was once again before us. Toni, the gay one, joined the rank in which the Singer marched soon after we had left Budy. She had a proposal for the Singer — let her try and get into a German block. There she would be safe from Luśka and all those horrible Poles. She assured the Singer that it was quite practicable, there always were some non-Germans in the German blocks. Toni would help her. She knew a block senior who was fond of having talented people round her. She had artists who painted her portraits, an actress who could recite, she would be sure to enjoy having a singer in her block. The Singer did not say a word. She seemed to have gone dumb, not one word passed her lips. She only nodded and kept on nodding even when the offended Toni had finally left her side and had gone back to her own rank in the van of the squad.

It was night when we arrived in Birkenau. We were pushed to Block 7, a Polish one, which was inhabited by one thousand women prisoners. In the commotion and darkness (there was no electricity in the block as yet) Luśka had lost the Singer. She scurried here and there trying to find her and was mobilizing the remainder of the Budy squad to wreak vengeance on her, but in vain. And next day she had changed her mind.

Next day we learned that neither Emma nor anyone of those who were in the ambulance were alive. They had not passed the gates of Birkenau. They were taken from Budy straight to the gas chamber.

WANDA KOPROWSKA

DAYS OF HORROR.

They came. I had expected them and so was not quite so shocked by this visit at night. It happened at 3^{30} a.m. sharp, February 12, 1943. I myself opened the door as Stach was not at home. They searched the whole flat and behaved in a terrible way. The four revolver muzzles did not frighten me as much as I thought they would. Two of them stood watch over me in the kitchen, the two others went into the bedroom. Jacuś was no longer asleep but he was not scared seeing the revolvers. He only turned his dear childish eyes towards me. What were his feelings then? He knew why they had come. Why, every evening he used to pray God to preserve his mummy and daddy. They wakened Jurek, brutally jerking off the counterpane from his cot. He opened his eyes but must have been very sleepy because he pressed his head again into the pillow, did not fall asleep, however.

The Germans, after having ransacked the entire flat, permitted me tò enter the bedroom. Jacuś was silently looking at me. And I? I just stood and saw how they threw all our clothes from the wardrobe, how they turned out the pockets in search of something. Then they asked me about Stach's documents. I told them my husband always carried his documents on him.

One of the *Gestapo* members went to a small table on which an album with photographs was lying, took out Stach's picture and looked at his fellows with triumph. Afterwards they told me to come to the table and started asking questions which I did not answer. They took down what they wanted, anyway. They asked me, "What does your husband do?" I answered he worked at the blast furnaces in the iron-foundry "Katherine". "Is that so? You were well off and still wanted to meddle with politics! Get dressed. And dress the children". It was only then that I grasped the tragedy of my situation. "Gentlemen! The children? Why the children?"

"Get dressed and don't talk back!" I heard them growl.

What was I to do? Their attitude was threatening. I came to Jacuś who stood with his shirt in his hand and was helplessly saying, "Mummy, I don't know where my shirt is. I'll dress myself but I don't know where my shirt is". Poor mite. Now he, too, got nervous. The *Gestapo* officials drove us on. I kept thinking hard how to let my neighbours know that I was being arrested. When one of the men brutally rushed us, I said I could not manage to dress the children so quickly and would he permit me to waken my neighbour? He shook his head but not very convincingly, so I repeated my request and he consented. I went to Mrs Nowak escorted by him. The wakened Nowaks could not at first understand what was the matter and particularly why the children should be arrested, too. But I did not think of anything. I only wanted them to know that I was arrested and to tell Stach. And also that Mary should be informed at once. I did not think twice but sent Mrs Nowak to Mary. And my dear Mary came rushing at once and began begging them to leave the children with her. "Why do you want to take them, what did the little ones do? Do leave them with me, please". She folded her hands as in prayer and begged them, but they stubbornly repeated, "No, the children too".

Her begging was of no avail.

We were led out and the door of the flat was sealed. I looked at the proceedings with indifference. Kazik came out to say goodbye to us. I am very grateful to him for this kindness. His words had kept me alive for many long months. When saying good-bye he whispered to me to be comforted. "As soon as the dawn breaks I'll begin trying to save you. At least I'll save the children". This promise kept me going. I was sure they, nobody but they, would save my children, would let my parents know. Even today I do not know how it had come to pass, but I am certain it was chiefly Mary's doing that my children were saved. Our farewells were brief, wordless almost, but we understood each other. I only managed to whisper to her, "Save Stach, too".

I left with my priceless belongings. My children were everything to me, my greatest treasure. And it was only this treasure I took when I left my home. They did not even allow me to take some little shirts for the children and they threw away everything from the baby carriage.

It was frosty outside. I covered up Jurek in his carriage, Jacuś took my hand and so our sad procession went forth.

The hand of Jacuś trembled in mine, Jurek was slowly falling asleep.

Thus we arrived at the house formerly occupied by a Polish club, now the seat of the *Gestapo*. Here we were taken over by other representatives of the German authorities. I had to hand over money and keys. A sign was put next to my name on the list and it was underlined with a red pencil. I was ordered to go with the children towards a wall of the room, near which several people were sitting while in the corner, on the dirty floor, some men were lying on their bellies. Jacuś looked straight into my eyes and kept asking, "Why, mummy, why?" "We are Poles, my son..." He understood and took my hand in silence. He was only eight then and Jurek was 18 months old. My heart was bleeding but I had to be strong.

Suddenly the door opened wide and Stach was led into the room. This was a terrible moment for me. He walked in and impatiently glanced around. He saw us... His head dropped on his chest. I knew what he must have felt at the moment. Jacuś had seen his father, too. He came to me and whispered, "Mummy, it's daddy. His hands are bound", That whisper nearly broke my heart... After a moment Stach was led to the group of men and was told to lie face downwards beside his companions in adversity.

A member of the *Gestapo* advanced towards the middle of the room, read my name, checked it and left after a while.

Later on people began flocking to the room from all sides. There were mothers with children, old people and youngsters. The room was filling. A lady with two children stood nearby. One child was a boy, as old as Jacuś, the other a girl, a little older than Jurek. The boy cried bitterly when he saw his father lying face downwards on the dirty, spittle covered floor.

Then several men were called, Stach among them. Their hands were manacled and they were escorted from the room, five at a time, under strict guard. Where to?... I remember what Jacuś did at that time. He must have guessed my feelings because he began comforting me, "Mummy, it doesn't matter. Nothing will happen to daddy, he is so healthy". Poor child, he was visibly nervous. Jurek ran about the room, quite pleased to have so much space for himself. And my heart was getting heavier and heavier. It almost burst my rib-cage. A dreadful pain constricted my chest, but I tried hard to keep myself in check. I could not swallow, so dry was my throat. My thoughts were chasing about, seeking some escape.

Again several men were called, their hards were bound and they were led out. This procedure was repeated again and again every few minutes.

Finally only women with children were left behind and a couple of men. Suddenly we heard somebody at the table saying the wives of the detained should come nearer, that is to the table. I was in the first group. Our personal data were taken down and we were told to go back to our seats. The other ladies whispered we should certainly be released. But I had a presentiment... I tried to persuade myself that the release was what should happen but my intuition told me to be prepared for another eventuality. I was right...

Another group of women was called to the table and... they were not allowed to go back to their children. Oh God, where to seek some help, how to save my children from those thugs?... And then I recalled what my mother had once said when Jewish women had been separated from their children and I felt indignant at their passiveness. "Wanda", she said, "should anything like that happen to you, which God forbid, you would also leave the children quietly, for their sakes and for your sake". I kept repeating feverishly though wordlessly my mother's remark. And I was right. The mothers who cried so loudly had their children taken away from them by force and they had to watch how their babies were thrown aside like kittens. There were also kicks and blows in plenty. I decided to prepare Jacuś for what was to come. First of all I put Jurek to sleep so that he wouldn't cry when I'd have to leave them. And then I wanted to tell Jacuś what was in store for him. I did not know how to start... what to say... Mothers who had gone through similar terrible experiences will understand my unhappiness. I did not know whether to beg or to defend my children even at the cost of my life. I nearly lost my reason. Nobody can grasp or describe my despair or the despair of so many other mothers.

The moment of separation was coming nearer and nearer and I felt some torpor descending upon me. I began to pray. It was a strange prayer but somehow courage returned. I lifted the chin of my son and told him, 'Jacuś, they may take me, too... "He did not let me finish the sentence. "I don't want you to go, no, I don't want it!" He cried and repeated the same words over and over again. I waited for a while and then began again, "Sonny, you must listen to what mummy is telling you. If you keep crying they will take Jurek away, too". This helped and dried his tears. Jacuś grew calmer and still swallowing the last tears he said, "Yes, Mummy, I am listening". So I went on, "Jacuś, if the Germans ask you where you want to go, tell them you want to be with Mrs Szczepańska. You remember your name and you know how old you are, don't you? And you know your brother's name and his age". "All right, Mummy", he said, still swallowing hard. But he wanted to hear what I had to say, he felt that he had become the only guardian of his little brother. He fought hard for self-control... And I was strangely calm, too, not a tear, who would have believed it, knowing me, but it had to be so... I gave Jacuś my last instructions what he would have to do when Jurek awoke and I would be away. I looked straight into his dear eyes while he repeated, "Yes, Mummy". Today, when recalling that dreadful moment of leave-taking I cannot help crying. Jacuś nestled close to me... What were his thoughts?

The dreadful momnet had arrived... Women were called to the table. How horrible! If I could only vanish, together with my children! It is far from easy to survive such partings.

I was half consciously noticing what went on around me. Jacuś drew closer to me and then I heard his whisper, "Mummy, take a piece of bread, you must be hungry". I did not want to disappoint him, so I broke off a piece of bread and started eating. But I was unable to swallow the morsel. I hid the bread in my muff.

And then my name was called... I kissed Jacuś, calm and cold, as if turned to ice. I kissed Jurek, too, and walked out of the room.

One hundred allegedly healthy and strong women were told to stand aside, their camp numbers were taken down and the day was settled when we were to leave the quarantine. We would leave that dirt at last. We did not know what work we were expected to do but we did not care. As long as we left that awful block and those mean people behind us! The lack of any kind of occupation was killing under such circumstances. The doctor had several times examined us; he looked at our legs with particular attention. Those with varicose veins were rejected and only young women passed the test. The Jewish women prisoners who were helping at the examination told us we would go to a very bad part of the camp, we wouldn't be able to stand the life there long and we were the first Poles to go there. Some of us got nervous but we calmed down when we heard that only political prisoners were to go there. And really, they started checking the colours of our triangles and rejected two with green ones. We could not be worse off anywhere than we were here. The day came when we marched out, it was April 4, 1943, a very cold, rainy and dreary day. The hundred selected women were driven to the sauna (bath). Again that dreadful bathing amidst blows and pushing. The same cold water and then dressing. This time we were given chemises and very dirty panties, a striped camp dress reaching down to the ankles almost, an apron, a blouse and a white linen kerchief to cover the head with. I was terribly cold and completely drenched by the rain. The women in the first five ranks brought us the bread rations. Before we had reached the gate the bread stuck to us, it got so soggy. We were escorted by SS men with dogs. They cursed all the time, displeased with the weather and the long march. They vented their bad humour on us, driving us on and baiting the dogs to jump on us. Our feet stuck in the muddy clay and would not move. The wooden clogs were an awful nuisance. They were heavy and too large and so fell off with each step while the paper strings with which they were fastened were continually breaking. What tortures! Perspiring and breathless we reached at last our journey's end. Some yards before our goal we noticed the first buildings. They were small, partly demolished houses, once inhabited but empty now. Immediately behind them, at the roadside, there stood a one storied building (once the school house) and next to it a green, windowless barrack. These buldings were surrounded by a barbed wire fence. This was "Budy", our camp. The same which awakened fear in the hearts of all women prisoners in the base camp, a place ruled entirely by German women prisoners with black triangles.

We hardly got any impression of the place at first. They made us wait in the rain in front of the gate for three quarters of an hour. The rain lashed our faces and bodies, streaming down into the shoes. Finally the supervisor, a German woman prisoner came and was so kind as to open the gate. She counted us and let us stand in the small roll-call square. She was accompanied by the block senior, called Sonia, a terrible beast in a rather handsome human body. She had been a prostitute before coming to the camp. She was never seen without a horsewhip which she used to beat us all the time. She arrogantly spoke to us but we did not understand a word of her speech. Her hoarse voice made the particular sounds unintelligible.

The next woman with a function in the camp was the room senior, a Jewess, Henrietta. She said that she expected much from us, we had to obey her orders, otherwise she would know where to send us and there was no return from that place. We would soon learn all about that! She also told us we were the first Poles to have come to Budy and our fate would be very sad indeed. After these speeches we were led to the garret to get our blankets. Each one of us got a clean blanket which pleased us no end. Then we were given leave to enter the barrack and we had our bunks assigned to us. There was one bunk for two women. The interior of the barrack made a pleasant impression on us, and particularly those three-tiered bunks. Melita and I, we took a bunk in the second tier. It proved to be rather narrow for two persons. We somehow managed to climb up to it. The barrack seemed roomy, but then the work squads were not yet back from work. 234 women lived in the barrack, 34 Germans, some Czechs, Russians and Yugoslavs, and all of them were political prisoners. I saw that my companions were pleased and so I felt pleased, too.

I spent 12 nightmarish months at Budy. The first weeks were horrible. Henrietta's words had come true. During that time we thought we were living in hell. We slept little, were hungry and beaten, had to work so hard that we could hardly bear it and we got such conflicting orders from the same capo that we were full of despair and quite nonplussed by them. We had come to Budy after the revolt of the Frenchwomen who had been murdered, all of them, but the black capos, the murderesses of the Frenchwomen had stayed on. They were our immediate supervisors. On the day of our arrival we came to know them all when the squads had returned from work. We, the newcomers, stood apart from the others during the roll-call. A woman of the name of Runge was the supervisor. She was very good-loking and just as mean. She kept us standing at the roll-call for two hours. It was raining cats and dogs and the rain beat our faces and streamed down our legs. All that time we watched the behaviour of the capos. Shivers of dreadful anticipation were running down our spines. After 2 hours of the hopeless standing soup was issued to the other inmates but not to us. We went hungry to bed. It was quite dark in the barrack, we only heard the cursing of the German women. They fell upon us and drove us to the bunks. Drenched as we were we lay down half-dead. At 3 a.m. we were wakened and driven out to attend the roll-call. There we stood again till the dawn.

On the first day we were driven out of the barrack earlier than usually.

We were allocated to different agricultural squads. The capos selected women for their squads. Three capos ran along the ranks and led away the women they had selected. I was allocated, together with some companions of mine. to an agricultural squad working in the fields.

A certain Trude Richter from Bytom was the capo of our squad. She was middle-aged, of middle height, a light blonde with fish-like, but piercing eyes. She would bore her eyes into a person's face like two sharp pins. She could bear no opposition, even if she was completely wrong. She was the highest authority in her squad, the fount of all knowledge, or so she, at least, thought. But she was also completely illiterate. We were obliged to obey her intricate commands, listen to her obscene vocabulary... Her whip helped us to carry heavy stones or beams. When we were demolishing the farmhouses left by the peasants, eight of us had to lift an enormous beam and then the whip of our "Protectress" gave us the necessary strength. We almost crawled on our knees, our insides were upside down, but the beam was lifted and taken to the place she had shown us.

There were as many as three supervisors in our squad: Anita, Friede and Emmy, a chosen trio of the most criminal types. They were prisoners, too, all of them with black triangles. They were the capo's helpers, but she used to beat them if they transgressed her orders. The starved, beaten, emaciated women prisoners kept working hard. Some were carrying bricks from one place to another, others were putting them into stacks. This was not the hardest kind of work but I avoided it as much as possible. To drag oneself from one spot to another was more irksome for me than pulling down a chimney. And we had to do it, too. One had to feel for the weakest spot of the chimney, take a firm stand and push hard and then the chimney would tumble down. Of course, one had to find the method for oneself. The capo, even when she knew how things should be done, would never tell you. She just gave the order to pull down a chimney and that was all. When she had told me to do it I started looking for a ladder as I thought I should have to take it to pieces beginning from the top. There were moments when I thought I could not stand it any longer but the "pleasant" shouts of our capo gave me new strength. My eyes nearly left their sockets, the pickaxe fell from the numbed fingers, my nose almost touched the ground and my stomach seemed to stick to the back. And the day was dragging on without end.

We went to work without food and it was only at noon that we got a priece of bread. In the evening there was some watery soup. Runge was fond of quietness, so she would issue our food only after two hours of waiting. There had to be absolute silence during the roll-calls which was rather difficult to exact with 300 hungry women present. 300 starving, tormented, hard-working skeletons wanted to eat and hunger does not induce quiet. There were various symptoms. Some women fainted, other sighed, some again cursed the day they were born. All this mounted to a perceptible murmur and as Runge had sensitive ears she punished us by not giving us any soup. Only when the women had grown quite faint did the murmur subside and then Runge conducted the rollcall. Then, one after another, we went to get half a litre of watery soup and 3 potatoes which most often were rotten. When we entered the barrack it was usually quite dark. Nobody felt like eating then. Sleep was most important.

There was a water well in the middle of the yard but no one dared to come near it and get some water... We went without washing for weeks. There was no question of washing or laundering and yet we were expected to be clean. One was also beaten for being dirty.

Once we were digging ditches. The whole squad, some 120 women, was employed at this work. The capo would assign our tasks according to her whim. We were led into the road which was flanked on both sides by overgrown and too shallow ditches. We had to clean them from grass, make them deeper and cover their slopes with turf. I had tried all kinds of work there. At first I used to dig, together with others, then I covered the slopes with pieces of turf which I made fast by means of a wooden mallet. The work would not have been so hard if we had not been expected to do so much of it. The ditches were to be absolutely clean, the pieces of turf had to be faultlessly arranged which was not attainable as they were of different sizes and shapes. The weather turned cold and rainy. On such dreary days the capo became more nasty than ever. She was cold, too, so she tried to get warm by beating us.

We breathed more freely when the sunny days had come. Then we started to work in the fields. The women with functions in camp were the only ones to boss us in the fields, while during our work in the camp everyone would boss us, even the room seniors.

Our first task in the fields was to plant lupine. It was not sown but planted. In the rows, made by the machine, we had to make a deeper hole with our hands (not on any account with a stick!). The clods of earth were still frozen. Into each hole we planted five or six seeds of lupine, covered them well with earth and pressed the earth down. This was done from 6 a.m. to 7 p.m. non stop! And always bending down. We could straighten our backs only during the lunch-break which lasted 20 minutes. If the weather was fine it was not so bad, but it was awful in rainy weather. The boss used to beat us without mercy if one more seed was planted and yet the seeds would stick to our wet hands which were covered with clay. The cold fingers lost the sense of touch but we had to hurry nevertheless, if anyone remained behind she got beaten. How many tears fell into this earth! It was made fertile by our tears, sweat, blood, no wonder the lupine made a pretty show. No one can describe the hard work that the planting of the lupine meant for us. First the planting, then the weeding, later on, when the plants had attained a height of 10 centimetres, the hoeing. And then the fields were ploughed. So much work... what for? The ploughed fields were again covered with a different fertilizer which was brought there and put into equal mounds. We had to break up the mounds and scatter the fertilizer over the fields.

Scattering it was very hard work indeed, and we had very little strength left. Three women with pitchforks stood at each mound. Since very few had ever done it before, they were beaten the more. The fertilizer had to be spread evenly, in thin layers. Otherwise, when the *Oberscharführer* [1]) came and noticed some clods, the whole field had to be done anew. We had to accomplish this task very quickly. After spreading the fertilizer the field was again ploughed and harrowed but this was done by men. We planted potatoes on the field later on.

The 9th of May was a day to be remembered in the history of my camp life. It was a Sunday, a nice and sunny, though cold day. We wore no blouses any more.

During the morning roll-call my number and three others were called. We were to go to the Political Section in Auschwitz, escorted by a very young *SS*-man, a boy really. He allowed us to have a wash in a ditch by the roadside.

I found myself in the Political Section for the second time. We waited a while outside, in front of the barrack, close to the crematorium. Then a *Gestapo* officer came and told us the officials from Katowice were waiting for us at Birkenau. We knew the officials and so could guess what they wanted with us. We did not wait long at Birkenau. Melita was the first to be called in. She came out after 20 minutes perhaps, as red in her face as a peony. I got nervous when I saw her but had no time to ask her what had happened as I was called in immediately after. I entered a smallish room in which I found two officers of the *Gestapo* and the interpreter, a Jewess. First they asked me about my personal data and then,

---

[1]) Officer's rank in the *SS*.

"When were you arrested and why?" I quietly answered all the questions giving the exact date of my arrest and telling them I did not know why I had been arrested. I had been taken together with my husband and children. "I'll tell you why", said the *Gestapo* official. "You are in camp because you consciously helped your husband, Stanisław Koprowski, in his anti-German and therefore illegal activities. Have you children? Where are they?" The last question I was unable to answer, I did not know then where my little ones were. "Have you anything to say in your defense? Nothing?" What was I to say? They would not believe my words anyway. "Speak up, you can't hurt you husband, defend yourself. He's..." and the *Gestapo* official drew his hand across his throat in an unmistakable gesture. I whispered, "When?"

"The 16th of April", was the answer.

I grew cold.

And then I heard, "Why should you rot in the camp, you can live. Tell us only who had drawn you into this filthy mess?" Oh, I thought, so that's it. Stach being hanged must be a lie, they want to scare me. I drew myself up and looked the *Gestapo* official up and down. He then gave me a terrific blow in my face. Once, twice, thrice, my head was wobbling from side to side. I tasted blood in my mouth, my ears were singing. Frightened, I felt that something clattered in my mouth. That were my teeth which had come loose. But I did not believe that Stach was dead. He was alive, surely, he'd got to be alive!

The *Gestapo* official calmed down after some time and gave me my statement to sign and some other paper. It was my sentence to remain in camp for the rest of my days. Was it irony? What did they expect? To rule for ever? I signed both papers and left. My thoughts went to Stach. What was in store for me? Will God let me return home? O God, let me bear everything, make me strong.

My companions went through with similar "formalities". We waited three long hours for our escort, trembling with cold and excitement.

The planting of potatoes began in the middle of May and the whole squad went to work in the fields. The capo assigned the tasks; some carried potatoes, others planted them. I belonged to the latter group. We worked together with Melita, carrying a basket of potatoes and walking behind the machine which was making holes in the ground. We dropped one potato into each hole and then pressed the earth down with our feet. One need not bend down when planting potatoes, so this work did not exhaust us. Trude made those women who got parcels from home do the planting. The rest was employed in breaking up clods of earth in the ploughed marshes which were not yet quite dry. We all wanted to do the planting as the work was not so hard and, besides, the capo did not beat us there quite so often on account of the men prisoners who were working nearby. And the men brought us some potatoes stolen from the vaporizer and meant to be fed to pigs. They did it very circumspectly. They gave the potatoes to the capo to divide them among us. But the way she divided them! She gave them to those she favoured and only one potato to each woman at that, and the rest she ate herself, sharing them only with her friends. Melita and I never got one single potato. This was, however, before I got the first parcel from home.

Till then I had had no news from home. We were finally allowed to write to our families and on May 29 I got a letter from my mother, but unfortunately she had written it in Polish. It contained only the first and the last sentence, the rest was cut out. I have kept this letter till now, it is my greatest treasure. How much did I suffer then on account of it! I received it during the roll-call. We had another supervisor at that time. Her name was Hasse, the well-known "chimney sweep", so called because she had sent many women to the gas chambers, the "chimney". Her appearance was sufficient to frighten anyone. It was she who handed me this letter with an expression which clearly said, "There you are, read it, but you won't learn much!" I thought my heart would break when I saw the letter. I could not by any means control loud sobs. I wept and folded it to my heart. I had waited for it so long, had counted the days... I had hoped to get some news about my children and all was cut out... I kissed the letter and my tears fell on it. Oh, mother, why did you forget that I was allowed to get only letters written in German? I could write another letter not earlier than next month. How should I bear the waiting? I wept the whole next day.

Then another letter came. But it was written in Polish too, so all I got was the envelope. It was only the third letter that brought me some news. All I could guess from it was that my children were in a safe place, perhaps with my parents. And I learned that Stach was in the Mauthausen camp.

*

The conditions in which we worked were still very hard, but things seemed to have improved somewhat in our barrack since we got a new block senior, Eve, a German with a black triangle. She had seemed to be of a better disposition and she did not get so mad as Sonia had done. She did not care much what was going on in the block. She liked to drink, though nobody knew where she managed to get the vodka from. But when drunk, and this was often, she used to be unbearable. She had big green eyes and so we called her "green-eyes". We did not like her although she was not as bad as Sonia. And we soon came to hate her with our deepest hatred.

Once she came to the block completely drunk. She was called because one prisoner, an elderly woman from Radom, got sick. She had been in the hospital and had returned two days ago not at all cured. She developed high temperature, tossed about and did the strangest things. We could not control her or calm her, so one of us went to the block senior to get some sleeping pills for her. Instead of the pills the block senior herself arrived and began to laugh heartily when seeing the antics of the delirious woman. And then... She grasped the unlucky woman by her hair and dragged her to the well. She ordered her helper to throw water over the victim, one bucket after another. The block senior was cruelly laughing all through this operation. The poor patient finally fell down and never regained consciousness. She was taken to the hospital where she died the next day.

Such was our "mild" block senior. We looked on with joy when Hasse smacked her face. These were our only pleasures.

*

After the inspection by Drechsel conditions had improved considerably. The washing was always done on Saturdays. Till then we had not known what warm water meant and now it was being warmed in cauldrons in the kitchen. Dinner was not cooked that day, it is true, but this did not matter.

The washing was of a very primitive kind. I made use of the water whenever I could. I bribed the capo to be able to do so, of course, only when Trude was in a good temper. Later on, when parcels kept arriving, I used to give Trude the toilet soap and she would let me wash.

We had been getting parcels from home since a few weeks. We were more happy than we could say. In the first parcel I got a loaf of bread, sliced and smeared with lard. Some sugar, some jam, three cloves of garlic and three onions. I don't know what else there had been in the parcel but I found some empty paper bags in it. The bread was not taken, however, and that was the important thing. After getting the first parcel I wrote home asking to have the loaf sent whole, not sliced. The next parcel was different. I got a whole loaf of bread, some sugar, lard, cakes, about 20 dekagrammes of sausage, garlic and onions. I was getting parcels of this kind till June 1944, twice a week. So I had plenty for myself and for others. I never kept my parcels hidden but gave away things to those that were hungry.

My first nameday in the camp was rather strange. I got a special parcel the day before with a lot of cakes and sweets. We were then planting cabbages and turnips as far as Harmęże, close to Birkenau.

I took my parcel with me when going to work so that I could share it with my companions in the lunch break. When we were passing a nursery orchard Marysia Kopczyńska left the ranks and picked an apple-tree blossom which she gave me with her good wishes. I was so touched by this gesture that I promised to keep the blossom for remembrance. We had half an hour's break at noon. I prepared some sandwiches, cut the cake and invited my best friends to the "table" that is to a spot on the grass near the fire. But we had to be very careful lest Trude catch us feasting.

The parcels meant everything to us. If it had not been for them many of us would have never again seen their families. They not only assuaged the hunger in the camp, they also served to bribe the supervisors who would then allow us, for instance, to wear two chemises in winter.

*

The spreading of compost was the worst kind of work. It had been my job for a long time. We all heard about compost but had no idea what hard work it entailed. And in Auschwitz particularly where everybody was so exacting. Those edges, for instance. It would seem that a heap of manure was a heap of manure and it did not matter what it looked like. But it was not so. The compost had to be arranged in a perfectly even way, forming exact rectangles with absurdly straight edges. It was my task for weeks to make them perfectly even. I volunteered for this kind of job. I am not sure whether everybody knows how the compost was prepared. The bottom consisted of straw and the sides were of straw which was less rumpled. Then the Jews brought the manure in buckets and poured it on the straw. Turf was put upon it, human ashes were strewn next and then again liquid manure in which we waded ankle deep. The edges of the compost were circa 10 meters long and its height came to almost 6 meters. When it was found that the stack was tall enough it was again covered with straw and turf, its top and sides were again strewn with human ashes. From afar the compost stacks looked like immense cakes.

*

The spring was so lovely but we felt worse and worse. So many were constantly leaving our squad. All sorts of diseases had made their appearance. Mrs Wirtek and Mrs Gałuszka were the first to leave Budy. They went to the hospital and were not fated to return from it. Mrs Wirtek had two children. She was strong but the disease proved to be stronger. I clearly remember Mrs Gałuszka. Our capo had sent her to wheel the wheelbarrows as punishment. She was working there a few days only, when they brought her from work half-dead. She had diarrhoea and next day was taken to the hospital together with Mrs Wirtek. They always stuck to each other and they died together.

Then Marysia Masłowska was taken, never to return any more. The disease took more and more victims and chose them at random. Others went, too, — Irka Woźniak, Hela Solarska, Janka Stolarska, Melita Bargieł, Mrs Lis. Melita came back looking horribly unwell. We were again working together.

We were now busy with the haymaking. This work was responsible for many casualties. We went to work a little farther than Rajsko, that means a distance of ten kilometres one way. The thirst was tormenting us and there was not a drop of water anywhere. We used to get up at 3 a.m. and went to work as early as 4^{30}a.m. We returned to the barrack at 9 p.m. This was extremely hard on us. We were unable even to eat the food they sent us from home. The work and lack of sleep were exhausting. The eyes would not open, the eyelids were swollen. It was only two weeks since the haymaking had begun and we were at the end of our tether. The mechanism of the body ceased to work and there was no help for it.

I remember the day when I told myself — I have had enough, I can't go on. We were just then working behind Rajsko, on a very sultry day. I had felt ill since the very morning, my head and feet were heavy, the body was aching all over. Even the blouse seemed to oppress me and the thirst was a torture. I noticed a small pond among trees, the surface of its water was covered by a thick skin. I removed some of the green skin and put my mouth to the water, forgetful of everything. Somebody jerked me violently back from the desirable liquid. It was Trude standing in front of me. I saw her through a kind of haze and heard her threatening voice as if coming from afar, "You'll go to the hospital tomorrow". She knew all prisoners were afraid of going to the hospital. But I did not care any more. I only wished to lie down, to stretch my aching body. I felt very feverish. Every moment seemed to stretch into infinity and the evening was so distant. I did not work that day, my nearest companions did the work for me. But I had to follow them and pretend I was working to escape the beating. I did not go to Rajsko the next day. There was hay to be collected not far from the camp, on a very damp terrain. I could wet my lips with water from time to time. I felt fire in my chest. That day we returned very late to the barrack and I fell upon the bunk half-dead. I was so glad it was Sunday next day.

But the next morning it was pouring. The *Oberscharführer* was afraid the rain would spoil the hay, so he ordered us to go to work, all of us. We went to the banks of the Soła river to save the hay at the cost of our own lives which had less value than a bundle of hay. We had been working four hours and when the hay was safe and secure, we returned to the barrack. I was brought back by my companions. Next day I was taken to Birkenau, together with Hela Jagło, Marysia Dutkiewicz and another woman. Things had changed at Birkenau since the last five months. A messenger girl escorted us to the out-patients clinic which was situated in a barrack immediately behind the barbed wire fence. Some women doctors and women journalists working as doctors were busy there. Here, one got assigned to the hospital if one had backing. After having examined us the doctor, a German journalist in fact, sent us to Block 29.

Its interior looked tidy enough at the first glance, if one did not probe further. We were told to undress as soon as we reached the entrance gate. Then they called us inside the block and told us to sit down (sitting down was a must) on a brick chimney pipe running right through the middle of the whole block and leading to the stove. The chimney pipe was ice-cold. Here we were to wait for our beds. Some minutes later the women doctors, prisoners too, had arrived. One of them was a Czech, another a Jewess, the third, Dr Mancy, a Hungarian. There were very many women sitting on the chimney pipe, seriously ill all of them. The doctors put thermometers under our armpits and left us to look after other patients. Then they would return and assign the patients to the different hospital wards, just as they fancied. The Czech doctor approached me and looking with surprise at the thermometer asked who had sent me here with such an insignificant temperature.

It was barely 38,4 degrees Centigrade which was a trifle not deserving to be cured in the hospital. I got frightened as the vision of a hospital bed seemed to dissolve before my eyes. I looked straight into the doctor's face and said, "Doctor, I am very ill indeed." She sensed the appeal, looked at me again, told me to show my tongue, looked into my eyes and decided that I was really ill. She called the ward senior and told her to lead me to ward II. I asked the doctor to let Hela and Marysia go with me and she consented. When I saw the ward senior I thought I had seen her before but I was too weak to do any thinking at the moment. We were put, all three of us, upon a bunk in the third tier, the highest, right under the roof. We were, of course, not given any nightgowns, this was not customary there. The straw pallet was dirty, full of spots, there were no blankets, but the dirty bed seemed heavenly to me. It was a tight squeeze for the three of us, but we were so happy not to have to go haymaking any more. The ward senior came again to see how many of us there were and if there was any room for others. It was then I recognized her, it was Marysia Januszkiewicz.

"How did you get here?" — I asked.

"What is that to you? Move along and don't rave", was the answer.

"You remind me of someone I knew when I was free", I continued.

"Freedom's gone phut. Who do I remind you of?" — she asked.

"Marysia Januszkiewicz", — I answered briefly.

She started and immediately her face, her voice, her behaviour, had changed. She looked at me sharply and then shouted at the top of her voice, "Is it you, Wanda? You here? How? Since when? I wouldn't have recognized you". She began sobbing violently. Then she ran down, brought me a nightgown, all the time feverishly repeating, "I won't let you go to the typhus ward, you would never leave it alive and you've got to live. I'll ask the doctor, she is so kind-hearted. You'll stay here". And so I learned that I had typhus.

Marysia had been in Auschwitz ever since its beginnings. She had a very low camp number. She looked well, as a ward senior she belonged to the camp elite. It is to her that I owe my life. She was like a sister to me. First of all she told the doctor all about me and the doctor let me stay where I was, under her care. All she could do was to come often and see whether my organism would conquer the disease. She had no drugs to dispense. That ward was for convalescents only. Hela had stayed on with me. I had also asked for Marysia to remain with us, but to no avail. She had to go to the typhus ward. Our doctor said, however, she would certainly leave it alive, her case was not so serious.

I do not remember what had happened next. After the first strong impressions I fell asleep and slept for three long weeks. Who had cared for me during that time, changed my underwear, protected me from lice? Marysia, for sure. But she would not even listen when I thanked her. The first day of my awakening was very strange indeed. I thought I was in a mill, there was such a noise in my ears and a mist before my eyes. Suddenly I heard a faint voice calling my name. I did not know where it came from, I did not realize where I was. That faint voice again... I looked down and saw Marysia Dutkiewicz standing below our bunk. I did not grasp the meaning of this. Is Marysia well again, why it was only yesterday she left for the typhus ward.

"No, Wanda", explained Marysia, "it wasn't yesterday, it was three weeks ago. You have fought the disease during that time. Death was near, but we managed to drive it away. You are past the danger now."

Three weeks! I must have been very dangerously ill indeed, since Marysia was so glad to see me recovered. But I could hear her words only faintly and, oh, horror, I could not see well, either. I was unable to move and something was biting me terribly. I was unable to raise my hand and scratch myself. I told Marysia about my predicament. She brought me a clean pajamas and dressed me. I then glanced at Hela who looked like a corpse. She had recovered from typhus more easily than I did, but now pneumonia had set in. She wanted to get up every few minutes and when asked where she wanted to go she kept saying she wanted to go to her children and take some bread to them. I told her to lie down and not to rave. Hela lay down but she only waited for me to pay less attention to her and then repeated her attempt to get away. I could hardly imagine what would have happened if she really had tried to get down the bunk. She would have fallen down from that height and who could have helped her down? I was still so weak that I was unable to turn over... But luckily Hela looked down from our bunk and the distance between it and the floor seemed to have frightened her. Finally she lay down and fell asleep. I could lie back quietly and think. Marysia was no longer there to help me, she was no longer in our ward. Mrs Mela had taken her place. Marysia Dutkiewicz was lying nearby and crying without stopping which made us very nervous. We were sufficiently unhappy, all of us, as it were. My nearest neighbours were Wanda Kwaśnik and Mrs Ula Kmita. They were not ill. Wanda had had angina and Mrs Kmita stayed on in the hospital thanks to some backing. They were both very nice and helped us a lot, being always ready to do anything for us if we needed it. It was thanks to their help that I was slowly recovering. I could not sit up as yet, but I was always washed, thanks to their care.

*

It was then that I got a letter from home with the picture of my children. The Jewess Mala brought it for me to have a look at the picture and to return it at once. Did I really see the picture then? The tears kept welling from my eyes when I tried to look at the dear little faces. I had only a few seconds' time to see the photo. I sat up in my excitement but soon lay down again on the pallet. I did not want to give up the photo, they had to take it from me by force. High temperature was the result of that excitement and after several hours I woke thinking that my children's picture was just a dream. I became fully conscious only after several weeks.

*

As a convalescent I could observe what was going on in the hospital. The death rate was alarming, the number of corpses was terrifying... And the corpses were not left in peace, not even they.

Rats were gnawing them before they got cremated. The rats in Birkenau were a calamity. They were as big as cats, fattened upon dead bodies. But they also attacked the sick. If a corpse lay on its right side, the other side would be just a mass of clean bones. The cheek, neck, breast, all fleshy parts were devoured by the rats. Nobody dared to disturb them. The nurses were afraid to come near them since they were not to be frightened away, not even by sticks. Whole families of them used to pass by and one had to avoid them as they would not run away when seeing people.

Special squads were assigned the task of carting the corpses away, they were called in German *"Leichen—"* or *"Himmelskommando"* (mortuary squads). They consisted of Jewish women, easily recognizable by the leather gloves they were entitled to wear. They came with stretchers made of two boards, covered with a dirty and stinking blanket which they used to cover the corpse with. If the corpse lay on a groundfloor bunk the procedure was simple, but if it was the second or third tier the spectacle was gruesome. One of the women would climb up to the bunk and throw the body right down upon the floor so that the head thudded on it. The corpse was then placed upon the stretcher and carried to the mortuary, whence trucks conveyed all corpses to the crematorium. But only bare skeletons were usually leaving the mortuary. Whole truck loads of bones — the flesh was eaten away by rats.

*

I could not stand life in the hospital any longer. My nerves would not bear it. Oh, to escape from it, to run away as quickly as possible.

*

I had returned to my family after many, many experiences. There was Ravensbrück a munitions factory at Finów, Ravensbrück again and finally (through the Red Cross) Sweden. This was freedom at last.

*

We had arrived at Częstochowa at 9 p.m. I knew that my parents had a telephone at home, so I wanted to let them know I had arrived. I went to the station master to make a call, but his telephone was not for outside use. So we went to the Left Luggage Office. I got my connection and when my brother-in-law came to the telephone, they handed me the receiver. At first I could not hear anything, there was such a commotion at the other end of the line. Then I heard, "Wanda, is that you, really and truly you? All right, we'll be coming for you at once". And then, "Wanda, I've dreamt of you today". And finally, "Mummy dear". I started to cry so much that I had to put down the receiver. I went to say good-bye to my companions. After a while I saw from afar my brother-in-law, then my sister with Jacuś, my son. My brother-in-law went to fetch a horse-cab. I said a final good-bye to my companions and went home. From my sister I learned that the children had been with them only since liberation.

My parents were waiting for me at home. My mother kept embracing me and then shoving me back to look at me and make sure it was really I. Jurek was already asleep, indifferent to everything that was going on. I went to his bed, knelt down and my mother spoke to him, "Jurek, get up, Mummy's come." The little head was raised for a moment, one big, dark eye became visible and then back to the pillow again! That was all I could see of him. Now I began coaxing, "Sonny, won't you look at Mummy? I know I am a stranger to you, so you don't want to see me, but look what I've brought you. A nice donkey which bows and lies down, all by itself". Now another eye appeared and looked at me a little longer. And then he said, "Did you come by ship?" He showed me a ship standing by his bed. So I began a tale of the ship that had been sailing over the seas till it came to Poland and brought Mummy back. The child sat up and listened, his lips partly open. The worst was over. I was full of joy that Jurek had accepted me at once and called me Mummy the very first day.

When my maternal heart was satisfied we began talking and relating and asking questions. Stach was not present, he was at work in Bobrek near Bytom where he lived. He would come the next day and we would start a new life together.

*

Danuta Czech, M. A.

MOST IMPORTANT EVENTS IN THE HISTORY OF THE CONCENTRATION CAMP AUSCHWITZ-BIRKENAU.

1940.

25.1. Chief of the *SS*-Head Office notified the *Reichsführer SS* Heinrich Himmler that a concentration camp would soon be established near the town of Oświęcim.

21.2. Inspector of concentration camps, *SS-Oberführer* Glücks informed the *Reichsführer SS* of the local inspection during which it had been settled that the former Polish military barracks at Oświęcim would be a suitable locale for a quarantine camp after making certain sanitary and building additions.

18,19.4. *SS-Hauptsturmführer* Rudolf Höss, then commandant of the custody camp of the Sachsenhausen concentration camp, stayed at Oświęcim as head of the second commission, the task of which was to assess the possibility of establishing there a concentration camp.

1940

27.4.	Following the report forwarded by Höss after his inspection, Himmler issued the order to establish a concentration camp at Oświęcim and to enlarge it, using prisoners as man-power.
29.4.	Glücks nominated R. Höss commandant of the Auschwitz Concentration Camp (*KL* Auschwitz) at Oświęcim.
30.4.	R. Höss arrived at Oświęcim with 5 *SS*-men to supervise work connected with organizing the camp.
20.5.	The *Rapportführer* of *KL* Auschwitz, Gerhard Palitzsch (detailed as Höss's subaltern by the Inspector of the Concentration Camps) brought from the *KL* Sachsenhausen 30 German prisoners chosen by himself, criminal offenders all of them. Their camp numbers were from 1 to 30 and they were located in Block No. 1. They were destined to have functions in the camp in the so-called "prisoners camp self-government". Prisoner No. 1, Bruno Brodniewicz had the function of the camp senior, others were to be block seniors, capos, *etc.* At the same time 15 *SS-men* from the *SS* calvary detachment in Cracow were sent to *KL* Auschwitz as its garrison.
14.6.	The first transport of Poles, political prisoners, in the strength of 728 men arrived here, sent from the prison in Tarnów by the commandant of the Security Police in the *General Gouvernement*. The prisoners got numbers from 31 to 758 and were located, for the period of quarantine, in the building of the tobacco monopoly, situated near the railway siding and separated from other buildings by a barbed wire fence. Transports of prisoners, citizens of various countries under Nazi occupation, began steadily arriving since that date. Further 100 *SS*-men were sent to strengthen the garrison, together with *SS* officers and *SS* N.C.O.'s of different rank, who were detailed to various posts in the camp administration
circa 5.7.	An old munitions bunker, formerly part of the garrison buildings, was converted to serve as a crematorium. Prisoners did all the work connected with its rebuilding. The crematorium was originally equipped with 2, later with 3 ovens, each with two retorts.[1]
6.7.	Escape of prisoner Tadeusz Wiejowski. This was the first escape from *KL* Auschwitz. The escape was ascertained during the evening roll-call. A punitive roll-call of all prisoners was ordered, which meant that all prisoners were kept standing from 6 p.m. to 2 p.m. on the next day (7.7.), i.e. for 20 hours.
July.	As retaliation for helping the first escapee, T. Wiejowski, the Polish civilian population, living in the neighbourhood of the camp was deported. This was also done to prevent the possibility of further escapes. Many families were taken to forced labour camps in the Sudeten region, others to the *General Gouvernement*.
15.8.	Arrival of the first transport of prisoners from Warsaw with 1,666 men. The transport consisted of 513 prisoners, formerly committed

---

[1] This was the so-called crematorium I, active since November 1940.

1941

	to the Pawiak prison and 1,153 men taken during police round ups[2]) in the streets of Warsaw. They got numbers from 1513 to 1899 and from 1901 to 3173.
August.	A penal company (*SK*) of prisoners was organized and located in one room of Block No. 3. In September the penal company was transferred to Block No. 11, the so-called "Block of Death".
22.11.	The first execution took place in the camp. 40 Poles, selected out of 4 lists presented by the police in Katowice were shot by order of *Gruppenführer* Heydrich, Head of the Security Police and Security Guard. The execution was to be an act of retaliation for alleged acts of terror and attacks upon the German police in Katowice. The execution was conducted by *SS-Obersturmbannführer* Fritzsch, was witnessed by *SS-Untersturmführer* Täger; the executioners were 2 *SS*-men from the firing squad, supplied for that day by the *SS-Totenwachsturmbann* Auschwitz. The bodies of the 40 men were immediately after cremated in the camp crematorium.
19.12.	Archbishop Prince Adam Sapieha sent to the Parochial Office of the town Oświęcim a letter addressed to the commandant of the concentration camp asking for permission to conduct religious services for Roman Catholic prisoners during the Christmas holidays. Commandant R. Höss declined to grant the request, stating that the camp regulations did not foresee religious services being conducted in the camp. He gave his permission, however, to supply all prisoners with circa 6,000 food parcels of 1 kilogramme each as Christmas gifts.
31.12.	The last camp number of that year, No. 7879, was issued to a prisoner brought from Katowice.[3]
1941.	
circa 7.1.	Dr Otto Ambros, member of the Board of *IG-Farbenindustrie* and manager of the *Buna* productions, acquainted himself during his stay in the Planning Office in Katowice with maps of the adjacent terrains and came to the conclusion that Oświęcim was the most suitable place for building new chemical plants (the so-called *Buna-Werke*) by the *IG-Farbenindustrie*.
18.2.	Hermann Göring, Marshal of the *Reich*, ordered all Jews from Oświęcim to be deported, so as to provide living quarters for civilians employed in the construction of *Buna-Werke;* Poles were to be left there for the time being, until the construction was finished; all prisoners of *KL* Auschwitz were to be used as man-power in the *Buna-Werke*.

---

[2]) Police round ups were organized by the Nazis in various towns and settlements of the General Gouvernement.
[3]) This means that during the time from May 20, 1940 to December 31, 1940, 7,879 prisoners were committed to *KL* Auschwitz.

1941

22.2. Chemical plants connected with the *Buna-Werke* were to be built at Dwory near Oświęcim, as the department of the *Leuna-Werke*.

1.3. *Reichsführer SS* Heinrich Himmler arrived at *KL* Auschwitz for his first visit of inspection. He was accompanied by *Gauleiter* Bracht, presidents of the regency, High Commander of the *SS* and Police in Silesia, Schmauser, executives from the *IG-Farbenindustrie* and Inspector of Concentration Camps, Glücks. After inspecting the camp and the entire zone of interests, Himmler issued the following orders to commandant Höss: to enlarge the camp at Oświęcim to the capacity of accommodating 30,000 prisoners, to build in the area of the village Brzezinka a camp for 100,000 prisoners of war, to supply the concern *IG-Farbenindustrie* with 10,000 prisoners who would build industrial plants at Dwory near Oświęcim, to foster agriculture, etc. in the entire terrain and to establish artisan workshops in the camp. He also demanded the construction of large armaments works in the vicinity of the camp, so as to enable the *SS* to lead in the field of rearming the German army.

8.3. Deportations of peasant population from villages lying in the zone of interests of *KL* Auschwitz were begun.[4])

26.3. Prof. Dr Ing. Zunker from Wrocław, after conducting investigations concerning water and pond conditions in the area adjoining the camp, pronounced in his written report the water used in the camp not fit for gargling even. He conducted the investigations with a view to establishing there farms raising cattle, fowls, fisheries, etc.

27.3. A conference took place with the following participants: commandant R. Höss, *Sturmbannführer* Kraus of the *SS* Economic Administration Head Office and Ing. Faust, Ing. Floeter, Ing. Murr, Dr Dürfeld of the *IG-Farbenindustrie*. At the conference it was resolved that:
1) *KL* Auschwitz would supply about 1,000 prisoners in 1941 for the construction of *IG-Farbenindustrie* works at Dwory,
2) about 3,000 prisoners would additionally be supplied in 1942. Should the concern demand it, the number would rise to 8,000,
3) these numbers would rise in the following years,
4) prisoners would go to work by train. The camp would build a railway bridge on the river Soła,
5) work hours would be from 10 to 11 hours in summer and 9 hours in winter,
6) the daily wages of a skilled worker would amount to 4 *RM*, for unskilled labour to 3 *RM*.[5])

7.4. In accordance with the resolutions passed at the conference of the representatives of the *SS* Economic Administration Head Office

---
[4]) Peasants from the following villages were uprooted: Pławy, Rajsko, Brzezinka, Babice, Broszkowice, Harmęże, Bielany, Osiek, Polanka.
[5]) From the cash receipts of the administration of *KL* Auschwitz it appears that the wages paid for workers by *IG-Farbenindustrie Buna-Werke* went into the till of the camp administration. The prisoners did not get any part of the wages.

1941

and *IG-Farbenindustrie* (of March 27, 1941), the prisoners of *KL* Auschwitz began their work in the *Buna-Werke*. The prisoners went to, and from, work on foot, both ways 10 kilometres each day.

23.4. Commandant Höss, in retaliation for a prisoner's escape, selected 10 prisoners from Block No. 2 and committed them to a bunker in Block No. 11. The prisoners were not given any food and all died of starvation in the period from 27.4. to 26.5. The same kind of punishment had been many times meted out in the camp.

6.6. The first transport of prisoners from Czechoslovakia (60 men) arrived from Brno. They were given camp numbers from 17045 to 17104.

circa 30.6. Commandant R. Höss was summoned by *Reichsführer SS* Himmler who personally discussed with him the technical aspects of solving the Jewish problem. R. Höss got his instruction from Himmler to conduct mass extermination of the Jews and was ordered to forward within four weeks a complete plan of the construction of installations for the mass killing of people.

circa 18. 7. Several hundreds of Soviet prisoners of war were brought to the camp and located in Block No. 11. The prisoners were employed to extract sand from pits. In the course of a few days the entire group had been killed while at work, either by shots from small calibre weapons or by blows with spades and pickaxes.

28.7. A special commission had arrived, announced by Himmler's order, with Dr Horst Schumann [6]) as its participant. The commission took over the invalids, cripples and chronic cases, selected under the pretext of transferring them to another camp and using them for easier work. Persuaded by the *SS*-men, some prisoners volunteered to go of their own free will. On Dr Schumann's recommendation *Rapportführer* Hössler took the transport of 575 prisoners to the Hospital for Mental Cases in Königstein [7]) in Saxony. According to Hössler's report, rendered to commandant R. Höss, those prisoners were gassed in a bathhouse into which carbonic oxide was let in.

August. In order to get rid of the sick, who were unable to work, the method of killing prisoners with injections was introduced, e.g. hydrogen peroxide, benzine, evipan and phenol were injected. At first intravenous injections were administered, later injections into the heart with phenol exclusively. The first attempts at killing with injections took place in the cellar of Block N. 28 where the mortuary was located, later the killing was done in the hospital blocks No. 20 and No. 21.

3.9. First attempt of mass murders of people by means of the gas Cyclon B, in *KL* Auschwitz. Into the emptied bunkers of Block No. 11, appro-

---

[6]) Dr Horst Schumann had lived in Ghana (Africa). In 1966 he was extradited to the German Federal Republic and is awaiting trial there.

[7]) The reports of the Resistance Movement Camp Organization stated that the prisoners were taken to Dresden.

ximately 250 sick prisoners from hospital blocks were brought. Then circa 600 Soviet prisoners of war (officers and commissars sent from the camps for prisoners of war by order No. 8, July 7, 1941) were driven in. The windows of the bunkers were shovelled shut with earth. When the SS-men had thrown the gas Cyclon B into the bunkers, the doors were screwed up tight. The next day *Rapportführer* Palitzsch, wearing a gas mask, opened the doors in the particular bunkers and found that some sick persons and prisoners of war were still alive. So another dose of Cyclon B was thrown in and the doors were sealed again.

5.9. In the evening several scores of prisoners from the penal company and from among the prisoners orderlies in the hospital blocks were brought to Block No. 11 and were given gas masks. They were told to descend to the cellars, to open the bunkers and to carry out the corpses of the gassed into the yard of Block No. 11. Under the supervision of SS officers: Fritzsch, Mayer, Palitzsch, the camp physician Entress and others, the prisoners removed the uniforms of the Soviet prisoners of war from the corpses, together with watches, rings, etc. The corpses were carried out for two successive nights and were carted to the crematorium in carts drawn by prisoners. The entire camp was obliged to stay indoors (*Lagersperre*) [8]) and the prisoners who had performed the above mentioned tasks were told to keep the secret under penalty of death.

28.9. The first transport consisting of 22 Yugoslavs, men, arrived from Veldes. Their camp numbers were from 21131 to 21152.

7.10. 2,014 Soviet prisoners of war were brought from the prisoners' of war camp in Lamsdorf (at present Łambinowice). The prisoners were located in nine blocks which had been separated from the camp as early as September and were surrounded by barbed wires charged with an electricity current of high voltage. These blocks formed a separate camp for the Soviet prisoners of war in KL Auschwitz. 9, 983 prisoners of war were located there up to November 15, 1941. Simultaneously with their being brought to the camp the construction of KL Auschwitz II had begun in the spot indicated by *Reichsführer SS* Himmler on March 1, 1941, that means on the site of the uprooted village Brzezinka, situated at a distance of $2^1/_2$ kilometres from KL Auschwitz I. Having arrived at KL Auschwitz, *SS-Gruppenführer* Dr Ing. Heinz Kammler, Chief of the SS Economic Administration Head Office, recommended to begin the construction of a camp for 200,000 p.o.w.'s, instead of a camp for 100,000 p.o.w.'s as had been planned in March. Soviet prisoners of war and camp inmates were driven to build that camp.

---

[8]) Closing of the camp. Prisoners were not allowed to walk about the camp at that time.

1941

11.11. The first execution by means of small-calibre weapons, with shots in the back of the neck, took place under the so-called "black wall of death" in the yard of Block No. 11. 151 prisoners, Poles, were executed.

16.11. The first Holy Mass was secretly said on Sunday. The Mass was said on the first floor of Block No. 4 in the corner of the room, a narrow and dark aisle between three-tiered bunks.

November. A special *Gestapo* commission from Katowice with Dr Rudolf Mildner at its head began to make a selection among the Soviet prisoners of war.

November. Due to the high death rate among the Soviet prisoners of war and to the low capacity of the ovens in crematorium I, corpses were buried in mass common graves at Birkenau (Brzezinka).

29.12. Arrival of the last transport in the year 1941. The newly arrived prisoners got camp numbers from 25093 to 25149 [9]).

1942.

19.1. The strength of *KL* Auschwitz, as of evening roll-call, amounted to 10,142 prisoners and 1,490 Soviet prisoners of war.

January. For the first time mass killing with gas Cyclon B was begun, the victims being Jews from Upper Silesia. The gassing took place in a cottage, the so-called bunker No. 1, at Birkenau, specially adapted for the purpose. The corpses were buried in common graves in the adjoining meadow.

1.3. On Sunday the camp of the Soviet prisoners of war, within the base camp Auschwitz I, had been liquidated. 945 prisoners of war, who were still alive, and many camp inmates were transferred to the camp Auschwitz II, still under construction, at Birkenau. Both camps in Auschwitz and Birkenau formed one administrative unit.

13.3. 1,200 convalescents and sick persons, not expected to recover soon and get back to work, were taken from the camp hospital in *KL* Auschwitz to Birkenau, where they were located in the so-called "isolation station" in sector BIb. The sick were thrown out into the square in front of the block where they were killed by the SS men with bludgeons. The bodies of the murdered persons were taken back to *KL* Auschwitz.

19.3. 144 women were brought to *KL* Auschwitz and shot in the yard of Block No. 11.

26.3. The first transport of women prisoners from *KL* Ravensbrück arrived at *KL* Auschwitz. The 999 women were given successive camp numbers from 1 to 999, they were placed in one part of the camp, divided by

---

[9]) 17,270 prisoners were committed to *KL* Auschwitz in the course of 1941.

a wall from the rest of the camp.[10]) This section of the camp consisted
of blocks Nos. from 1 to 10.
Two hours later the first transport of 999 Jewish women from Slovakia was brought to the camp. Their camp numbers were from
1000 to 1998. It was the first transport sent to *KL* Auschwitz through
the *Reichssicherheitshauptamt*, so-called *RSHA* (Reich Security
Head Office) IVB4 (Jewish Section)[11]) The Jewish women were given
Soviet uniforms, left after the Soviet prisoners of war had been killed
off. The *RSHA* transports from Slovakia kept arriving till October,
1944.

30.3. First transport from France (Paris) of 1,112 Jews (*RSHA* transport)
arrived. The Jewish prisoners were given camp numbers from 27533
to 28644.

27.4. First transport of Polish women, politica prisoners, was brought
from the Montelupi prison in Cracow and from the prison in Tarnów.
The 127 women got camp numbers from 6784 to 6910.

4.5. First selection of prisoners who were to be gassed took place at
Birkenau. The selection was conducted by an *SS*-man, hospital
orderly. The selected persons were taken by trucks to the bunker
where the gassing took place. The barrack, called the "isolation station", was surrounded by a wall and prisoners doomed to death by
gassing were brought there from all over the camp. The barrack was
constantly overcrowded. Time and again the trucks would come and
then about 90% of the inmates were taken away. 1,200 prisoners
were usually accommodated in the barrack.

9.5. The prisoners' penal company was transferred from Block No. 11
in *KL* Auschwitz to Birkenau where it was located in barrack 1 in
sector BIb.

27.5. 168 prisoners from the so-called "group of artists" were executed
in the yard of Block No. 11 under the wall of death. They had been
brought from Cracow on April 24 and 25, as hostages after an attempt
on the life of an *SS* officer of high rank in Cracow.

30.5. Prof. Dr. C. Clauberg in his letter to the *Reichsführer SS* Himmler
offered to experiment in sterilizing the women prisoners of *KL* Auschwitz and asked to be given necessary apparatus for the purpose.

10.6. Approximately 50 prisoners of the penal company tried to run away
while at work. During the chase 13 prisoners had been killed, while
9 managed to escape. The next day after the morning roll-call in the
penal company about 320 prisoners were left in the camp and over
a hundred of them went to work in the *Königsgraben*. About 10 a.m.
Schutzhaftlagerführer Aumeier had arrived with several *SS*-men
and demanded that the 320 prisoners disclose the names of the orga-

---

[10]) The women's camp had been located there till August 15, 1942, when it was transferred to Birkenau.
[11]) *SS-Obersturmbannführer* Adolf Eichmann stood at the head of the Jewish Section.

1942

nizers of the revolt. Since there was no reply, he called 20 prisoners from the ranks and he himself shot 17 from among them, while *SS-Hauptscharführer* Hössler shot the 3 remaining ones. In the afternoon over ten prisoners of the penal company were brought from the camp hospital, their clothes and shoes were removed and their hands were bound in the back with barbed wire. In the evening the entire column of circa 320 prisoners was taken to bunker 1 at Birkenau and was killed there with gas. All together 30 prisoners of the penal company were shot and 320 were gassed on that day.

20.6. 4 prisoners escaped from *KL* Auschwitz: Kazimierz Piechowicz, No. 918, Józef Lempart, No. 3199, Stanisław Gustaw Jaster, No. 6438 and Eugeniusz Bandera, No. 8502. The escapees were dressed in *SS* uniforms, had weapons taken from storehouses and left by a stolen *SS* car.

30.6. Because of the great number of *RSHA* Jewish transports, doomed to extermination, bunker 2 was set in action. It was another cottage in a wood clearing, west to the subsequently built crematorium III and it was suitably adapted for the purpose.

1.7. The Central Building Office of the *SS* and Police Auschwitz approached the firms: *Hütte Hoch und Tiefbau, A.G.* and *Schlesische Industriebau Lenz & Co.A.G.* in Katowice, who had already constructed buildings in *KL* Auschwitz before, with the proposal to make offers for the construction of new crematoria in the camp. The firms were to undertake the building while the installations of the gas chambers and the ovens in the crematoria were to be forwarded by the firm *Topf and Sons* from Erfurt, who were also to install them on the spot.

7.7. The *Reichsführer SS* conferred with *SS-Brigadeführer* Prof. Dr Gebhardt, *SS-Brigadeführer* Glücks and *SS-Brigadeführer* Prof. Dr Clauberg to put *KL* Auschwitz at his disposal for conducting experiments in the sterilizing of people and animals. The *Reichsführer SS* also expressed his wish to be informed as to the results of the experiments with a view to applying them for the sterilization of Jewish women.

8.7. *RSHA* transports from Paris brought 1,170 "Aryan" prisoners with camp numbers from 45157 to 46326. They were French communists and people of various nationalities deported to *KL* Auschwitz in the operation under the code word "Night and Fog" (*"Nacht und Nebel"*).

10.7. The *Reich* Security Head Office notified the *Gestapo* that a special section for women prisoners had been established in *KL* Auschwitz under the name: *Konzentrationslager* Auschwitz-*Frauenabteilung* — Auschwitz-Oświęcim, Ost Oberschlesien (Concentration Camp Auschwitz — Women's Section — Auschwitz-Oświęcim, Eastern Upper Silesia).

15.7. The firm *Lenz* declined to construct a crematorium in Birkenau because of shortage of man-power. Therefore the Central Building Office of the *SS* and Police in Auschwitz accepted the offer of the

	firm *Hütte* (tendered on July 13, with a construction estimate for 133,756,65 *RM*) and recommended the firm to start building at once.
circa 15.7.	A sub-camp at Goleszów was established in the area of the cement works, then called *"Golleschau Portland-Zement Aktiengesellschaft Oberschlesien"*. The cement works belonged to the numerous *SS* enterprises and profited by the slave labour of the prisoners from the concentration camp. The prisoners worked in the cement works and in the 4 quarries which belonged to it.
17.7.	The first *RSHA* transport from Holland brought 2,000 Jews from the camps of Westerbork and Amersfoort. Among them were 1,303 men and boys and 697 women and girls. After a selection on the ramp 1,251 men were committed to the camp and were given camp numbers from 47088 to 47687 and from 47843 to 48493. 300 women entered the camp with numbers from 8801 to 8999 and from 9027 to 9127. The remaining 449 persons, old people, children, mothers with children and sick persons, were killed in the gas chamber. *RSHA* transports from Holland were arriving till September, 1944.
17.7.	*Reichsführer SS* Himmler inspected *KL* Auschwitz again, his visit lasting two days. In his suite were: *Gauleiter Bracht*, *SS*-Gruppenführer Schmausser and *SS-Gruppenführer* Kammler. On the first day of his inspection Himmler and his suite were taken round the entire camp zone, he saw the camp farms, the draining work, the construction of a dyke, laboratories and plant cultures at Rajsko, the cattle breeding farms and tree nurseries, After inspecting Birkenau he watched the process of extermination of a Jewish transport from Holland which had arrived that day. He was present at the unloading of the transport, at the selection of people fit for work, at the gassing in bunker 2 and at the emptying of the bunker, filled with corpses. He then visited the *Buna-Werke*. The next day, after having finished his tour of inspection, he ordered Höss to step up the tempo of building Birkenau, to liquidate Jews unfit for work, to develop the armaments industry. Himmler awarded R. Höss the rank of *Obersturmbannführer* in recognition of his achievements.
23.7.	Commandant R. Höss ordered the camp to be strictly out of bounds for *SS*-men in connection with the typhus epidemic, rampant in the camp [12])
31.7.	After the morning roll-call prisoners called out from the ranks the day before were shot in the yard of Block No. 11 under the wall of death, with the exception of Prof. Marian Gieszczykiewicz, who was kept by his friends in the camp hospital under the pretext of illness. At 9 a.m. *Rapportführer* Palitzsch gave the order to bring Professor M. Gieszczykiewicz regardless of the state of his health. Profesor Gieszczykiewicz, though well in fact, was put undressed on a stretcher,

[12]) On July 25, the daily register shows 203 cases of deaths among the prisoners.

1942

was covered with a blanket and brought to the yard of Block No. 11 by two prisoners, orderlies from the hospital. Palitzsch uncovered the professor, verified his camp number and shot him twice in the head.

31.7. Janusz Skrzetuski-Pogonowski, prisoner with camp number 253, employed in the surveyors' squad which worked outside the camp area, received and brought to the camp an illegal consignment of 1,000 ampoules of various medical remedies, sent for the prisoners' camp hospital by the secret organization "Aid for Prisoners of Concentration Camps".

1.8. Chief of the Office B Group in the *SS* Economic Administration Head Office consented to issue to the firing squads on days of executions supplementary food rations, i.e. 100 grammes of meat, 1/5 of a litre of vodka and 5 cigarettes per person.

5.8. The first *RSHA* transport from Belgium, from the camp in Malines, arrived with 1,000 Jews. After the selection 426 men were committed to the camp as prisoners with camp numbers from 56433 to 56858, and 318 women with camp numbers from 14784 to 15101. The remaining 256 persons were killed in the gas chamber. *RSHA* transports from Belgium were arriving till August, 1944.

15.8. A sub-camp at Jawiszowice was established. The prisoners from *KL* Auschwitz, transferred to the sub-camp, were working in the pit coal mines at Brzeszcze and Jawiszowice, taken over during the war by the *Hermann Göring* Concern. This was the first case in the history of concentration camps of employing prisoners underground.

16.8. The women's section in the base camp Auschwitz I was liquidated and the women were transferred to Birkenau, sector BIa.

18.8. The first *RSHA* transport of Jews from Yugoslavia came to Auschwitz. After selection 87 men were committed to the camp as prisoners with camp numbers from 59604 to 59690. The rest were killed in the gas chamber.

19.8. The strength of the men's camp amounted to 22,925 prisoners, together with 163 Soviet prisoners of war.

28.8. 948 Jews were brought from the camp in Drancy by an *RSHA* transport. Children and mothers with children were in the majority. After the selection 27 men were committed to the camp with camp numbers from 62093 to 62119, and 36 women with camp numbers from 18609 to 18644. The remaining 885 persons were killed in the gas chamber. *RSHA* transports from France kept arriving till August, 1944.

29.8. Under the pretext of quelling the typhus epidemic the camp authorities decided to destroy typhus carriers, i.e. lice together with the sick and the convalescents. From the prisoners' camp hospital 746 patients and convalescents were selected, loaded upon trucks and taken to Birkenau where they were killed with gas.

1942

16.9. Commandant R. Höss, together with *SS-Untersturmführer* Hössler, *SS-Untersturmführer* Dejaco and in the presence of *SS-Standartenführer* Blobel from Eichmann's office, visited and inspected the installations for burning corpses in the extermination centre for Jews in Chełmno on the Ner. The purpose of the visit was to find ways to empty all common graves at Birkenau (where the decomposing bodies were liable to poison the waters and cause epidemics), to burn the corpses and obliterate all traces of crimes.

After his return to *KL* Auschwitz Höss ordered to start burning the corpses in the open. At first they were burnt on piles of wood, upon which approximately 2,000 bodies were placed, then corpses previously buried were burnt in pits. To make them burn more quickly the corpses were sprayed with crude oil, later methanol was used. The corpses were burnt continuously, day and night.

25.9. *SS-Obergruppenführer*, Prof. Dr Ernst Robert von Grawitz, Chief Surgeon of the *SS*, Chief of the *SS* Sanitary Head Office and chairman of the German Red Cross, visited *KL* Auschwitz. He inspected the overcrowded hospitals for prisoners, the mortuaries, the makeshift installations for disinfecting water at Birkenau, he observed the extermination process of the Jews and the burning of corpses in pits.

26.9. Deputy Chief of the *SS* Economic Administration Head Office, *SS-Brigadeführer* August Frank issued an order to the commandants of *KL* Auschwitz and *KL* Lublin (Majdanek) to proceed with the cashing of effects of the exterminated Jews. In his order he recommended to forward all cash in German banknotes to the Reich Bank, foreign currency, gold and other precious metals, also jewellery, were to be sent to the *SS* Economic Administration Head Office, likewise watches, alarm-clocks and fountain-pens, which after being repaired, would be consigned to the troops at the fronts. Clothes, underwear, shoes, materials, various articles of personal use and household goods were to be sent, for a consideration, to the *Volksdeutsche Mittelstelle*.

30.9. The Head of the Employment Section in *KL* Auschwitz, *SS-Obersturmführer* Heinrich Schwarz, got permission from the *SS* Economic Administration Head Office to go by car to Friedland near Wrocław in order to inspect the processing of human hair, done by the firm of Held.

5.10. In order to free the concentration camps in the Reich from Jewish prisoners, the *Reichsführer SS* Himmler ordered to transfer them to *KL* Auschwitz and *KL* Majdanek.

5.10. In the evening, a German woman prisoner and former prostitute, with the function of capo in the women's penal company at Budy, consisting mainly of French Jewesses, called a guard for help, suspecting the Jewish women of planning to start a mutiny and to escape in a body. The *SS*-men, together with the German capos, attacked the Jewesses and slaughtered them, shooting some and killing others with rifle-butts, bludgeons and poles. One of the women capos murdered the prisoners with an axe. During that action about 90 women prisoners, French Jewesses, were murdered. The next day, after the arrival at Budy of commandant R. Höss and later, of the functionaries of the Political Section, all wounded women were killed by phenol injected into the heart, thereby remowing witnesses of the murders committed. 6 German women prisoners, capos, among them Elfriede Schmidt, who had been murdering the women prisoners with an axe, were committed to a bunker in Block No. 11, pending the investigations held by the Political Section. The place of the crimes and the corpses had been photographed. The prints were put at the commandant's disposal and the plates were destroyed in his presence.

28.10. The first *RSHA* transport from the ghetto-camp in Theresienstadt in Czechoslovakia brought 1,866 Jews. After selection 215 men were committed to the camp with camp numbers from 71060 to 71274, and 32 women with camp numbers from 23275 to 23306. The remaining 1,619 persons were killed in gas chambers. *RSHA* transports from Czechoslovakia were arriving till October 1944.

circa 30.10. At Monowitz, in the area of the *Buna-Werke*, an Auschwitz sub-camp was established. It was built by *IG-Farbenindustrie* for prisoners brought from *KL* Auschwitz to work there.

30.11. The action of burning corpses extracted from the mass graves at Birkenau came to an end. According to commandant R. Höss, 107,00 corpses had been buried in the mass graves.

1.12. The first *RSHA* transport of Jews was brought from Bergen in Norway, in the strength of 532 persons. 186 men were committed to the camp as prisoners with camp numbers from 79064 to 79249. The remaining 346 persons were killed in gas chambers.

3.12. About 300 prisoners, employed in the special squad burning corpses, were brought from Birkenau to the Auschwitz base camp. They were led into the gas chamber of crematorium I and gassed there. Thus the witnesses of the burning of circa 107,000 corpses were liquidated.

10.12. The first *RSHA* transport of Jews from Germany arrived on that day. After selection 137 men were committed to the camp with camp numbers from 81263 to 81399. The rest was killed in gas chambers. *RSHA* transports from Germany were arriving till September, 1944.

13.12. 314 men and 318 women, Poles deported from the Zamość district, were brought and committed as prisoners to *KL* Auschwitz.

16.12. The Chief of Office IV of *RSHA* and deputy of the Chief of the Security Police and Security Service, *SS-Gruppenführer* Heinrich Müller, prepared a plan of deporting to *KL* Auschwitz 45,000 Jews so as to provide man-power for the munitions factories of that region.

---

[13]) Children of both sexes were also in this transport and were committed to the camp as prisoners, too.

1942

The plan foresaw the deporting of 30,000 Jews from the Białystok district, 10,000 from the Theresienstadt ghetto, 3,000 from Holland and 2,000 from Berlin. From among the Jews brought to Auschwitz only 10 to 15 thousand able-bodied workers were to be selected and allowed to live. Due to a period of military leaves and transportation difficulties connected with it, it was decided to start with the deportations on January 11, 1943, and to finish them on January 31, 1943.

28.12. Prof Dr Carl Clauberg began his experiments in sterilizing, using women prisoners from the women's hospital at Birkenau as experimental material.

30.12. A collective transport of women prisoners was brought to the camp. They got camp numbers from 27864 to 27905. This was the last transport of women committed to the camp in 1942.[14])

30.12. 39 men prisoners were brought from Katowice and given camp numbers from 85158 to 85196. This was the last transport of men committed to the camp in 1942.[15])

1943.

25.1. A selection was made in the bunkers of Block No. 11, during which 51 prisoners, suspected of having taken part in illegal activities against the *SS* in the camp and of preparing an escape, were singled out. Among them were officers of higher ranks, such as Col. Edward Gött-Getyński, Col. Jan Karcz, Col. Karol Kumaniecki, also members of the intelligentsia from the Auschwitz base camp and the Monowitz sub-camp (*Buna-Werke*). They were executed by shooting in the yard of Block No. 11 under the wall of death that same day.

27.1. 230 women, political prisoners, were brought from Romainville (France). They got camp numbers from 31625 to 31854. Among them were: Danielle Casanova, Marie Politzer, Helene Soloman-Langevin, Ivonne Blech, Raymonde Salez, scientists, political, social and cultural leaders, antifascists.

29.1. Ing. Prüfer of the firm *Topf and Sons* from Erfurt inspected the crematoria II, III, IV and V, under construction at Birkenau, and stated that finishing the construction of crematorium V depended on weather conditions, but the rest of them would be finished and ready to work in the time between February 15, and April 17.

29.1. The *Reich* Security Head Office ordered to arrest all Gypsies living in the *Reich* and in the occupied countries and to liquidate them in concentration camps.

7.2. Scientists from the Weigl Institute in Lwów were brought to the camp together with their families. Among them were: Dr Ludwik Fleck, Dr Jakub Seeman, Dr Umschweif and Dr Abramowicz. Together with their wives and children they were located in the base camp, in the

---

[14]) In the period since the establishment of *KL* Auschwitz for women, i.e. since March 26, 1942 till December 31, 1942, 27,905 women were committed to the camp.
[15]) 60,047 men prisoners were committed to *KL* Auschwitz in the course of 1942.

1943

prisoners' camp hospital, and were employed in the SS Institute of Hygiene, which was at first situated in Block No. 10 and then at Rajsko near Oświęcim. On February 11 they were given camp numbers and treated as prisoners since then.

10.2. Chief of the Office DII (employment of prisoners) in the SS Economic Administration Head Office, *SS-Obersturmbannführer* Gerhard Maurer, arrived at the camp. During a conference with the management of the *Buna-Werke* he promised to increase the number of inmates of the Monowitz sub-camp up to 4,000—4,500. As there were too few guards, he recommended to employ the prisoners only within the factory itself.

23.2. 39 prisoners, boys aged from 13 to 17, were brought to the Auschwitz base camp from the camp at Birkenau, selected there to undergo training as hospital orderlies. In the evening they were killed with phenol injections into the heart. The injections were administered by the second hospital orderly, *SS-Unterscharführer* Scherpe. The boys had come to the camp with the transports of Poles deported from the Zamość district.

26.2. The first transport of Gypsies from Germany came to the camp. There were several families with children in it. They were located at Birkenau in the still unfinished sector BIIe, later going by the name of "camp for Gypsy families". The Gypsies got camp numbers different from those of other prisoners, beginning with "Z-1" for men, and "Z-1" for women.

1.3. 80 prisoners, boys of Polish and Jewish nationality, aged from 13 to 17, were brought to the Auschwitz base camp from the camp at Birkenau. In the evening they were killed with phenol injections into the heart, administered by the second hospital orderly, *SS-Unterscharführer* Scherpe.

8.3. At a conference in Essen, the participants of which were: Alfred von Bohlen, Prof. Houdremont, Prof. Dr E. Müller, Dr Löser, Dr Korschan and others, it was resolved to speed up the tranfer of the workshops of *Friedrich Krupp, A.G.*, producing aeroplane parts and fuses,[16]) to *KL* Auschwitz.

13.3. The first transport from Mińsk (Soviet Union) arrived with 187 prisoners who got camp numbers from 107585 to 107771. Transports from Mińsk were arriving till June, 1944.

15.3. The Resistance Movement Camp Organization sent a report to Cracow in which it was stated that the official number of deaths of people gassed or killed with phenol injections amounted to 20,000 registered prisoners in the period from January 15 to March 15, 1943.

---

[16]) Negotiations connected with the building of workshops for the *Krupp concern* in *KL* Auschwitz were going on since July, 1942, between the representatives of the *Krupp* concern and the *SS* Economic Administration Head Office.

20.3.	The first *RSHA* transport from Salonika (Greece [17]) arrived with circa 2,800 Jews. After selection 417 men with camp numbers from 109371 to 109787, and 192 women with camp numbers from 38721 to 38912, were committed to the camp. The rest were killed in gas chambers. *RSHA* transports from Greece were arriving till August, 1944.
22.3.	The Building Office of the *SS* and Police *KL* Auschwitz finished the construction of crematorium IV, together with gas chambers, and handed it over for use to the commandant of *KL* Auschwitz.
31.3	The Building Office of the *SS* and Police *KL* Auschwitz finished the construction of crematorium II with one large gas chamber at Birkenau and handed it over for use to the commandant of *KL* Auschwitz.
circa 1.4.	Commandant R. Höss, in compliance with the request of the *SS* Economic Administration Head Office, put Block No. 10 at the disposal of *SS-Brigadeführer* Prof. Dr Clauberg. The block was to be an experimental station in which Clauberg intended to conduct experiments in sterilizing women prisoners. At the same time about 20 women prisoners of various nationalities were transferred to the experimental block in the character of doctors, nurses, etc.
4.4.	The Building Office of the *SS* and Police *KL* Auschwitz finished the construction of crematorium V with gas chambers, and handed it over for use to the commandant of *KL* Auschwitz.
30.4.	Commandant R. Höss informed the *SS* garrison that the *Führer* conferred upon him the Cross of War Merit of the First Class with Swords. The same decoration was also awarded to *SS-Hauptscharführer* Otto Moll, chief manager of the gas chambers and crematoria.
3.5. 10.5.	The strength in the experimental Block N. 10 amounted to 243 women prisoners, used for experimenting, and 22 nurses (women prisoners, too). Danielle Casanova, communist and heroine of the French Resistance Movement, died of typhus in the women's camp at Birkenau.
25.5.	The camp surgeon, *SS-Hauptsturmführer* Josef Mengele selected 507 Gypsies(men) and 528 Gypsy women, suspected to be ill with typhus and condemned them to die in gas chambers. Among then were Polish and Austrian Gypsies brought to the camp on May 12.
6.6.	Ing. Weinhold, director of the *Krupp* concern, arrived at *KL* Auschwitz from Essen with a staff of 30 technicians. The next day they began fitting machinery and technical apparatus in a rented hall in the area of *KL* Auschwitz. The members of Krupp's technical staff signed a pledge never to divulge any matters in any way whatsoever connected with *KL* Auschwitz.
7.6.	Prof. Dr Clauberg stated in his report to Himmler that his method

---

[17]) In the time from March 20 to May 16, 32, 141 Jews had come to *KL* Auschwitz in 18 registered transports. 10, 568 were committed to the camp (6,422 men and 4,146 women), 21,573 were killed in gas chambers. Further transports from Greece were arriving till August 1944. The total of deported people amounted to circa 65,000.

1943

of sterilizing women without resorting to operations was nearly ready and required only certain improving touches. Thanks to his method, he asserted, a trained surgeon working in a suitably equipped surgery would most probably be able, with the assistance of a staff of 10, to sterilize several hundreds or even perhaps several thousands of persons per day.

21.6. Professor of the Warsaw University, member of the Polish Academy of Sciences and Letters, Dr Zygmunt Łempicki, prisoner in the camp, died of typhus.

25.6. The Building Office of the *SS* and Police *KL* Auschwitz finished the construction of crematorium III with gas chamber at Birkenau and handed it over for use to the commandant of *KL* Auschwitz.

28.6. Chief of the Building office of the *SS* and Police Auschwitz reported to the *SS* Economic Administration Head Office that the crematoria could cremate the following amounts of corpses in the course of 24 hours:

I	old crematorium (base camp)	340 corpses
II	new crematorium (Birkenau)	1,440 corpses
III	new crematorium (Birkenau)	1,440 corpses
IV	new crematorium (Birkenau)	768 corpses
V	new crematorium (Birkenau)	768 corpses
	Total	4,756 corpses.

7.7. Commandant R. Höss ordered a complete closure of the camp on account of the typhus epidemic in the camp at Birkenau, to which also *SS*-men on duty there had succumbed. He ordered the *SS*-men on duty to be isolated and each day after leaving duty to be medically examined and deloused.

8.7. In accordance with the request of *SS-Obersturmbannführer* Maurer of the *SS* Economic Administration Head Office, 1,500 Jewish prisoners, men and women, were brought from *KL* Majdanek to work in the *Buna-Werke* and at Jaworzno. The camp doctors, after examining the draft found that.:

49 prisoners should be sent to the camp hospital with phlegmons, utter exhaustion and hernia,
277 prisoners were temporarily unfit for work due to exhaustion,
424 prisoners could be employed at the *Buna-Werke* after a quarantine of four weeks,
  5 women prisoners died after arrival,
  2 women prisoners had shot wounds,
 80 women prisoners were unfit for work, among them 28 aged from 15 to 17,
  2 women prisoners had had pneumothorax,
 44 women prisoners had more or less severely wounded limbs,
  5 women prisoners had abscesses on their shins,
  1 woman prisoner had inflammation of connective tissue.

The remaining 611 women were suffering of scabies.

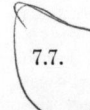

13.7.	All Jewish prisoners (excepting the Jews from Poland and Greece) were told to write letters to their families, asking them for food parcels. They were ordered to state in the letters that they were well and were to give as their address *Arbeitslager Birkenau, Postamt Neu Berun* (Labour Camp Birkenau, Post Office New Berun).
16.7.	During inspection of the camps of the English prisoners of war at Libiąż near *"Janinagrube"* and the forced labour camp for Jews at Ławki near Wesoła, connected with *"Fürstengrube"*, it was decided to establish Auschwitz sub-camps there. The inspection was conducted by commandant R. Höss and the representatives of *IG-Farbenindustrie*.
19.7.	A joint gallows was erected in the base camp in front of the camp kitchen and after the evening roll-call 12 prisoners from the surveyors' squad, previously committed to bunkers in Block No. 11, were hanged. The executed men were suspected of illegal activity against the camp authorities, of contacts with the civilian population and of helping the escapees from the camp.
3.8.	The camp Employment Section presented the *Krupp* concern at Auschwitz with a bill No. 2/43 for the sum of 21,306 *RM*, this being the equivalent for the wages of prisoners who had worked there from July 1 to July 31.
21.8.	A selection was made in the women's camp at Birkenau. 498 Jewish women prisoners were selected and killed that same day in the gas chamber. There were 441 Greek Jewesses among the gassed. The camp leader, head supervisor Maria Mandel had signed the list of names of the selected persons.
29.8.	An *SS* surgeon made a selection among the prisoners in the men's camp at Birkenau. 4,462 Jewish prisoners were selected and killed that night in the gas chambers.
2.9.	A sitting of the Summary Court was held in Block Nr 11 in KL Auschwitz, during which 63 men and 30 women, brought from Silesia and waiting trial, were sentenced to death.
4.9.	An Auschwitz sub-camp, going by the name of *"Janinagrube"*, was established at Libiąż, near the coal mine. Circa 300 prisoners, mainly Jews, to be employed in the coal mine, were sent to the sub-camp which formerly housed 150 English prisoners of war.
7.9.	The firm *Friedrich Krupp A.G.* Auschwitz was notified that the fuse factory at Zaporoże [18] owned by the firm *Union* (from Werl in Westphalen) would have to be evacuated to Oświęcim. The firm *Krupp* was offered either to take over the production of the firm *Union* or to hand over their production to the firm *Union* or possibly establish a merger.

---

[18]) A town in the Ukrainian Republic. The capital of the Republic, Kharkov was liberated by the Soviet Army on August 22,1943.

1943

8.9. 5,006 Jews from the ghetto-camp in Theresienstadt were brought by *RSHA* transport. There were 2,293 men and boys, with camp numbers from 146694 to 148986, and 2,713 women and girls with camp numbers from 58471 to 61183. The next day they were located in the recently opened camp at Birkenau, sector BIIb, later going by the name of "Family Camp Theresienstadt". They got better treatment than other prisoners. They were allowed to keep their possessions, they lived together with their families, their hair was not shorn, they could write letters to their relatives once a fortnight and could receive parcels. The children could play in a garden and got better food at first. In spite of that the death rate was high. Approximately 1,145 persons had died up to March, 1944.

9.9. A transport of the *"Einsatzkommando 9"* [19] (*E. Kdo 9*) from Witebsk (Soviet Union) brought 459 men prisoners, camp numbers from 149467 to 149925 and 753 women prisoners, camp numbers from 61417 to 62169.

15.9. The Chief Command of the Army, the Central Department for Munitions and the Minister of the Reich for Armaments and Munitions decided that the firm *Union* (evacuated from Zaporoże) would take over from the *Krupp* concern in *KL* Auschwitz the factory, machines, installations and production.

16.9. The Political Section undertook an action of quelling the Camp Resistance Movement and terrorizing the prisoners. They arrested and committed to bunkers in Block No. 11 prisoners' who were former army officers, physicians, lawyers, artists and political leaders, and who were suspected of having established a secret military organization in the camp.

The arrests in the camp continued till September 29. The majority of the arrested were shot on October 11.

18.9. A woman prisoner from a Katowice transport gave birth to a girl in the women's camp at Birkenau. The girl was not killed, but officially entered into the camp register with the camp number 62695, with which the infant was tattooed. Children born in the women's camp since its establishment till June 1943 were killed by the *SS* sanitary orderlies with phenol injections into the heart. In the beginnings of the camp new-born children were drowned in a bucket filled with water.

1.10. The firm *Union* took over from the management of *KL* Auschwitz a production workshop (rented till then by the *Krupp* concern) together with machines and installations from *Friedrich Krupp, A.G.* They started with the assembly of their own machinery and with the production of fuses.

---

[19]) Small units evolved from the so-called *"Einsatzgruppe"*, i.e. special detachment of the *SS*, security police and military police; their tasks were to liquidate communists, partisans, Jews and Gypsies near the front line areas.

1.10.	An Auschwitz sub-camp was established in Brno (Czechoslovakia) and 250 prisoners were transferred there. The prisoners were employed building the Academy of Technology of the SS and Police.
4.10.	11 boys, born in the women's camp at Birkenau in the time from June 27 to October 4, were registered in the men's camp. Their camp numbers were from 155909 to 155919. They remained in the women's camp.
7.10.	An *RSHA* transport brought 1,200 Jewish children from the ghetto camp in Theresienstadt. They originally came from the ghetto in Białystok (Poland) from where they had been deported during the uprising in the ghetto, that is in the time from August 16 to August 23, 1943. 53 guardians, doctors, men and women, arrived with them. All were killed that same day in gas chambers.
8.10.	On the eve of the Jewish religious holiday of *Yom Kipur* the *SS* doctors made a selection in the women's camp at Birkenau and in the men's camps. They selected several thousands of Jewish prisoners, men and women, who were driven to gas chambers on that day and gassed.
10.10.	327 prisoners from the men's quarantine camp at Birkenau were killed in the gas chamber. Among them were 270 Russian prisoners, brought from Witebsk on that day.
23.10.	The first *RSHA* transport with Jews from Rome arrived. After selection 149 men were committed to the camp, with camp numbers from 158491 to 158639, and 47 women, with camp numbers from 66172 to 66218. The rest was killed in gas chambers. The *RSHA* transports from Italy were arriving till August 1944.
23.10.	1,700 Jews were brought by an *RSHA* transport from *KL* Bergen-Belsen. They had been informed that the transport would go to Switzerland. When they arrived at the ramp in Birkenau and saw they had been deceived, one woman wrested the revolver from the hands of an *SS*-man and wounded *SS-Oberscharführer* Schillinger and *SS-Unterscharführer* Emmerich. Other women attacked the *SS*-men with their bare hands. The *SS-men* demanded assistance and having got it, quelled the riot with guns and grenades. Those Jews who were not killed on the spot were gassed in the gas chamber of crematorium III. *SS-Oberscharführer* Schillinger died on his way to the hospital.
1.11.	The Camp Employment Section presented bills for the period from October 1 to 31, to the firm *Union* for the sum of 35,781 *RM*, to the *IG-Farbenindustrie* for the sum of 488, 949 *RM*.
5.11.	The first *RSHA* transport from Riga (the Latvian Republic) arrived with Jews. After selection 120 men were committed to the camp as prisoners with camp numbers from 160702 to 160821, and 30 women, with camp numbers from 66659 to 66688. The rest was killed in gas chambers.

1943

~~11.11.~~
19.11. SS-*Obersturmbannführer* Artur Liebehenschel took over the commandant's office of KL Auschwitz from R. Höss, commandant to date.[12]
A selection was made in the women's camp at Birkenau in result of which 394 Jewesses were killed in the gas chamber.
22.11. A. Liebehenschel, in accordance with the recommendation of the SS Economic Administration Head Office, divided KL Auschwitz into three independent concentration camps:
1) KL Auschwitz I — base camp
   commandant: SS-*Obersturmbannführer* Liebehenschel
2) KL Auschwitz II — Birkenau
   commandant: SS-*Sturmbannführer* Hartjenstein
   1 camp leader of the men's camp: SS-*Untersturmführer* Schwarzhuber
   1 camp leader of the women's camp: SS-*Untersturmführer* Hössler
3) KL Auschwitz III — outside camp
   commandant: SS-*Hauptsturmführer* Schwartz.
28.11. From Viljandi (Estonia) 334 Soviet prisoners of war were brought, all of them highly disabled veterans. They were all killed in the gas chamber on December 10.
2.12. The first *RSHA* transport from Vienna (Austria) brought Jews of whom, after selection, 13 men were committed to the camp with camp numbers from 165331 to 165343, and 11 women with camp numbers from 69471 to 69481. The remaining persons were killed in gas chambers. *RSHA* transports from Austria kept coming till September, 1944.
10.12. A selection was made in the women's camp at Birkenau during which the SS camp doctor, assisted by SS-men, selected circa 2,000 Jewish women, ill with typhus or supposed to be ill with typhus. They were killed that day in gas chambers.
14.12. The building of the property storehouse was finished at Birkenau. The confiscated property of the prisoners was stored in it. It was situated near crematoria IV and V, was called „*Canada*" by the prisoners and consisted of 30 barracks, in which the effects, looted from the Jews brought to KL Auschwitz to be exterminated, were collected, sorted and temporarily stored. Prisoners employed in the storehouses were accommodated in 5 further barracks, where the administration of that section was also housed.
15.12. A selection was made in the men's quarantine camp at Birkenau and 338 selected prisoners were killed with gas.
16.12. The Chief Surgeon of the surgical ward of the prisoners' camp hospital KL Auschwitz made a report covering the period from September

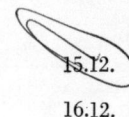

---

[20]) A. Liebehenschel, member of the SS, No. 39,254, was previously Chief of the Office DI in the Economic Administration Head Office (political matters) and was followed there by R. Höss, who took over this post on December 1,1943.

	16 to December 15, 1943, in which he stated that 106 operations involving the castration of prisoners were undertaken during that time, (amputations of testicles, operations of genitals, removal of ovaries and oviducts).
29.12.	3 Gypsies, men, and 5 Gypsies, women, were brought from Germany. The men got camp numbers from Z-9006 to Z-9008, the women from Z-9724 to Z-9728. This was the last transport of Gypsies to be committed to the camp in 1943.[21]
29.12.	5 women prisoners were brought from Katowice. They got camp numbers from 73978 to 73982. This was the last transport of women to be committed to.the camp in 1943.[22]
30.12.	4 men prisoners were brought from Katowice and they got camp numbers from 171349 to 171352. This was the last transport of men to be committed to the camp in 1943.[23]
December.	8,931 women prisoners with camp numbers perished in the women's camp at Birkenau in the course of December. 4,247 out of this total were killed with gas.

1944.

15.1.	An SS doctor selected 363 men prisoners in the men's quarantine camp at Birkenau. They were killed with gas.
20.1.	The total strength of the camp amounted to 80,839 prisoners, men and women. *KL* Auschwitz I 18,437 prisoners *KL* Auschwitz II 22,061 men prisoners 27,053 women prisoners *KL* Auschwitz III 13,288 prisoners. At the Monowitz sub-camp there were 6,571 prisoners, included in the above total.
2.2.	The first *RSHA* transport of Jews from Trieste to arrive at the camp. After selection 4 men with camp numbers from 173154 to 173157 and 1 woman with camp number 75045 were committed to the camp. The *RSHA* transports from Triéste kept arriving until September 1944.
3.2.	247 Jewish prisoners, brought from the Auschwitz sub-camp *Neu Dachs* at Jaworzno, were killed in the gas chamber.
12.2.	60 Poles were brought from Radom and immediately shot under the wall of death in the yard of Block No. 11.
21.2.	Jews from the Jewish labour camp (Judenarbeitslager) at Płaszów (near Cracow) were brought to the camp and after selection 260 men were registered in the camp with camp numbers from 174000 to 174259. The rest were killed in gas chambers.
February.	Head of the Jewish Section IVB4 in the Reich Security Head office

---

[21]) 9,008 Gypsies, men, and 9,728 Gypsies, women, were committed to *KL* Auschwitz in the time from February 26 to December 31,1943.
[22]) 46,007 women prisoners were committed to *KL* Auschwitz in 1943.
[23]) 36,156 men prisoners were committed to *KL* Auschwitz in 1943.

9.3.	*SS-Obersturmbannführer* Adolf Eichmann visited *KL* Auschwitz. In *KL* Auschwitz II he visited the "Family Camp Theresienstadt". After a six months' quarantine in the "Family Camp Theresienstadt" at Birkenau, during which about 1,145 persons had died, 3,791 Czech Jews (brought with an *RSHA* transport from the ghetto-camp in Theresienstadt on September 8,1943) were killed in gas chambers. Circa 70 persons were left to live, among them doctors and twins, the latter to be used for medical experiments. *SS* doctor Josef Mengele conducted experiments on twins. Only those Jews, who had come with *RSHA* transports on December 16 and 20, 1943, were left in the "Family Camp Theresienstadt" at Brzezinka.
5.4.	In an *SS* Economic Administration Head Office report, addressed to the *Reichsführer SS* Himmler, it was stated that:

Auschwitz I   housed   16,000 prisoners
Auschwitz II   housed   15,000 prisoners(men)
                and   21,000 prisoners (women)
Auschwitz III   housed   15,000 prisoners
_____
                 Total   67,000 prisoners.

Out of this total 18,000 were the sick and the disabled, 15,000 prisoners were located in sub-camps, scattered all over Upper Silesia. In connection with this state of things, in spite of fences and charged wires, watch towers and an inner and outer line of bunkers, in case of danger, the precautionary measures being insufficient, the camp would be threatened by 34,000 prisoners, while the strength of the garrison amounted to 2,300 *SS*-men, with a police company, 130 men strong, as reinforcement. From this report we can gather that the camp authorities and the *SS* Economic Administration Head Office were seriously considering the possibility of a mutiny of the prisoners and of an armed uprising in *KL* Auschwitz, in spite of their extreme watchfulness and continual liquidation of prisoners suspected of taking part in conspiracies against the *SS*.

5.4.	A Jewish prisoner from the "Family Camp Theresienstadt", by name of Siegfried Lederer, escaped and got to Czechoslovakia. As member of the Czech Resistance Movement he penetrated into the ghetto in Theresienstadt and there informed the Elders of the Council of the Jewish Community about the fate of the Jews in *KL* Auschwitz.
74.	Two Jewish prisoners, Alfred Wetzler and Rudolf Vrba, escaped from Birkenau's quarantine camp and the "Family Camp Theresienstadt". They managed to get to Czechoslovakia and joined the partisans. Dr Rudolf Vrba wrote a report on *KL* Auschwitz for the papal nuncio in Slovakia which was received in Vatican by the middle of June.

---

[14]) The total of persons brought to the camp was 4,964.

1944

9.4. The first evacuation transport from *KL* Majdanek arrived with 2,000 prisoners among whom 119 were dead. The transport had been 8 days on the move, without medical care or water. It was directed to *KL* Sachsenhausen where it was not admitted because the camp was overcrowded. 86 prisoners died the day after the arrival.

circa 10.4. In order to obliterate the traces of crimes in *KL* Auschwitz crematorium I was made into an air-raid shelter and the "black wall of death" in the yard of Block No. 11 was demolished.

circa 16.4. 6 British prisoners of war who had been working in the *Buna-Werke* were shot. The reason of the shooting was: it was stated that they shirked their work. The remaining British prisoners left their work in protest.

29.4. A paper "On the action of Rentgen rays upon human reproductive glands" by *SS* doctor Horst Schumann was forwarded to the *Reichsführer SS* Himmler. The paper was based on experiments conducted by Schumann in the camp of Birkenau. Schumann asserted that the method of castration operations was much quicker, surer and cheaper than castration with Rentgen rays.

8.5. *SS- Obersturmbannführer* A. Liebehenschel was transferred to the post of commandant of *KL* Majdanek and of the labour camps in Warsaw, Radom, Budzyń and Bliżyń.
Ex-commandant of *KL* Auschwitz, *SS-Obersturmbannführer* Höss, to date Chief of Office DI in the *SS* Economic Administration Head Office, became the commandant of the *SS* garrison until further notice. He was at the same time nominated by *Reichsführer SS* Himmler plenipotentiary for the extermination of the Hungarian Jews.

11.5. *SS-Hauptsturmführer* Richard Baer [25]) took over the commandantship of *KL* Auschwitz I.

13.5. In order to camouflage the actual number of prisoners registered in *KL* Auschwitz a new series of camp numbers was introduced for Jewish prisoners, for both sexes separately. Both series began with A-1 and were intended to end with A-200,000, then the next series with the letter B was to follow.

16.5. For the first time a long closure of the barracks was imposed in the camps of Birkenau. The prisoners were not allowed to leave the barracks. Several freight trains had arrived at the three-track siding bringing the first *RSHA* transports of Jews from Hungary. The Jews were marshalled into columns and were marched straight to the gas chambers without undergoing selection. Since that day from 2 to 5 transports of Hungarian Jews were daily arriving. One single

---

[25]) R. Baer, *SS* member No. 41255. Previously to his nomination for the commandantship of *KL* Auschwitz he had been aide-de-camp of Pohl, Chief of the Economic Administration Head Office. He went into hiding after the war, pretending to have been a woodman, was arrested on December 20, 1956. Died in the Frankfort prison June 26, 1963.

1944

transport used to consist of 40—50 freight vans. There were about 100 persons in each van. The next transports underwent a selection. They kept arriving until September, 1944.
Eichmann arrived at KL Auschwitz at the time of the incoming of the first Jewish transports from Hungary. He personally checked and speeded up the extermination action.

24.5. The Resistance Movement Camp Organization, watching closely over the activities of the camp authorities, ascertained that the number of the Hungarian Jews killed with gas rose to above 100,000.
The SS-men on duty at the liquidation of the Jews stayed for 48 hours at their posts and then had a break of 8 hours.

25.5. Several hundred persons from an evening transport of the Hungarian Jews tried to escape, hiding in a wood near the crematoria and in ditches. The camp leader of the women's camp. Hössler, took charge of the chase. All escapees were shot in the floodlit area.

May. In the period between May 16 and May 31 the camp authorities had obtained 40 kilogrammes of gold and white metal from the teeth of Jews killed in the gas chambers[26]

15.6. The Resistance Movement Camp Organization stated in its report that 300,000 Hungarian Jews were brought to the camp in the time from May 16 to June 13.

15.6. The Resistance Movement Camp Organization notified its base in Cracow that the camp authorities were requested (in result of the situation at the fronts) to evacuate Aryan prisoners, chiefly Poles and Russians, from KL Auschwitz.

24.6. Mala Zimetbaum, camp number 19880 (a Jewess from Belgium) escaped from the camp at Birkenau together with a Polish prisoner, Edward Galiński, camp number 531. After two weeks they were captured and committed to bunkers in Block No. 11. In September Galiński was hanged and Mala cut the veins at her wrists under the gallows.

27.6. Two Polish men prisoners, Konstanty Jagiełło, camp number 4507 and Tomasz Sobański, camp number 13609, made their escape from the Birkenau camp. They joined the partisans in the vicinity of the camp, cooperating with the Resistance Movement Camp Organization.

2.7. The camp authorities decided to liquidate the "Family Camp Theresienstadt". Its strength amounted to over 10,000 men, women and children. To camouflage the crime, the camp doctor Dr Mengele made a selection and sent 3,080 peple, young, healthy and fit for work, to various camps in the Third Reich. Among them were men, women and youngsters.

11.7. The liquidation of the "Family Camp Theresienstadt" was begun. About 3,000 women and children were taken to gas chambers during

---

[26]) Besides Jews from Hungary, the transports also brought Jews from Belgium, France, Holland and Italy, at that time.

the day. In the night of July 11/12 the remaining 4,000 men and women were gassed

12.7. The strength of the camp amounted to:

Auschwitz I	— 14,386 prisoners (men)
Auschwitz II	— 19,711 prisoners (men)
and	— 31,406 women prisoners
Auschwitz III	— 26,705 prisoners (men)
Total	92,705 prisoners

This total does not include Hungarian Jews, men and women, who were not registered in the camp registers, being regarded as "transitory Jews", located for the time being in the so-called "transit camp" which the prisoners had called *"Mexico"*. There they waited to be gassed or to be sent to other concentration camps.

28.7. An evacuation transport from *KL* Majdanek, 1,000 men and women prisoners strong, arrived at *KL* Auschwitz with only 452 men and 156 women. The remainder was shot during the evacuation. *KL* Majdanek was liberated by the Soviet Army on July 24,1944.

2.8. The Gypsy Family Camp at Birkenau was liquidated and the remaining 2,897 men, women and children were killed in gas chambers.

In the period from February 26,1943 to July 21,1944 (date of the arrival of the last Gypsy transport at *KL* Auschwitz) 21,667 Gypsies (10,818 men and 10,849 women) were committed to the Gypsy Family Camp at Birkenau. On April 15, May 25 and August 2,1943,2,991 Gypsies (1,884 men and 1,107 women) were deported to *KL* Buchenwald, Flossenburg and Ravensbrück. It follows that over 15,000 persons had perished up to August 1, 1944.

12.8. Arrival of the first transport of civilian population, arrested in great numbers after the armed insurrection in Warsaw. There were 1,984 men and boys in this transport, who got camp numbers from 190912 to 192895, and 3,175 women and girls. Further 7,936 persons were brought with the next transports arriving on September 4,13 and 17.

15.8. From the last, not yet liquidated ghetto in Poland, in Łódź, there came the first transport of Jews, 70,000 of whom were destined to be exterminated in *KL* Auschwitz. After selection 244 men were committed to the camp as prisoners with camp numbers from B-6210 to B-6453. The rest were killed in gas chambers.

16.8. An *RSHA* transport from the isle of Rhodes brought Jews. 346 men and 254 women were, after selection, committed to the camp as prisoners. The rest, among them 1,202 men, were killed in gas chambers.

22.8. The strength of *KL* Auschwitz amounted to 105,168 prisoners, men and women, and about 30,000 Hungarian Jews, not registered in the camp, but located in the transit camp at Birkenau. The garrison of the camp amounted to 3,250 soldiers, 70% of them being *SS*-men, 30% *Wehrmacht*, that is soldiers of the Germany Army.

30.8.	The strength of the special squad, consisting of Jews employed at burning corpses in the crematoria, amounted to 874 prisoners.
4.9.	The Resistance Movement Camp Organization sent to Cracow secretly taken photos from Birkenau, illustrating the burning of corpses in the open and the spot in the wood where people undressed before going to the alleged baths, while in reality the went to be gassed.
5.9.	In an *RSHA* transport Anna Frank [27]) (author of the well-known diary) came from Westerbork together with her family.
circa 5.9.	The Resistance Movement Camp Organization forwarded information to Cracow, asking to send it on to London, disclosing the fact that the ex-commandant of *KL* Auschwitz, R. Höss had arrived at the camp in order to investigate technical possibilities of liquidating the camp at Birkenau, together with prisoners, buildings and crematoria, so as not to leave any traces.
13.9.	During an air-raid of the American Air Force bombs fell not only upon the *Buna-Werke* but also upon the camps. In Auschwitz I 2 blocks of the *SS* living quarters were demolished and 15 *SS*-men were killed while 28 were seriously injured. One building containing the clothes workshop was also demolished and 40 prisoners were killed there, while 65 were seriously injured and 13 were trapped among the ruins and died there. Two bombs fell on Auschwitz II. The one damaged the railway track and the embankment of the railway siding leading to the crematoria, the other demolished the anti-air-raid shelter situated among the tracks and killed about 30 civilian workers. In Auschwitz III — the *Buna-Werke* — the damages were slight. The number of injured persons amounted to 300.
circa 25.8.	After the action of deporting Jews from Hungary and from the ghetto in Łódź had been finished it was decided to reduce the strength of prisoners employed in the *Sonderkomando* cremating corpses in the cremation pits at Birkenau. About 200 prisoners of the *Sonderkommando* were transfered to *KL* Auschwitz and killed with gas in the chamber in which clothes used to be disinfected.
30.9.	After the liquidation of the "Family Camp Theresienstadt" at Birkenau, the first from among eleven transports from Theresienstadt arrived at *KL* Auschwitz. 2,499 persons came with it. The next ten transports kept arriving until October 30. The total of those brought to be exterminated amounted to 18,402 men, women and children. 15% of them were committed to the camps as prisoners, the rest were killed in gas chambers.
September.	A delegate of the International Red Cross arrived at *KL* Auschwitz. He conversed with the commandant of the camp in the presence of *SS* officers. As he later mentioned in his report, "they had been polite, but had little to say". He was not allowed to enter the camp,

---

[27]) Anna Frank with her sister Edith was deported from *KL* Auschwitz to *KL* Bergen-Belsen and died there of typhus.

	neither could he talk with prisoners. He was not able to verify whether the rumours about gassing the prisoners were facts.
September.	6,296 prisoners, mainly Poles and Russians were deported from *KL* Auschwitz to concentration camps in the Reich in the course of September.
1.10.	The camp commandant of *KL* Auschwitz took charge of a new camp for women established in the area adjacent to the camp. The manageress of the new women's camp was supervisor Volkenrath. The strength of the camp amounted to 3,785 women.
3.10.	17,202 Jewish women, inmates of the transit camp at Birkenau, were transferred to the women's camp Auschwitz II. The total strength of the women prisoners at Birkenau amounted to 43,462 on that day.
7.10.	On Saturday morning the Resistance Movement Camp Organization notified the leader of the battle group of the special squad that according to information received the camp authorities had decided to liquidate shortly the entire special squad. In result of the information the special squad members, employed in crematorium IV proceeded at noon to set fire to crematorium IV and to throw grenades they themselves had manufactured. This became the signal for the squads employed in crematoria II, III, and V, to raise mutiny and to begin an armed action against the *SS*-men on guard duty. The squad of crematorium II killed 2 *SS*-men and 1 German capo, and after cutting through the wire fences, escaped to Rajsko. There they were caught and killed. The squads of crematoria III and V were unable to enter into the action as the *SS*-men on guard duty there immediately got the situation in hand. The squad of crematorium IV, which had started the mutiny, escaped to a small wood in the vicinity of the crematorium and defended itself as long as the scant reserves of arms and munitions had lasted. About 750 prisoners from the special squad fell in battle, among them were the organizers of the mutiny: Zelman Gradowski, Józef Warszawski, Józef Deresiński, Ajzyk Kalniak, Lajb Langfus and Lajb Panusz. Further 200 prisoners were shot in the evening. 212 prisoners were left to live out of the 663 members of the special squad. The deputy commander of the camp spoke to them, threatening that all prisoners in the camp would be shot, should another attempt at mutiny be made. During the mutiny the prisoners had killed 3 *SS*-men and had wrecked crematorium IV.
9.10.	3 Jewish women prisoners were arrested in the women's camp Auschwitz. I. Their names were Ela Gartner, Toszka and Regina (the family names of the two latter have not been identified till now). Being employed in the „*Union-Werke*", they were accused of having stolen explosives from the magazine of the „*Union-Werke*" and of having transmitted them to the camp at Birkenau. The next day 2 other women prisoners were arrested in the women's camp Auschwitz II.

	one of them was Róża Robota, who had worked in the Prisoners' Property Store, adjacent to the area of crematorium IV and so could smuggle the explosives to the special squad.
10.10.	14 prisoners of the special squad [28]) were arrested and committed to the bunkers of Block No. 11. Among the arrested there was one of the organizers of the mutiny — Jankiel Handelsman. The remaining 198 prisoners were divided into three squads, with 66 men in each, and detailed to crematorium II, III and V. The squads continued to work in two shifts, each shift consisting of 33 prisoners.
27.10.	A group of prisoners who were organizing an escape from the camp were betrayed by the driver, *SS-Rottenführer* Johann Roth, and committed to bunkers in Block No. 11. Among them were the members of the Resistance Movement Camp Organization: Ernst Burger (Austrian), Czesław Duzel, Piotr Piąty, Zbigniew Raynoch, Bernard Świerczyna (Poles) and the liaison of the organization, *SS*-man Frank. The arrested men took poison and Zbigniew Raynoch and Czesław Duzel died in consequence. 2 Austrians, Rudolf Friemel and Ludwig Vesely, who cooperated with the organizers of the escape, were also detained in bunkers. After the arrests the *SS*-men went to Łęki (7 kilometres from the town of Oświęcim) where two former escapees (who had escaped from *KL* Auschwitz in June, 1944), Konstanty Jagiełło and Tomasz Sobański were waiting for the escaping prisoners. With them were Franciszek Dusik and Kazimierz Ptasiński from the partisan group acting in the neighbourhood of the camp. Konstanty Jagiełło was shot. Franciszek Dusik, Julian Dusik, Wanda Dusik and Kazimierz Ptasiński were arrested. Tomasz Sobański had managed to escape.
October.	In the course of October 5,065 men prisoners and 13,095 women prisoners were deported to concentration camps in the *Reich*.
October.	From notes taken by one prisoner of the special squad it transpired that 43,635 persons were killed in gas chambers in the time from October 6 to October 25.
7.11.	The commandant of the *SS* garrison *SS-Sturmbannführer* Baer issued the order that all *SS*-men and soldiers of the German Army should prove their identity on request, as it had been ascertained that members of the Polish Resistance Movement (The Country's Army) had appeared within the camps's zone of interests in *SS* or German Army uniforms. The Resistance Movement Camp Organization had notified its head quarters of the order as early as November 11.
11.11.	In Lichtewerden (Czechoslovakia) an Auschwitz sub-camp for women prisoners was established, adjoining the thread spining factory, owned by the firm *G.A. Buhl and Son*. 300 Jewish women prisoners were transferred to this sub-camp from *KL* Auschwitz.

[28]) All the arrested prisoners perished in the bunkers in result of tortures to which they were subjected during the investigations conducted by the Political Section.

25.11. Concentration camp Auschwitz I was renamed concentration camp Auschwitz, and concentration camp Auschwitz III was renamed concentration camp Monowitz. Concentration camp Auschwitz II was incorporated into the base camp, i.e. concentration camp Auschwitz.

26.11. *Reichsführer SS* Himmler gave the order to destroy the crematoria in *KL* Auschwitz. A final selection of the special squad was made and 170 prisoners [29]) were laid off. 30 prisoners were left to attend to the ovens of crematorium V.

1.12. A "wrecking squad" was formed to wreck crematorium III at Birkenau. 100 women prisoners worked in it, dismantling crematorium III.

5.12. A special wrecking squad was formed at Birkenau and its task was to clean and cover up with earth and turf the pyres and pits in which corpses were burnt during the extermination action of the Hungarian Jews.

18.12. Head of the Security Police in Katowice Thümmler, D. P. R. elaborated an organizational scheme of the Polish Resistance Organization in the Silesian District, known as the Country's Army. He also described the methods it was using in its work. He gave some data concerning its strength, the commanders of its several battle groups or their pseudonyms. He stressed the role of the Oświęcim District Command of this organization in keeping in touch with the Military Council of the Camp which had the camp matters in its care and had personal ties with the district commanders. The Security Service of the *Reich*, though having all facilities of investigation at its disposal, was unable to identify and make known the leaders of the Resistance Movement Camp Organization and of the Military Council of the Camp, in spite of arrests in the area adjoining the camp and in the camp itself, in spite of the torturing of the prisoners during inquiries and in spite of executions.

26.12. The Soviet airplanes bombed military targets in the vicinity of the camp and dropped bombs at Birkenau upon the *SS* hospital. 5 *SS*-men were killed.

27.12. *SS-Rottenführer* Johann Roth, who prevented the escape of 5 prisoners on October 27, was thanked by the Chief of the *SS* Economic Administration Head Office, Oswald Pohl and received Pohl's photograph with the latter's signature.

30.12. After the evening roll-call the following prisoners, leaders of the Resistance Movement Camp Organization in *KL* Auschwitz, were hanged: Ernst Burger, Rudolf Friemel, Ludwig Vesely, Piotr Piąty and Bernard Świerczyna. This was the last execution in the base camp. The three Austrians and two Poles loudly denounced the *SS* and fascism before they died.

---

[29]) Nothing is known about the fate of those 170 prisoners. No document, stating where and how they had died, has so far been found.

1945

6.1.   4 Jewish women were hanged in the women's camp Auschwitz for helping the prisoners of the special squad in raising mutiny on October 7, 1944, by transmitting to them explosives from the magazine of the *"Union-Werke"*. Two of them were hanged during the evening roll-call in the presence of women prisoners and those men prisoners who worked the night shift in the *"Union-Werke"*. The two remaining ones were hanged after the prisoners' squad working the day shift in the *"Union-Werke"* had returned to the camp. Their names were Ella Gartner, Róża Robota, Toszka and Regina. This was the last execution in the women's camp.

17.1.   The last evening roll-call took place. The strength of the camp was as follows:

KL Auschwitz	— 15,317 men prisoners
and	— 16,577 women prisoners
KL Monowitz	— 10,223 men prisoners
in the sub-camps	— 22,800 men prisoners
and	— 2,095 women prisoners
Total	— 67,012

17.1.   In the evening SS-men started burning camp registers and dossiers in the various offices of the camp and in the hospital blocks. The SS camp physician, Dr Mengele packed his materials collected by experimenting on twins and departed with them for Berlin. At night preparations were begun for the evacuation of the prisoners from the various camps. The Resistance Movement Camp Organization gave the following facts in its last report: "Dear Comrades, We have lived to see the evacuation. The SS in panic — drunk. We manoeuvre as well as our political possibilities permit, to make the march on foot as bearable as possible and to save the sick, allegedly staying behind, from being liquidated. Such designs had existed, perhaps they still do exist." [30]

18.1.   The evacuation of KL Auschwitz had started in the small hours. At short intervals columns of 500 women prisoners with children were leaving the camp, escorted by SS-men. Columns of men prisoners were leaving Birkenau in the afternoon. The last group left the base camp Auschwitz after midnight. The route of the evacuation march led to Pszczyna, from where the prisoners were directed by two routes to Wodzisław in Silesia.[31] The first columns of women prisoners had reached Wodzisław on January 21, while men prisoners got there on January 22. All were loaded into uncovered vans, used to

---

[30] Quoted after "Materials Concerning the Camp Resistance Movement," v. III. p. 207. Archive of Państwowe Muzeum w Oświęcimiu.

[31] On both evacuation routes the SS-men shot weak prisoners who could not continue marching on foot. In 23 mass graves, lying along these routes, 510 men and women prisoners were buried.

carry coal, and were taken to concentration camps in the *Reich*. The prisoners from *KL* Monowitz were led in their evacuation march in groups of 1,000 persons. Their evacuation route led to Gliwice which was the rallying point for other Auschwitz sub-camps, too. On January 21, the prisoners rallying in Gliwice were taken by trains to the concentration camps Buchenwald, Dachau and Sachsenhausen.

19.1. The sick, the weak and children had remained in *KL* Auschwitz. There were 4,428 women prisoners and girls and 169 boys in the women's camp at Birkenau. In the men's camp at Birkenau circa 2,000 prisoners, in the base camp circa 1,250 prisoners, at Monowitz circa 850 prisoners. In the small hours the Soviet airplanes bombed industrial targets in the town of Oświęcim. The power station was wrecked and so the prisoners had to go without light, water and food.

20.1. *SS-Sturmbannführer* Kraus received from the Head of the *SS* and Police of the Wrocław District, *SS-Obergruppenführer* Schmauser, the order to liquidate all prisoners who could not be evacuated on foot. The *SS*-men, who were plundering the camp at Birkenau, had led from the camp about 200 Jewish women prisoners and shot them outside the camp gates. On leaving the camp they blasted crematoria II and III.

23.1. In the evening the *SS*-men set fire to a pyre with the corpses of prisoners, lying beside crematorium V, then they set fire to 30 barracks-magazines with looted property, the so-called *"Canada"*. The barracks were burning for several successive days.

24.1. *SS-Sturmbannführer* Kraus arrived at the camp with an *SS* detachment. He shot 3 prisoners in the camp kitchen.

25.1. A detachment of the *SD* (Security Service) arrived at the camp. Together with the SS detachment they intended to liquidate the prisoners who were still alive. While they were forming columns of prisoners they were notified by liaison that the Soviet Army was liable to encircle them. So they left the prisoners in columns and hurriedly drove away in cars.

26.1. The *SS* detachment, detailed to obliterate traces of crimes, blasted the last, i.e. the fifth crematorium at Birkenau at 1 a.m. Fighting was already going on in the neighbourhood of Oświęcim.

27.1. The first Soviet soldier from a reconnoitering detachment appeared in the grounds of the camp hospital in *KL* Monowitz in the morning. In the afternoon Soviet soldiers entered the town of Oświęcim. There was a fight going on in the foreland near the Auschwitz base camp. 2 Soviet soldiers fell at its gates. At 3 p.m. small groups of Soviet scouts entered the camps at Birkenau and Auschwitz and were joyfully welcomed by the liberated prisoners. After clearing the adjoining terrains of mines, the 92nd Infantry Division (of the 59th Army of the Ukrainian Front) commanded by Col. M. Winogradow, entered the camps. In the grounds of the former *KL* Auschwitz there lay approximately 600 corpses of men and women prisoners, who had either died or been killed. When the Soviet Army had entered the camp, there were about 1,200 men prisoners at Auschwitz, still living, about 4,000 women prisoners and 1,800 men prisoners at Birkenau and about 650 men prisoners at Monowitz. They were ill and exhausted, so that the lives of many of them could no more be saved.

INDEX OF FAMILY NAMES.

Abramowicz, Dr 198
Ambros Otto, Dr 15, 187
Aumeier 32, 192

Baer Richard (SS) 208, 213
Bałaban Kuba 90, 91
Baraś Jan (Komski) 85
Bach-Zelewski Erich, von (SS) 2
Bailey 103
Bargieł Melita 178
Bendera Eugeniusz 83, 193
Beger Bruno, Dr 17
Bicz Bolesław 67, 71
Biegański Wł. 98, 100
Billroth 103
Binnig (SS) 112
Bischof Karl (SS) 5, 22
Blalock 103
Blech Ivonne 198
Blobel (SS) 196
Bohlen Alfred, von 199
Bończa 72
Bracht 4, 188, 194
Brand Rudolf, Dr 18
Brandt Karl, Dr 105
Brewda Alina, Dr 111, 115
Brodniewicz Bruno 186
Burger Ernst 90, 213, 214

Caesar Joachim (SS) 51
Casanova Danielle 198, 200

Chróścicki Tadeusz 85
Clauberg Carl, Prof. Dr (SS) 17, 97, 98, 108, 110, 111, 112, 113, 114, 115, 117, 192, 193, 198, 300
Claude Bernard 100
Clausen 72
Crafford 103
Cushing 103
Cyrankiewicz Józef 89
Czech Danuta 35, 185

Dawidowski Roman 30
Denda Ludwig 87
Deresiński Józef 212
Ding 110
Drechsel 176
Dusik Franciszek 94, 213
Dusik Julian 94, 213
Dusik Wanda 94, 213
Dutkiewicz Maria 179, 181, 182
Duzel Czesław 90, 213
Duzel Czesław 90, 213
Dürrfeld, Dr 15, 188
Dziama 72

Eichmann Adolf 18, 20, 192, 196, 207, 209
Eicke Theodor 58
Eisfeld (SS) 2
Emmerich 28, 41, 204

Entress *(SS)* 190
Eisebach Mendel 90

Faust 15, 188
Fejkiel Władysław, Prof. Dr 97, 109, 119
Fleck Ludwik, Dr 198
Floeter 188
Foltański 73
Fortuna Adam 87
Franco 7
Frank Anna 211
Frank August *(SS)* 196
Friemel Rudolf 90, 214
Frietzsch *(SS)* 187, 190

G. Tadeusz, Dr 65
Galiński Edward 209
Gałuszka 177
Garncarz 73
Gartner Ela 212, 215
Gawalewicz Adolf 131, 132
Gebel, Dr 112, 113, 115
Gebhardt, Prof. Dr 193
Gecel Abraham 90
Genzgen 110
Getyński Edward Gött vide Gött Getyński Edward
Gieszczykiewicz Marian 194
Gilewicz 72
Gliński Bogdan 68
Glücks Richard *(SS)* 2, 4, 62, 185, 186, 188, 193
Gött Getyński Edward 198
Gradowski Zelman 212
Gravitz Ernst Robert, Dr *(SS)* 196
Gromaszewskij J.W. 109
Grzywacz B. 110

Hagen 110
Hałoń Kazimierz (Wrona) 87, 89
Handelsman Jakiel 213
Handzlik Helena 94
Harat Andrzej 87
Hartjenstein *(SS)* 205

Hasse 174, 176
Heydrich *(SS)* 8, 187
Himmler *(SS)* 2, 4, 6, 35, 66, 111, 185, 186, 188, 189, 190, 192, 194, 196, 200, 207, 208, 214
Hirt 110
Hitler 7, 17, 56, 108
Horsley 103
Houdremont 199
Höss Rudolf *(SS)* 2, 3, 4, 10, 15, 19, 20, 21, 22, 24, 26, 29, 30, 31, 35, 36, 37, 42, 57, 58, 59, 62, 65, 66, 67, 68, 71, 73, 74, 111, 112, 113, 185, 186, 187, 188, 189, 194, 196, 197, 200, 201, 202, 205, 208, 211
Hössler *(SS)* 31, 74, 189, 192, 196, 205, 209
Hunter 104

Iwaszko Tadeusz 77, 89

Jagiełło Konstanty 87, 90, 209, 213
Jagło Helena 179
Januszewski Mieczysław 85
Januszkiewicz Maria 180
Jaster Stanisław Gustaw 83, 193

Kagan Raja 74
Kajtoch Janina 86
Kalniak Ajzyk 212
Kammler Heinz, Dr *(SS)* 5, 21, 190, 194
Karcz Jan 198
Kartamyszew A.J. 109
Keitel 8
Klein Sława 115
Kmita Ula 182
Koino 104
Komski vide Baraś Jan (Komski)
Kopczyńska Maria 176
Koprowska Wanda 161
Koprowski Stanisław 173
Korschan, Dr 199
Kostrzewski J.K. 104

Kowalczyk August 85
Kraus *(SS)* 188, 216
Kremer, dr *(SS)* 18, 31
Krzywicki Janusz 128
Kubiak Maximilian 68
Kubiczek Stefan 94
Kuczbara Bolesław 85, 86, 87
Kulig 83, 94
Kulig Wawrzyniec 94
Kulikowski 73
Kumaniecki Karol 198
Küsel Otto 85, 86
Kwaśnik Wanda 182

Langevin Helene Salomon vide Salomon Langevin Helene
Langfus Lajb 212
Lempart Józef 83, 193
Liebehenschel Artur *(SS)* 205, 208
Lis 178
Lisowski-Paolone 72
Löser, Dr 199

Łempicki Zygmunt, Dr 201

Majcisz 73
Majewski Stefan 90
Mancy, Dr 179
Mandl Maria 202
Markiel Władysław 94
Martus 114
Masłowska Maria 178
Maurer Gerhard *(SS)* 13, 14, 15, 14, 15, 31, 73, 199, 201
Mayer *(SS)* 190
Mengele Josef, Dr *(SS)* 17, 200, 207, 209, 215
Mildner Rudolf, Dr 8, 191
Moczutkowski 104
Moll Otto *(SS)* 33, 200
Mordowicz Czesław 92
Motyka Lucjan 88
Mozart 149
Mrugowsky 110
Mrzygłód Stanisław 65

Murr 188
Müller E., Prof. Dr 199
Müller Heinrich *(SS)* 197
Münch, Dr *(SS)* 16

Nitsch 104
Nowaczyk Jan 82, 83, 94
Nowak 162
Nowak Jan 125
Nowakowski Lucjan 89

Ohrt 73
Olbrycht J. Prof. Dr 110, 112

Paderewski 136
Palitsch Gerhard *(SS)* 3, 32, 186, 190, 194, 195
Panusz Lajb 212
Paolone-Lisowski vide Lisowski-Paolone
Pettenkofer 104
Pęcalski Edward 30
Piąty Piotr 213, 214
Piechowicz Kazimierz 83, 193
Pogonowski Janusz Skrzetuski vide Skrzetuski-Pogonowski Janusz
Pohl Oswald *(SS)* 14, 208, 214
Politzer Matrie 198
Posmysz Zofia 135
Prüfer 21, 22, 198
Ptasiński Kazimierz 213
Pyś Edward 90

Rajcer 73
Rajewski Ludwik 72
Rapacz 73
Rascher 110
Raynoch Zbigniew 90, 213
Richter Trude 169
Rickord Philip 109
Robota Róża 213, 215
Romberg 110
Rosenberg Walter vide Vrba Rudolf
Rosin Arnold 91
Roth Johann *(SS)* 90, 213, 214

Runge 168, 170
Rydygier 103

Sadczykow Jerzy 89
Salomon Langevin Helene 198
Salez Raymonde 198
Samuel, Dr 112, 113
Sapiecha Adam 187
Scherpe (SS) 199
Schillinger (SS) 28, 204
Schmauser (SS) 4, 188, 194, 216
Schmidt Elfriede 197
Schubert 136, 149, 153
Schumann 149, 151
Schumann, Prof. 110
Schumann Horst, Dr 189, 208
Schwarz Heinrich (SS) 196, 205
Schwarzhuber (SS) 205
Seeman Jakub, Dr 198
Sehn Jan, Dr 6, 30
Sellheim 114
Sikorski Władysław, gen. 86
Sikorski 73
Sievers Wolfram 18
Skrzetuski-Pogonowski Janusz 73, 195
Sławiński 73
Smoleń Kazimierz 1, 8, 55
Sobański Tomasz 88, 209, 213
Socha Staszek 133
Solarska Helena 178
Sommer Karl 13
Sorge Gustaw 57, 58, 59
Speer Albert 45
Stochmal 62
Stiewitz 72
Stoeckel 114
Stolarska Janina 178
Stópkowa Helena 85, 86
Szczepańska 166
Szklarz Lucja 85
Szopa Tadeusz 87
Szpiro Fiszel 64

Szumański 72
Szumowski Wł. 101, 104, 109
Szymański Rudolf 89
Świerczyna Bernard 90, 213, 214

Täger 187
Thilo, Dr (SS) 31
Thümmler 214

Umschweif, Dr 198
Uszyński Tadeusz 89

Vesely Ludwig 214
Vetter Helmuth, Dr 17
Vrba Rudolf (Rosenberg Walter) 91, 207
Vuysje, Dr 113

Wajndrach G.M. 109
Warszawski Józef 212
Weinhold 200
Wetzler Alfred 91, 207
Wiegand (SS) 2
Wiejowski Tadeusz 65, 70, 82, 186
Winogradow M. 216
Wirtek 177, 178
Wirths, Dr 17, 111
Wojnarek Szymon Zajder vide Zajder-Wojnarek Szymon
Wojtyga 73
Wolf (SS) 14
Woźniak 73
Woźniak Irena 178
Woźniakowski 72
Wójcik Stanisław 87
Wrona vide Hałoń Kazimierz

Zajdow-Wojnarek Szymon 87
Zelewski Erich Bach vide Bach-Zelewski Erich
Zimetbaum Mala 209
Zunker, Prof. Dr 188

INDEX OF GEOGRAPHICAL NAMES.

Africa 189
Altdorf (Stara Wieś) 52
Amersfoort 194
Austria 9, 205
Auschwitz (Oświęcim) 1, 2, 3, 4, 5, 7, 8, 9, 10, 11, 12, 14, 15, 16, 17, 18, 19, 20, 21, 23, 24, 25, 26, 27, 30, 31, 33, 35, 36, 37, 38, 39, 40, 41, 42, 43, 44, 45, 46, 47, 48, 49, 50, 51, 52, 53, 54, 55, 57, 58, 59, 62, 66, 67, 69, 71, 72, 75, 77, 78, 79, 80, 81, 82, 85, 86, 88, 89, 91, 92, 93, 94, 95, 97, 110, 111, 112, 113, 119, 124, 127, 129, 134, 135, 138, 140, 141, 142, 149, 151, 152, 154, 155, 157, 158, 160, 172, 177, 181, 185, 186, 187, 188, 189, 190, 191, 192, 193, 194, 195, 196, 197, 199, 200, 201, 202, 203, 205, 206, 207, 208, 209, 210, 211, 212, 213, 214, 215, 216, 217

Babice 51, 53, 188
Bajszowy 85
Belgium 9, 195, 209
Bergen 197
Bergen-Belsen 41, 44, 49, 204, 211
Berlin 5, 21, 58, 62, 198, 215

Będzin 47
Białystok 198, 204
Bielany 188
Bielsko 90
Birkenau (Brzezinka) 2, 3, 4, 5, 6, 7, 9, 16, 21, 26, 30, 39, 47, 48, 52, 55, 69, 71, 72, 77, 78, 80, 84, 88, 89, 90, 91, 92, 92, 93, 111, 112, 113, 160, 172, 176, 179, 183, 185, 188, 190, 191, 192, 193, 194, 195, 196, 197, 198, 199, 200, 201, 202, 203, 204, 205, 206, 207, 208, 209, 210, 211, 212, 214, 215, 216, 217
Blechhammer (Blachownia Śląska) 40, 48, 53
Bliżyń 208
Bobrek 53, 184
Broszkowice 86, 87, 188
Bruntal 41, 46
Brünn (Brno) 36, 41, 53, 189, 204
Brzeszcze 45, 94, 195
Buchenwald 42, 43, 45, 53, 54, 109, 110, 210, 216
Budy 51, 53, 69, 137, 140, 142, 143, 144, 152, 154, 155, 156, 160, 167, 168, 177, 196, 197
Budzyń 208
Buna-Monowitz vide Monowitz
Bytom 169, 184

Chełmek-Paprotnik 41
Chełmno/Ner 196
Chorzów 40
Chrzanów 44
Cracow (Kraków) 1, 18, 30, 40, 41, 43, 44, 45, 46, 47, 50, 88, 97, 104, 109, 110, 120, 131, 132, 137, 186, 192, 199, 206, 209, 211
Czechoslowakia 36, 37, 41, 46, 189 197, 204, 207, 213
Częstochowa 183

Dachau 58, 71, 110, 216
Dessau 20
Drancy 195
Dresden 189
Dwory 35, 42, 44, 46, 188

Erfurt 21, 193, 198
Essen 15, 199
Esterwegen 58
Estonia 205
Europe 26

Finów 183
Flossenburg 54, 210
France 7, 9, 192, 195, 198, 209
Frankfort 33, 208
Friedland 196

General Gouvernement vide Poland
German Federal Republic 97, 189
Germany 1, 8, 9, 13, 27, 32, 36, 37, 38, 39, 45, 47, 53, 54, 56, 91, 97, 109, 114, 130, 187, 197, 198, 199, 203, 206, 209, 212, 213, 214, 216
Ghana 189
Gleiwitz (Gliwice) 40, 42, 43, 47, 49, 53, 216
Golleschau (Goleszów) 43, 53, 194
Great Britain 7
Greece 9, 200, 202
Gross Rosen 40, 42, 44, 48, 49, 54

Halemba 39
Harmęże 36, 51, 53, 176, 188
Holland 9, 31, 194, 198, 209
Hungary 7, 9, 10, 92, 208, 209

Italy 9, 10, 204, 209

Japan 109
Jasło 133
Jawischowitz (Jawiszowice) 41, 45, 53, 195
Jaworzno 47, 48, 201, 206

Karlsruhe 53
Katowice 1, 8, 24, 39, 40, 41, 42, 43, 44, 45, 46, 49, 50, 52, 172, 187, 191, 193, 198, 203, 206, 214
Kharkov 202
Kobiór 52
Königstein 189
Krosno 133

Lagischa (Łagisza) 45, 47, 50
Lamsdorf (Łambinowice) 44, 190
Latwian Republic 204
Lędziny 43
Libiąż 87
Libiąż Mały 44, 202
London 2, 19, 21, 22, 87, 211
Lublin 196
Luxemburg 7
Lwów 198

Łagiewniki Śląskie 44
Ławki 42
Łęki 90, 94, 213
Łódź 210, 211

Majdanek 196, 201, 208, 210
Malines 195
Mauthausen-Gusen 43, 45, 49, 54, 65, 71, 175
Mińsk 199
Monowitz (Monowice) 3, 4, 5, 6, 39, 41, 46, 47, 53, 78, 80, 92, 93, 197, 198, 206, 214, 215, 216, 217

Natzweiler 17
Neu Berun (Nowy Bieruń) 202
Neustadt (Prudnik) 49, 53
Nordhausen 44
Norway 9, 42, 197
Nuremberg 8, 18, 56, 105

Opawa 49
Opole 40, 49
Osiek 188

Paris 192, 193
Płaszów 206
Pławy 51, 53, 188
Poland 2, 31, 84, 85, 184, 186, 187, 202, 204, 210
Polanka 188
Porąbka 91
Poręba Wielka 82, 83, 94
Przemyśl 133
Pszczyna 52, 215

Racibórz 49
Radom 175, 206, 208
Rajsko 36, 51, 53, 112, 178, 179, 188, 194, 199, 212
Ravensbrück 6, 183, 191, 210
Reich vide Germany
Riga 204
Rodos 210
Romainville 198
Rome 204
Roth b/Nürnberg 29
Rumania 81
Rydułtowy 41

Sachsenhausen 2, 3, 42, 54, 57, 58, 185, 186, 208, 216
Salonika 200
Saxony 189
Siemianowice 46
Silesia 4, 9, 31, 37, 45, 47, 50, 138, 188, 191, 193, 202, 207
Slovakia 9, 91, 192, 207
Sławięcice 40
Soła 1, 32, 88, 90, 179, 188

Sosnowitz (Sosnowiec) 47, 49, 53
Soviet Union 4, 7, 8, 9, 97, 199, 203
Stara Kuźnia 39
Strassburg 17
Sucha 84
Sudeten 37, 186
Svetla 46
Sweden 7, 183
Switzerland 7, 204
Świętochłowice 41, 47

Tarnów 124, 186, 192
Theresienstadt 197, 198, 203, 204, 207, 209, 211
Trieste 206
Trzebinia 50, 53
Tschechowitz-Dziedzitz (Czechowice-Dziedzice) 50, 53

Ukrainian Republic 202
United States 7, 92
Upper Silesia vide Silesia

Vatican 207
Veldes 190
Vienna 47, 137, 205
Viljandi 205
Vistula 1, 32, 84, 87

Warsaw (Warszawa) 6, 9, 87, 98, 109, 124, 125, 128, 131, 186, 187, 208, 210
Wesoła 202
Werl 202
Westerbork 194, 211
Westphalen 202
Wilczkowice 88
Witebsk 203, 204
Wodzisław Śląski 45, 215
Wrocław 1, 188, 196, 216

Yugoslavia 9, 10, 195

Zabrze 44
Zamość 197, 199
Zaporoże 203